Deaf Lives

Deaf People in History

Edited by

Peter W. Jackson and Raymond Lee

Supported by a Millennium Awards for All Grant

19 ♥ 93
BDHS

British Deaf History Society Publications

Published by the British Deaf History Society
288 Bedfont Lane
Feltham
Middlesex
TW14 9NU
ENGLAND

A branch of the
British Deaf History Society
Registered Office:
49 Whitton Close
Doncaster
DN4 7RB
ENGLAND

British Library Cataloguing Publication Data

ISBN 1-902427-08-4

Printed in England by:
Palladian Press, Unit E, Chandlers Row, Port Lane, Colchester, Essex CO1 2HG

Production Team:

Editors:
Peter W. Jackson
Raymond Lee

Editorial Team:
Anthony J. Boyce
Geoffrey J. Eagling
Doreen E. Woodford

Original Layout:
Christopher Marsh

Final Layout:
Maureen A. Jackson
Cheridah J. Sword

Contributors:

Martin Binysh
Anthony J. Boyce
David Breslin
Peter R. Brown
Serena Cant
Breda Carty
Arthur F. Dimmock
Geoffrey J. Eagling
Philip K. Gardner
Winifred Gilbert
Arthur Groom
Jack Hart

John A. Hay
Mary Hayes
Maureen A. Jackson
Peter W. Jackson
David Kettle
Philip Kilgour
Elaine Lavery
Raymond Lee
Rachel O'Neill
Donald Read
David Whiston
Doreen E. Woodford

Other Contributors (Workshop Participants):

Robert Anderson
Malcolm Beech
Rowena Clear
Carol Denmark
Clark Denmark
Richard Dunn
Ann Hart
Shirley Hay
John Lawler
Christopher Marsh
Ruth Morris (USA)
Denis Shilston
Ian Carmichael
Diane Warburton
John Warburton
Brian Whalley

Martin Atherton
Ian Clear
Sheila Cubis
Jean Dimmock
Harold Fallman
Ruth Fallman
Gynn Hayes
Mark Heaton
Peter Morley
Percy Morris (USA)
Issy Schliesselman
Jonathan Sterne
Noel Traynor
David Woolley
Angela Woolley

*To all those whose struggles and perserverance
contributed to the wealth of Deaf History
and
in memoriam of
Jean Dimmock, 1920-2000,
who loved 'people' and was a strength
in the development of
Deaf Literature*

Page

Picture Acknowledgements   ix
Foreword   xi
Introduction   xiii
1.   Agnew, William   1
2.   Alexandra, Queen   2
3.   Armour, Robert   3
4.   Arrowsmith, Thomas   5
5.   Ash, Harry   7
6.   Atkinson, Alexander   9
7.   Bain, Charlotte   11
8.   Baker, Daniel Thompson   12
9.   Banton, George   13
10.   Barnett, Algernon Joel Morris   14
11.   Bastin, Clifford   16
12.   Bather, Arthur Henry   18
13.   Beale, George   20
14.   Beale, Henry Blenkarne   21
15.   Bilibin, Alexander   22
16.   Blackwood, Alexander   23
17.   Bloomfield, Frederick Allen   24
18.   Blount, Hiram J.   26
19.   Bone, Edward   28
20.   Brojer, Mika   29
21.   Burke, James   30
22.   Burns, John   32
23.   Burns, Matthew Robert   33
24.   Burnside, Helen Marion   35
25.   Campbell, Duncan   37
26.   Carmichael, John   39
27.   Carr, Cyril   41
28.   Cavendish, William Spencer
        (6th Duke of Devonshire)   42
29.   Clemo, Jack   43
30.   Close, Samuel   44
31.   Cooley, Thomas   45
32.   Creasy, John   47
33.   Crosse, Richard   48
34.   Davidson, Thomas   49
35.   Dent, Rupert Arthur   50
36.   Docharty, James & Edwin   51
37.   Drysdale, Alexander   52
38.   Duff, John   54
39.   Dyott, John   55
40.   Edmond, Arthur   56
41.   Edward, George   57
42.   Edwards, Leslie   59
43.   Fagan, Lawrence   60
44.   Fagan, Robert   61
45.   Fairbairn, Sir Arthur Henderson   62
46.   Farrar, Abraham   63

47.	Fenning, Oliver	65
48.	Fleming, Sir John Ambrose	66
49.	Fyfe, David	68
50.	Gaudy, Sir John &	
	Gaudy, Framlingham	69
51.	Gawen, Joseph	71
52.	Geikie, Walter	72
53.	Gilbert, William	74
54.	Goodricke, John	75
55.	Gorham, Charles	77
56.	Gostwicke, Sir Edward &	
	Gostwicke, William	79
57.	Graham, Sir James	80
58.	Gray, William	81
59.	Griffiths, William A.	83
60.	Groom, Jane Elizabeth	84
61.	Gubbins, Beatrice	85
62.	Hague, Joseph	87
63.	Harvey, Felicia "Kate" Catherine	89
64.	Healey, George Frederick	91
65.	Heaviside, Oliver	92
66.	Hepworth, Joseph	94
67.	Herriot, James	96
68.	Hodgson, Edwin A.	98
69.	Hogg, George Edwin Hartnoll	100
70.	Hossell, Leigh	101
71.	Howe, James	102
72.	Hunter, William	103
73.	Isted, Ambrose	104
74.	Jennings, John	106
75.	Kickham, Charles Joseph	107
76.	Kirk, Edward Alfred	109
77.	Kitto, John	111
78.	Landseer, Thomas	113
79.	Lowe, John William	115
80.	Lucas, Samuel Bright	117
81.	Mackenzie, Francis Humberstone	
	(Lord Seaforth)	118
82.	Mackenzie, George Annand	119
83.	MacLellan, Archibald & Duncan	121
84.	Macleod, Murdoch	122
85.	Maginn, Francis	124
86.	Magson, Saul	125
87.	Maguire, Francis Ross	126
88.	Mahon, Thomas	127
89.	Martineau, Harriet	128
90.	McDonnell, Francis	130
91.	McDougall, William	131
92.	Miles, Dorothy	132
93.	Mitchell, William Frederick	134
94.	Morgan, Benjamin	135
95.	Muirhead, Alexander	137

96.   North, Samuel White   138
97.   O'Keeffe, Robert Jones   140
98.   Oxley, Kate   141
99.   Patrick , George Percy (Lord Carberry)   142
100.   Pattison, Thomas   143
101.   Paul, James   145
102.   Payne, Benjamin H.   146
103.   Pearce, Richard Aslatt   147
104.   Pitcher, Bernard   148
105.   Plantagenet, Princess Katherine   149
106.   Poole, Jane   150
107.   Popham, Alexander   152
108.   Princess Joanna   153
109.   Reynolds, Cyril   154
110.   Reynolds, Sir Joshua   155
111.   Roch, Sampson Towgood   156
112.   Rose, Frederick John   157
113.   Rowland, Edward   158
114.   Sambell, Philip   160
115.   Scott, Charlotte Angas   162
116.   Scott, George & Robert Menzies   164
117.   Shaw, Kathleen Trousdell   166
118.   Shirreff, Charles   167
119.   Smith, John   168
120.   Smith, John Guthrie Spence   169
121.   Spearing, John Thomas Alysius   170
122.   Steel, Elizabeth   172
123.   Strathern, Alexander Fairley   174
124.   Stryker, Emil   176
125.   Sutcliffe, Thomas   178
126.   Tait, George   180
127.   Tavaré, Frederick L.   182
128.   Thomson, Alfred Reginald   184
129.   Thorpe, Raymond Banks   186
130.   Tonna, Charlotte Elizabeth   187
131.   Trood, William Henry Hamilton   189
132.   Turner, Joseph   190
133.   Whalley, Daniel   191
134.   Widd, Thomas   192
135.   Williams, Richard Rowland   194
136.   Wilson, Arthur James   195
137.   Wise, Dorothy Mary Stanton   197
138.   Wood, John Philp   198
139.   Woodcock, Peter George Spencer   200
140.   Woodhouse, Stan   201
141.   Wright, David John Murray   203
Sources and References   205

The majority of pictures and photographs in this book
have come from the following sources:

The British Deaf History Society Archives
The Anthony J. Boyce Collection
The Arthur F. Dimmock Collection
The David Breslin Collection
The Geoffrey J. Eagling Collection
The John A. Hay Collection
The Peter & Maureen Jackson Collection
The Raymond Lee Collection
The RNID Library

The British Deaf History Society acknowledges the sources
listed below for the reproduction of the following pictures:

Algernon Barnett	*Arthur Groom*
John Carmichael	*The National Library of Australia*
William S. Cavendish	*The Chatsworth Settlement Trustees*
Walter Geikie	*Edinburgh & East of Scotland Deaf Society*
John Goodricke	*Royal Astronomical Society*
Thomas Landseer	*National Portrait Gallery, London*
Dorothy Miles	*Don Read*
William Mitchell	*National Maritime Museum*
Alexander Muirhead	*University of Oxford*
Sir Joshua Reynolds	*National Portrait Gallery, London*
Philip Sambell	*National Monuments Records Office*
Thomas Widd	*Mary Hayes*

The British Deaf History Society (BDHS) is proud to present *Deaf Lives* to everyone who is interested in the history of the Deaf. The BDHS is grateful to the Millennium Award committee for a grant that makes this book possible.

No book containing biographies of Deaf people throughout history existed and there was always a need for such a book. Since public access to the archives and public record offices were made widely available in the early 1970s, a great wealth of information in connection with the history of Deaf people was unearthed and this eventually led to work towards the preservation and publication of such information. Deaf researchers and historians came about and this led to a situation that was to give birth to the BDHS.

It was on 29 March 1993 when correspondence took place between John A. Hay of Edinburgh and Raymond Lee of Feltham, Middlesex. Outlining to Lee his research into the life and work of Thomas Braidwood, the man who established the first regular and private school for the Deaf in Edinburgh in 1760, Hay explained he felt he had located the whereabouts of the burial place of Thomas Braidwood. Hay indicated that it was somewhere in a cemetery adjoining the Presbyterian Dissenters' Meeting House on the south side of St. Thomas' Square in Hackney, and asked Lee to look into it. Three days later, Lee visited the former cemetery and found a gravestone belonging to the Braidwood family. It gave the names of five members of the family, including Thomas. From this small but significant find, it became clear to both Hay and Lee that a group was needed to begin the great work in unearthing, writing, preserving, researching and promoting Deaf history. On 14 April 1993, they both established the British Deaf History Society and invited people to its first workshop in Edinburgh on 30 October 1993. The BDHS was formally established on that day. Since then, it has grown steadily, obtaining charity status. The BDHS publishes *Deaf History Journal* three times a year, and helps to promote and develop awareness of Deaf history, advancing education in the history of Deaf people for the benefit of the general public through publications and workshops.

The BDHS has come a long way since 1993. As its present Chair, I wish to express how grateful the BDHS is to every individual who contributed to *Deaf Lives*. It must be remembered that these individuals, deaf and hearing alike, worked entirely on voluntary basis on top of their paid occupations. These contributors are the rock and pride of the BDHS. I would also like to thank both Peter Jackson and Raymond Lee for their hard work as joint editors of the project. For them *Deaf Lives* had not been an easy task and they had to work within a tight budget and limited finances. However, they both saw to the publication of the project and this in itself is a wonderful end to their hard work.

Deaf Lives marks a milestone in Deaf history. Its collection of biographies represents one story - a story about Deaf people who struggled long and patiently to rid of the shackles of enforced helplessness and isolation to achieve individual independence. It is an epic saga that occurred during different eras and different circumstances. The struggle is also portrayed against different educational, social, religious and political backdrops which often shunned the Deaf from social acceptance and integration. Thankfully, the current situation is more tolerant and accepting of the Deaf and this could not have come about without the struggle and contributions of the Deaf in the past.

This book does not complete work on Deaf history; more needs to be done. However, it is hoped that this book will encourage readers to undertake further research into Deaf history. *Deaf Lives* makes a fascinating read and it is also an essential source of reference for those on Deaf Studies courses. I trust this book will provide enjoyable reading for everyone for a long time to come.

Anthony J. Boyce
Chair, BDHS.

As the celebrations of the new Millennium got under way, it was clear that many other communities were commemorating or preserving their histories. The British Deaf History Society (BDHS) considered how Deaf History could be part of these celebrations. It was decided to create a project called *Deaf Lives* that would record the achievements and contributions of deaf people to history. The BDHS was fortunate enough to secure a grant from the National Lottery to enable the project to be carried out.

The *Deaf Lives* project started with a workshop and exhibition held in Vale Royal Deaf Centre, Northwich, Cheshire. In accordance with National Lottery criteria, the aim was to give as many people as possible opportunities to make personal contributions to the project that would eventually take the form of a book. The *Deaf Lives* project presented an opportunity for Deaf people to contribute positively towards the work. Apart from necessary editing, the editors have tried not to alter the style of writing of every individual Deaf contributor. It is hoped that the project will encourage many others to participate actively in future projects.

For a book that sought to recognise the contributions D/deaf people have made to history, three issues needed to be resolved at the outset; the first was how to define a contribution and the second was how to define a historical context. The third conundrum is perhaps something many D/deaf people could identify with; just what is a deaf person who achieved a contribution? Is it someone who was born deaf, someone who became deaf as a child, someone who lost their hearing later in life? The historical context had to be the British Isles and included emigrants to other countries, and immigrants into the British Isles, which of course included Ireland. Within this historical definition, the contribution made had to be significant to either the larger world inhabited by people who hear or be specific to Deaf Britain. One criterion resolved was that only persons who were dead could be considered for inclusion.

Initially, the scale of the undertaking was greatly under-estimated. Although many members of the BDHS were knowledgeable about the achievements of deaf people in history, it became clear that in many cases much of the information that they held was incomplete. To do proper justice to these people, an intense research programme had to be carried out, necessitating visits to all parts of the country from the Highlands of Scotland to Cornwall, from East Anglia to Ireland, and to many libraries and other public places in London. To compound the issue, the more members researched, the more "names" they discovered of past deaf achievers that were previously unknown. These, too, needed to be extensively researched. One of the biggest difficulties in many respects was to find suitable portraits or other pictures to go with each story. This was not always possible. In many instances, the pictures that could be obtained were of poor quality that needed a lot of time-consuming artwork to make them presentable in a book of this nature.

The final selection of articles may surprise some people, particularly as it was reluctantly decided due too lack of space that the majority of sporting achievements would be excluded, along with those persons whose claim to fame was confined to a single deed of heroism. One example of the latter was the story of Albert Tarr, who was the only deaf person ever to be posthumously given an award for bravery. To compensate for this, it was agreed that the BDHS would in the near future bring out a separate book devoted to deaf people who had received significant national awards for acts of heroism. In itself, this topic needed extensive research to do the subject justice and the editors were desperately pressed for time.

It was disappointing to find that apart from several persons of Jewish faith, all those selected for inclusion were white British people. There were none from the deaf British Black African-Caribbean or Asian ethnic minority communities who fitted the criteria as most of these people became active in the later half of the twentieth-century. Again, to compensate, the BDHS has resolved to set up a project to encourage deaf people from British ethnic minority communities to contribute to a book that traces their achievements and developments in recent history.

A word here about the difference between the capitalised Deaf and lower case deaf is needed to ensure that those not familiar with the usage do not get confused. The use of capitalised Deaf refers to those deaf people who have been raised, educated and conditioned in mainly "deaf" surroundings, in particular residential and day schools for the deaf. These deaf people use sign language as their main means of communication, and in a good number of instances, as their first language. Furthermore, they mix in company of other deaf people, sharing the same culture, mentality, attitude and approach. They differ in a large way from deaf people who have been raised in the hearing way and who have been conditioned to the hearing system, mentality, attitude and approach.

To distinguish the difference between these two groups, the sign-language using deaf became identified as Deaf, whereas the deaf who closely associate themselves with the hearing world became known as deaf, the d being in lower-case.

The use of D and d is not new. Deaf people as far back as 1880 used it to distinguish the two different groups; Thomas Davidson was the first to use the term "the Deaf" in a letter to *The Deaf and Dumb Magazine* (Feb. 1880 issue). However, as many editors of magazines for the deaf were hearing, they took to editing Deaf as deaf and the use was lost for some time. It is now in widespread use.

The editors feel that the end result of this book will very significantly achieve its aim of recording deaf people's achievements and contributions to history. We feel it will constitute a valuable resource for immediate and future generations of deaf people and students of Deaf Studies to refer to, as well as being an interesting book to have in one's own personal library. Our grateful thanks are due to all those who contributed in the debates and by submitting articles.

Peter W. Jackson
Raymond Lee
Editors.

William Agnew
1846-1914

William Agnew was born deaf in Glasgow. At an early age he was sent to be educated at the Glasgow Institution for the Deaf and Dumb, where he proved to be a remarkable scholar.

After his education, Agnew was employed as a bookbinder for nine years and then worked for a further four years with the Deaf printer, Alexander Strathern. At the age of 28, he became a writer with the well-known legal firm of Moncrief, Barr, Paterson and Co. in Glasgow.

Throughout his life, Agnew could not speak and relied entirely on sign language and fingerspelling, but was a highly articulate man – he penned a great number of articles in Scottish and national newspapers, giving his views on the introduction of oralism into British schools. He was a strong opponent of the oral system, believing that 'Knowledge is Power' and that to deny a really good education to Deaf people through the use of oral methods was to put them in the power of others.

A man of immense dignity and bearing who could converse (in fingerspelling) with Royalty and aristocracy on equal terms, William Agnew was a monarchist interested in all things to do with Royalty and in 1893 published a little known book called *The Deaf and Dumb Royalty.*

He was also a talented artist in his leisure time whose fame rested primarily on the series of paintings he did of Queen Victoria and Elizabeth Tuffield, nee Groves – 'The Royal Condescension' paintings of 1883, 1889 and 1890, 'True Nobility' (1897) and 'Post Office, Whippingham, I.O.W.' (1899). No trace exists of any of these five paintings, which are now much sought after by Deaf people.

'The Royal Condescension' painting of 1889 was exhibited at the Edinburgh Exhibition in 1890 and won an award; it was also specially exhibited to Queen Victoria at Lord and Lady Blythswood's house in Glasgow in 1891, at which time the Queen agreed to become patron of the proposed new Glasgow Institution's building fund. She also made a handsome donation although she had not been asked for money.

Through William Agnew's painting, and the notice it received, the building fund (Agnew's brainchild) got off to a splendid start, and Agnew's energy and his business contacts throughout Glasgow soon saw the fund grow quickly. The Grand Bazaar on 19-21 November 1891 realised over £6000 – much more than Agnew had hoped for. By the end of 1892, Agnew had met his target for the building fund, and work commenced on the new Institute. The new building was opened with great fanfare in January 1895, and the grateful Deaf members appointed William Agnew a director, a position he retained until his death after a long illness in 1914.

Peter W. Jackson

Alexandra, Queen Consort
1844-1925

There has never been a British monarch, or before the union of England and Scotland, an English or Scottish monarch, who was Deaf.

The nearest Britain came to having a Deaf monarch was in the case of Prince Albert Victor, eldest son of the Prince and Princess of Wales, later King Edward VII and Queen Alexandra. Prince Albert had inherited the hereditary disease, otosclerosis, from his mother who had herself inherited it from her own mother, Queen Louise of Denmark. However, Prince Albert Victor died of thyroid even before his father became King.

Born on 1 December 1844, Queen Alexandra is probably Britain's best known Deaf Royal. She was so beautiful that the Prince of Wales, who was then the most eligible bachelor in the world, fell in love with her photograph before he even met her. When Alexandra and the Prince of Wales finally met, the meetings they had were brief and chaperoned. It seemed that the fact she was deaf was withheld from the Prince who was determined to rush into marriage with this fabulous beauty.

The marriage took place at St. George's Chapel in Windsor Castle on 10 March 1863, but the Prince of Wales, who was notorious for his liking for loose women, grew to bitterly regret rushing into the marriage. The Prince often poked fun at her deafness and was impatient in her company. Alexandra never had a formal education and found she had very little in common with her husband, despite having four children by him. However, the young Danish Princess overwhelmed her new mother-in-law, Queen Victoria, with her beauty. The Queen was, however, heard to lament, "Alas! She (the Princess) is deaf and everybody observes it, which is a sad misfortune." Despite this, Queen Victoria and the Princess of Wales became very close. As Alexandra never learnt to lip-read and refused to use an ear trumpet, it is likely they communicated in fingerspelling. Queen Victoria was fluent in fingerspelling (she comforted a dying Deaf woman in the Isle of Wight for several hours at a time, and was also able to communicate with other Deaf people such as William Agnew) and probably taught Alexandra the British manual alphabet. With her fingerspelling skills, Alexandra would sometimes attend St. Saviour's Church for the Deaf in Oxford Street, London, where she enjoyed the services.

During her period as Queen Consort, and after the King's death as the Queen Dowager, Alexandra would sometimes purchase a number of works of Deaf art and sculpture, especially if the work of art was of herself. Several Deaf artists and sculptors therefore enjoyed her patronage. The Queen particularly favoured the young Deaf sculptress, Dorothy Stanton Wise.

Queen Alexandra died in 1925 at the age of 81.

Maureen A. Jackson

Robert Armour
1837-1913

Robert Armour was born in Kilmarnock in 1837. He became deaf through brain fever during infancy, and was educated at the Glasgow Institution for the Deaf and Dumb, under the famous headmaster, Duncan Anderson. He made rapid progress in his studies; in fact, Mr. Anderson was anxious to secure him as his first pupil teacher. His inclinations lay, however, in another direction, and he was apprenticed to a designer in the glass-staining trade. After serving seven years, he went to St. Helens, where he worked for Pilkingtons Glass Works. He did not stay long at Pilkingtons.

In 1860, Armour went to Liverpool, where he was destined to spend the remainder of his career. He obtained employment with a famous firm of glass-stainers, Messrs. J. A. Forrest and Co. and almost immediately began to identify himself with his fellow-deaf people in the area. These numbered some two hundred for whom no special provision existed at the time.

Prior to moving to Lancashire, Armour had, in the summer of 1856, while engaged at his trade at Glasgow, been brought into touch with James Herriot, the founder and first Superintendent of the original Manchester and Salford Adult Deaf and Dumb Benevolent Association. At that time Herriot was contemplating starting a similar society in Liverpool and offered the post of missioner there to Armour, guaranteeing his salary for three years. The latter declined the offer, explaining that his ambition lay in quite a different groove.

In 1864, George F. Healey started the Adult Deaf and Dumb Society in Liverpool. Robert Armour was one of the first members. He was to work with the Society, at first as a volunteer and then as a paid official, for many years.

Writing in *The Deaf and Dumb Times* of August 1891, Armour paid a splendid tribute to George Healey and his co-workers, who helped to form a Penny Savings Bank, a library and a Temperance Society, besides extending welfare work with local Deaf people in all directions.

The work continued on this voluntary basis until 1879 when Robert Armour was appointed missioner, it having become clear that volunteers could no longer conveniently perform the duties. Side by side with his own private work as a designer, Robert Armour had been engaged in much voluntary work and he also conducted services in three different places every Sunday. In dealing with a Mission like Liverpool, it should be remembered that it extended at that period to Birkenhead, Widnes, Warrington and the whole peninsula of north Cheshire, so it was a large area to cover on a voluntary basis.

Years afterwards, Armour wrote:- *I must confess that I then had little thought that after the lapse of nearly two decades be appointed to that very position (that had been offered by James Herriot).* But all this happened - he was missioner for thirty-three years at Liverpool!

Although his time was fully occupied by his work, he still found time to be a great reader, particularly from the French. As he was possessed of a retentive memory, there were few subjects upon which he was not well read. He was prominent in literary activities, his articles in the Press appearing under the *nom de plume* of "R.A." or "Robertus" and wrote about the life of Jean Massieu, which was printed in *The Deaf and Dumb Magazine* in 1876.

He was fortunate in having at Liverpool such prominent Deaf men as George Healey. The esteem with which he was regarded within Liverpool was shown in 1898 when he was presented with a gold watch by the Deaf people he served. He also had a portrait painted in oil by a Mr. C. D. Mackenzie and presented to him. For years, this adorned the walls of the Institute in Princes Street.

After over 33 years' service, Robert Armour retired from active work in October 1912. Barely twelve months later, on 9 November 1913, he died after a short illness, leaving four sons and one daughter to mourn their loss.

Peter W. Jackson

Thomas Arrowsmith
1771- c1830

Thomas Arrowsmith was born in Newent, Gloucestershire, the fourth of six children of Nathaniel and Elizabeth, née Cook. According to available church records, Thomas was christened on 23 January 1771 but his exact date of birth cannot be discovered to date. Thomas was born deaf and his early years were described in the book, *The Art of Instructing the Infant Deaf and Dumb*, published in 1819. The author of that book was none other than Thomas' younger brother, John Pauncefort Arrowsmith, who was christened on 30 December 1772 in Newent.

According to John Pauncefort, when Thomas was about four or five years old, he was taken by his mother to a local village (hearing) school and she demanded that he be educated. When the schoolmistress expressed difficulties that would occur due to the boy's deafness and lack of speech, she was told to teach Thomas to read and write and take matters up from there. It appears that Thomas did well at this "dame school" and was able to attain a good command of written English and understanding of the language, but his speech was nowhere as good as anyone hoped.

There is a void in Thomas' life after he left his local school when he was only about ten or eleven years old until 1789 when he entered the Royal Academy Schools - a gap of seven years. Certain deaf historians have come to a common consensus that Thomas attended Thomas Braidwood's Academy for the Deaf and Dumb in Mare Street, Hackney. A number of reasons point to this conclusion:

1. Thomas was well acquainted with a number of Braidwoodian pupils, particularly John Creasy and Mr. Harris, as he painted portraits of these persons. The only way he could have acquainted himself with them would have been as classmates.

2. John Pauncefort Arrowsmith's 1819 book, *The Art of Instructing the Infant Deaf and Dumb,* contained a strange and somewhat abrupt article praising the Abbé de l'Epée and his method of instruction using the systematic manual alphabet. This seems to indicate that the Arrowsmith family was disappointed with the education Thomas received in his latter childhood after leaving his local hearing school – and if that was the case, the Braidwood Academy for the Deaf and Dumb was the only available school in existence.

In 1827, Thomas Dodd of Manchester wrote of Thomas Arrowsmith in part three of *The Connoisseur's Repertory:*

Thomas ... was blessed with a quick and comprehensive mind and a natural turn towards attaining to a proficiency in the art of painting portraits and other subjects in miniature, in which practice he excels, and continues to do so to the present time. He first exhibited at Somerset House in 1792 with two subjects in miniature compass,

'Cain slaying Abel' and 'Mary Magdalene conversing with Christ'. In the following year, he applied himself to portrait painting and exhibited two portraits of gentlemen. In 1795 he reappeared at Somerset House in a miniature of himself and of six others of different individuals. In 1796, he produced a portrait of a bishop, and that of an old man. In 1797, miniature portraits of Mr. Harris, Mr. Flaxman and Mr. Weston, also of himself, Mr. Harris Jnr., and Mr. Creasy Jnr., the two latter his associates, who were also alike defective in speech and hearing. In 1799, a miniature of Mr. Luke Fitzgerald. Mr. Arrowsmith now resides in Manchester where his talents are duly appreciated.

Thomas Arrowsmith painted quite a large number of portraits, which included that of William Durning, Daniel Lambert, Carr Fenton and the banker Burrell of Liverpool amongst others. His last RA exhibited work was in 1829 and it was a portrait of Mr. Singleton, Professor of Mechanism.

Thomas married Elizabeth Carpenter at St. Marylebone, London, on 17 September 1812. Elizabeth was described as "illiterate" but this description seems to be a cover-up of the fact that she was actually a deaf person; it seems to be way wealthy families of that day behave as it was then seen by a certain group as a stigma to have a deaf and dumb person in the family. Within a year or two of the marriage, Thomas and Elizabeth departed for the north, living at various times in Lancashire, Liverpool and Manchester.

It appears from research that Thomas and his younger brother, John Pauncefort, were close and Thomas moved wherever John moved. John worked as a solicitor and he died at his house in Pembroke Garden, Liverpool, on 14 April 1829. What happened to Thomas and his wife afterwards is not yet known. Conflicting testimonies and rumours appeared that Thomas died in Manchester in 1829-30. However, there is evidence that Thomas, then aged 58 years, visited the Yorkshire Institution for the Deaf and Dumb on 17 December 1829 and he signed the Visitor book, entering his place of residence as London.

Raymond Lee

**Harry Ash
1863-1936**

The Deaf Awareness movement seems to be a relatively modern initiative: many believed the British Deaf Association at the beginning of the 1980s initiated it. In fact, the Deaf Awareness movement began 100 years earlier by a financially poor deaf man named Harry Ash.

Harry Ash, the son of a struggling engine and coach painter, was born in Bridgewater in 1863 and he lost his hearing at the age of eighteen months through scarlet fever. The other affliction Ash incurred as a consequence of that illness was near-sightedness. The Ash family suffered extreme poverty and they moved to Swindon in search of a better life. However, things went from bad to worse when the head of the family could not obtain gainful employment and therefore care for his family. In desperation the family moved to London.

At the age of 11 in 1874, Ash was sent to the London Asylum for the Deaf and Dumb under the headship of the Rev. T. J. Watson and thence to Margate. Educationally, Ash made rapid progress, learning under the signs system. Late in 1877, Ash was sent back to the Kent Road Asylum, where he became a head monitor until the day he left school.

Ash started to study foreign languages, starting with French outside normal school hours, later adding German and Dutch. Ash developed an interest in art, particularly glass-staining and sought an apprenticeship in that line, but without success. As a desperate measure, he worked with his father in the coach-building business that paid very little money. After some time, Ash was introduced to the Rev. Samuel Smith who was able to secure him employment as a draughtsman under one Mr. Dawson in Chiswick, London. But this did not last long as trade dropped off but Mr. Dawson obtained for Ash employment with a bookbinder, an occupation which he stuck with for seven years. Bookbinding did not interest Ash. He attended a school of Art in Regent Street and took to designing wallpaper patterns and went on to the School of Art in King's College to study figure drawings – he was to win three prizes during that time. In 1886, he married a deaf lady and returned to work as a pen and ink artist with Mr. Dawson in Chiswick. However, his first marriage did not last long – he married for the second time to Mrs. Tedder, a deaf lady from Plumstead in southeast London.

Ash was a man of great intelligence and an inventor; he had many ideas, all of which were acknowledged by the Admiralty, the London Fire Services and so on. However, Ash never made much headway career-wise and always remained on the borderline of poverty. He always felt people's lack of understanding of deafness and the Deaf were the root cause of deaf people not getting the breaks in life. With this in mind, he drew, wrote and printed his famous publications – the *Guide to Chirology* and *Comic Graphics* booklets which depicted signs, gestures and written versions in English in the hope that the public at large would be endeared by sign language and fingerspelling. Whilst Ash was working on his publications to generate public awareness of the Deaf, he harboured a dream to create and publish a dictionary of signs. His dream, alas, was not to materialise due to the fact that he had no one to assist him with the literary side and also that he could not obtain any financial backing.

Ash moved around often, having lived in Fulham, Chiswick, Watford and Southampton for a period of time. He never gave up on the idea of his book of signs and publications to generate Deaf awareness among members of the general public. Money, however, never found its way to Ash's pockets, nor did it land on his lap. He struggled along in life, perhaps forever wondering how many people were "well off" whereas he was not, in spite of all the hard work he put into life.

Ash was a pioneer in another way; he walked from London to Paris in 1883, just to prove that anyone can do it! In the annals of British Deaf History, he is indeed the first known and recorded deaf person to have walked from London to Paris.

The British Deaf Times (Nov-Dec.1934) recorded Ash's demise in September 1934:

> *Mr. Harry Ash, another well-known deaf and dumb personality, passed away in September last. He was intimately connected at one time with the late Messrs. Brown and Goodwin. Mr. Ash published several pamphlets from time to time illustrating the use of the Manual alphabet and signs with descriptive letterpress. He was somewhat near-sighted, but had an inventive turn of mind and tried to get the government to take up one of his inventions – one was and apparatus for saving lives at fires. Mr. Ash married, as his second wife, Mrs. Tedder of Plumstead, and lived at one time in Southampton and more recently at Fulham. He passed away at Bromley-by-Bow in East London, aged 71. The Rev. N. E. Westall, chaplain of All Saints, West Ham, officiated at the funeral.*

Raymond Lee

Alexander Atkinson
1806-1879

Born in Newcastle-on-Tyne on 29 August 1806, Alexander Atkinson was the youngest and fourth son of Joseph Atkinson, tailor, in the parish of St. Nicholas and Margaret, daughter of Alexander Stuart, cordwainer of the same parish. He was christened on 18 September 1806 at All Saints Parish Church, Newcastle. Atkinson was probably born deaf and dumb; it was quite a while before his deafness was discovered. Alexander learned to

Chessel's Court, site of the Edinburgh Institution for the Deaf and Dumb

communicate with his mother by fingerspelling and spent his early years sewing in his father's own tailoring workshop. When he reached the age of eight, his paternal grandfather died and left his considerable freehold property as well as his shipping and tailoring businesses to his family. It meant that Alexander's parents could afford to give him an education and chose Edinburgh. Alexander described this *"the priceless blessing of receiving a regular education"*.

On 1 June 1815, Alexander found himself at Chessell's Court, Canongate, where the Edinburgh Institution for the Deaf and Dumb was sited. John Braidwood, the grandson of the celebrated Thomas Braidwood, opened this school in 1810 and after a year, John left for the U.S.A. His assistant, Robert Kinniburgh, took charge of the school. Alexander was taken in as a parlour boarder. As revealed in Alexander's autobiography *Memoirs of My Youth*, he gave a very detailed account of his progress at school, his relationship with Robert Kinniburgh and his family and his adventures with his school friends whilst at school and travelling around Scotland. This afforded the present generation an insight into how the Deaf were taught and lived in those pioneering days. Alexander was at school for five years, leaving on 15 October 1820. He was Robert Kinniburgh's model pupil, the *"dux"* of his school, and was often used in public exhibitions from which Kinniburgh was able to profit in terms of income, new entrants and his growing reputation.

The next three months after leaving school saw Alexander settling down with his family after an absence of five years. His family learned sign language and communicated with him on general topics of the day. Alexander's inquiring mind soon turned to books to satisfy his thirst for more knowledge. It was at this stage that he, at the age of 15, started to write his autobiography in the form of a folio book. His sister, Annie, and his elder brother, Charles, supplied him with the family background and Charles corrected his written work now and then for grammatical errors. Up to the time after leaving school, he had already written fifty pages. This work, as it was, was left entire and had only been read by his own family.

During the summer of 1821, his brother Charles became a member of the Literary and Philosophical Society of Newcastle-on-Tyne. Alexander gave a fascinating account of his feelings towards Charles whom he showed no envy. He realised that there was an immense difference between him and his hearing brother, who had the ease and rapidity of understanding in his reading although Charles was five years older than him. Alexander formed a resolution that nothing would prevent him from reaching Charles' intellectual attainments.

On reaching his nineteenth year, Alexander was pondering on the kind of career he would have liked to embark upon. His parents suggested that he should learn some handicraft business but he preferred to aspire to a higher level. He thought of becoming a copying clerk in a lawyer's office or merchant's office but met resistance from his parents. He sought advice from Kinniburgh, his old master, but the reply was that in common with his previous parlour pupils, he ought to take up engraving. There was the seven year apprenticeship to reckon with and as he did not have the natural talent for drawing "*even on the slate*", he rejected this recommendation. Since he had the legacy from his maternal grandfather to receive when he reached his maturity, he thought that since there were no schools for the deaf existing in the north of England, he could set one up in Newcastle and drew up his grand plan, but once again he faced resistance and objections. Therefore instead of all the grand schemes which he dreamed of for his future, he reluctantly took up tailoring under his father.

In 1851, Alexander and his widowed 79 year-old father continued their tailoring business in Newcastle. Alexander was still a bachelor, a condition brought about by his duty to care for his ageing father, besides managing the family business. In 1865, he negotiated with the local engraver, John W. Swanton, regarding the publication of his autobiography and his book *Memoirs of My Youth* was the outcome.

Alexander died on 2 May 1879 at his lodging home. He was described on the death certificate as a hawker, aged 73 years.

Alexander's book is a classic in terms of both Deaf history and local history. His detailed descriptions and keen observations of local scenes in and around Newcastle-on-Tyne are clear and vivid. Surely, today's local historians in Newcastle would find them indispensable for their early nineteenth century studies. He also did the same when he was at school in Edinburgh thus affording a comparison between Auld Reekie and Canny Newcastle. Atkinson was the first born-deaf person to write an autobiography and the first of the deaf people to write a detailed account of his five years at the Edinburgh Institution for the Deaf and Dumb, showing a valuable link between the method of instruction used by Robert Kinniburgh and that used by Thomas Braidwood and his family.

Anthony J. Boyce

Charlotte Bain
1785-1846

The morning of Thursday 25 December 1806 dawned calm and fair, and boats from many little fishing villages along the Moray Firth prepared to go to sea. Among them were the three Stotfield boats carrying twenty-two men. This was the entire male population of the village except for three old fishermen too infirm to follow their calling and some boys still too young to go to sea. The men in the three boats had just taken their respective stations when a young girl came running down from the village to the shore in breathless haste; it was Charlotte Bain, a 21 year old uneducated deaf girl without speech. She instantly jumped into the boat in which her father was seated, and seizing him by the breasts of his coat, motioned him to return to the shore. The father, thinking it was some foolish notion she had taken to have him out of the boat, took no notice of her frantic signs, but she would let not him go and dragged him with almost superhuman effort out of the boat. Her father feared for her reason, and left the boat telling his fellow fishermen he would remain at home that day.

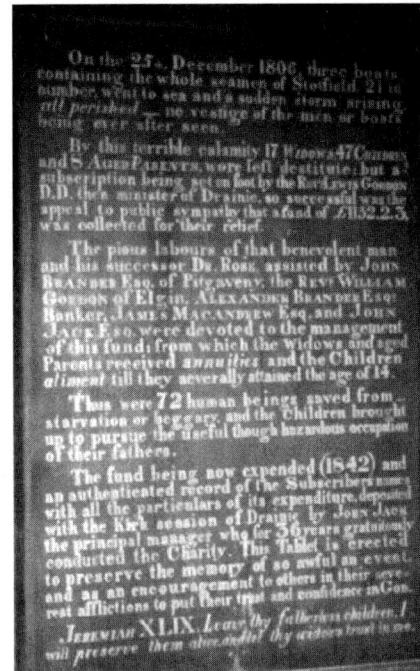

Stotfield Fishing Disaster Memorial in Drainie Church, Lossiemouth

Charlotte then employed every sign that she knew to tell the other fishermen that none of them should put to sea on that day, but to no avail. She then took her father's hat from his head, laid it upside down on the sand, rocked it backwards and forwards a few times, and then upset it. The fishermen understood what she meant, that there could be a capsize if they put out to sea, but they laughed at her, thinking she had mental hallucinations and left early in the morning for the fishing grounds a few miles out from Stotfield. They fished from small open boats, which had no deck and pulled up on a sheltered beach. They had the grave drawback of being easily swamped in rough seas. The Stotfield men put out their lines and made a good haul.

It was when they were returning home about noon that a fearful hurricane arose out of the south west. Mountainous seas broke over their boats, and in spite of the desperate efforts of the men to row back to the harbour at Stotfield, the gale carried the boats down the Firth to the open sea. Neither men nor boats were ever to be seen again. This terrifying storm raged with unabated fury for four hours until the wind veered to the north and gradually died away. Although there were other tragedies among the fishing fleets at other places along the coast, Stotfield was the only village to lose its entire fishing fleet, and the storm left 17 widows and 47 orphaned children.

When the extraordinary circumstances were known, Dummie Bain, as she was called, passed through the rest of her life as a seer. Young girls would come to her to have their fortunes read, to see what sort of husbands they would get, the number of children they would have and so forth, all of which circumstances she would signify by movements of her hands and fingers. With the general spread of schooling becoming available, her occupation as seer waned and Charlotte used her second sight in later years sparingly. She died unmarried on 5 August 1846.

Maureen A. Jackson

11

**Daniel Thompson Baker
1824-1878**

Daniel Thompson Baker was one of England's greatest artists. He was born in Fakenham in Norfolk on 13 June 1824. His father was a prosperous businessman with a good accumulation of property. Baker was the only deaf child in the family and he was first of all sent to a private hearing school run by his uncle, but attempts at educating him were unsuccessful.

Baker was then placed in the London Asylum for the Deaf and Dumb under Thomas James Watson and in a short time became intelligent and well educated. He was afterwards articled to one Mr. Ninham of Norwich to learn the profession of heraldic artists and in 1841, he returned to London as a pupil at the Heralds' College where he studied for 10 years. From there, Baker became a prolific artist and he had his own customers who included, amongst many, the Lord Mayors and Sheriffs of London and Sir Edmund Burke. His splendid emblazonments of arms on coaches, carriages and plaques were much admired and reported by *The Times* and other newspapers from time to time.

Baker opened his own heraldic art business and employed deaf apprentices. Amongst those were W. P. Pugh and W. A. Taylor, who were among the large number of successful deaf workers. From there, Baker extended his business by opening a shop for the sale of stationery and engravings.

Baker married twice, the first time in June 1846 to a hearing girl and his second marriage was to a deaf girl, Hannah Carter, in 1871. Baker died in September 1878.

Raymond Lee

George Banton
1812-1879

In 1876, George Banton, the last survivor of Dr. Joseph Watson's great Deaf teachers, retired from his post as teacher at the London Asylum. He had reached fifty years' service as a teacher.

George was born in Finsbury, Middlesex, on 7 July 1812. Eldest of five children, he was one of the three Deaf sons and two hearing daughters of George and Sarah Banton. When he was young, he was sent to the Private Academy for the Deaf and Dumb, run by Mr. Woodman at Kilburn, North-east London. He was not there for long before moving to the London Asylum for the Deaf and Dumb in the Kent Road, Southwark, in South-east London as a pay-list pupil in 1823. It meant he had to mix with the charity pupils.

In 1826, a sub-committee responsible for the appointment of teachers approached Joseph Watson, the headteacher at the Asylum. Watson was given authority to appoint four new teachers. George Banton was one of those chosen and began his training as a teacher. In the same year, his younger brother, William, entered the Asylum as a charity pupil.

In 1827, Banton became a qualified teacher and received a starting salary of £10 per year. In same year, his youngest brother, Edmund John, entered the Asylum as a charity pupil. Banton was a popular and conscientious teacher. In 1840, Thomas Watson, the second headteacher and son of Joseph, reporting on Banton's conduct, stated… *he performs his duties well and is a useful and conscientious teacher.*

As a Deaf man Banton attained a high position. He had a good and ready command of language and he was able to mix in good company. At the Asylum, he preferred as a rule to communicate by spelling on the fingers, although he used sign language which can be seen from a unique sentence, extracted from the 1890 short biography of Banton by John Platt Barrett in *Deaf and Dumb Institution Pamphlet* as follows:

> *A plan existed in his youthful days of signing each word separately, without reference to the meaning of the sentence as a whole…*

In 1875, Banton's health began to fail. Doctors who examined him believed he had a valvular disease of the heart, which caused him to experience fainting fits. A year later, due to his illness, he retired with a pension of £2 per week.

On his retirement, he went to live in Charnock Road, Clapton, until his death caused by a combination of epilepsy and disease of the heart in 1879. He was buried on top of his parents in their grave at Abney Park Cemetery in Stoke Newington, London.

Peter R. Brown

Algernon Joel Morris Barnett
1884-1953

Born deaf in London to Jewish parents, Algernon Barnett acquired fluent speech through the patience of his mother for whom he had great love and admiration. After leaving school, he worked in an art studio as a copy artist until the company went into liquidation and he was unemployed for a time during which he studied to become a layreader and frequented the deaf missions in the London area run by the RADD. Algernon later converted to Christianity. His mentor was the Reverend Albert Smith whose influence helped him to apply for the post of Missioner for the Deaf and Dumb in the Diocese of Northants & Rutland in 1928.

Algy Barnett (as he was known) was a unique character. He was a huge man with a permanent smile on his face, often oddly dressed with a bow tie at an awry angle and shoes that were rarely polished. On his head he wore a large homburg hat which he sometimes waved to get the attention of deaf people at a distance. His favourite was a green trilby with a feather in it which, sadly for him, he lost when the wind blew it out to sea from Southend pier on a day's outing with a group of Northampton Deaf people.

His ever-ready smile brought a comment from a police constable on patrol one dismal Sunday morning, "Good morning Mr Barnett, you have brought the sunshine". He was a household name throughout the diocese of Northants & Rutland, visiting every town and village, making collections from door to door to keep the mission in funds.

Algy had no transport of his own; he often planned his day by the bus timetable, being a well-known figure at the bus station and also at the Castle railway station in Northampton. He was once seen hurrying with sweat pouring down his face to catch a bus to officiate at a village funeral for a deaf person. In the age of modern office technology, he would be out of place. The typewriter, the computer, the minicom and the e-mail were not for him. He relied on pen and paper and Shank's pony to get from place to place.

During his time as missioner, the front door of the Green Street Building was rarely used and it was open only for Harvest Festival and other special days. To enter the building one went in the side door and another door on the left led to his office. Behind a large oak desk facing the person sat Algernon Barnett, ever ready to give him a welcoming smile.

Like the man himself, his office was unique; his desk cluttered with papers and photographs of many friends he met on his travels throughout Europe. On the walls were some of his paintings and ink drawings. His office must have been a cleaner's nightmare! Above the mantelpiece he had the poem "If" by Kipling. From this desk he organised holidays abroad on cruise ships, visiting countries in the Mediterranean for some of the elite Deaf of that time.

Being a large man, Algy almost filled the room when he visited some of the homes of local Deaf people. He also loved his food. He once recalled the time when he was gazing into a fish shop in Peterborough, and there was a touch on his shoulder. When he turned, it was the Bishop of Peterborough, who said, "Why are you looking into a fish shop and not a bookshop?" When in London, he would frequent Lyons Corner House and visit the Salad Bowl. At one time after he had finished one course, he had a second helping and the chair collapsed from under him, spilling all the food. After the waiter had cleaned him up and served him with a fresh plate, he apologised for the setback to his meal.

A Londoner born and bred, Algy often returned to the city of his birth. This came to the notice of one deaf gentleman who had never been to London in his life and Algy promised to take him. The day dawned and they set out by train from Castle station, it was one of those old steam trains with divided compartments and no toilet facilities. On the way the train stopped just beside a gentlemen's toilet and Algy felt he had to get off to have a "quick one". However, when he came out, the train was fading away into the distance. Meanwhile the poor deaf man on the train began to worry. When it drew into Euston and the deaf man saw all the hustle and bustle of the city, his heart sank even more. Suddenly, he saw a huge man waving his homburg hat at the end of the platform. It was Algy. He told his client that when he saw the train fading away from the station, he contacted the stationmaster explaining the situation, whereupon the stationmaster rang the signal box and the express from Scotland stopped especially to pick up Algy to get him to Euston in time.

On special Sundays, such as Harvest Festival, Algy always invited special hearing preachers such as Vernon Jones, F.W.G. Gilby and Henry Fry. The Rev. F.W.G. Gilby was remembered for his "split personality" as he used to sign to a deaf person and speak to a hearing person at the same time on two different topics.

Algy was responsible for organising the annual Midland Deaf regional dinner and dance at the Guildhall where people flocked from all parts of the Midlands and London. The last big "do" at the Guildhall proved too much for him as he was far from well, and he died a few weeks later on 14 February 1953 as he would have wished, sitting on his office chair.

St. Peter's Church was packed for his funeral. The Bishop Spencer Leeson paid tribute to his work in a moving service. Algernon Barnett never married. His "wife" was his work with Deaf people, and he served Northants and Rutland for 25 years right up to his death. After his successor, the Reverend Ken Earle, took over, it was obvious there were going to be big changes. The office was stripped of its "gaiety"; the walls were repainted, and except for one or two pictures, was almost bare. It looked as if the "warmth had gone with the showman and Jack Frost had taken over".

And for the first time on the desk was a typewriter and a telephone, and on the road was a motor-car - all the things that Algy Barnett never had.

Arthur Groom

Clifford Bastin
1912-1991

A schoolboy prodigy, Cliff Bastin's name was paramount in football supporters' discussions of the 1930s. The *Arbiter* rated Bastin as one of the most brilliant footballers of modern times. Cliff's career began while playing for Exeter schools and his prodigious skills were soon to be seen. He was selected to play for England Schoolboys versus Wales when only fourteen. Soon after he joined the local side, Exeter City, and made his league debut when he was fifteen. Cliff scored six goals in seventeen league games as a seventeen-year-old. Herbert Chapman signed him for Arsenal in 1929 for £2,000. He appeared as an inside right but later he converted to his famous left wing position. By the end of his initial season at the club, Cliff featured in 21 league games and scored seven times.

In the 1929-30 season, he was the youngest player to appear in a FA Cup Final in which Arsenal beat Huddersfield. When the team won the league championship in the next season, Bastin's partnership with the legendary Alex James on the left flank started to flourish. Not only was he ever present, the youngest at the age of 18-19 to be so for the club, he contributed with no less than 28 league goals. This included a hat trick against Derby.

In 1931-2, Bastin won the first of his 21 England caps and was then only nineteen. He became the youngest player ever to win an England Cap, League Championship and FA Cup medal in one season and became known as Boy Bastin because he had done everything in the game while still a boy.

In the 1932-3 season, Bastin set a record, which undoubtedly will stand for all time for a winger, when he scored staggering 33 league goals. No other winger in history of the game, before or after, has come remotely close to equalling this total. The reason that Bastin was so deadly was that, unlike any other winger, he stood at least ten yards in from the touch line so that his alert football brain could thrive on the brilliance of James threading through defence splitting passes with his lethal finishing job.

In the same season, it also became abundantly clear that Bastin was having problems with his hearing. He and James used a kind of sign language on the field, but this type of silent communication was of their own making. Herbert Chapman, the man who was Bastin's mentor and whom he idolised, died in 1934. Nevertheless, Bastin bagged 20 goals in 36 league appearances in that year. Arsenal dropped to the sixth place in the 1935-6 season. This was partly due to the fact that the new manager, George Allison, was in a quandary as to who to replace Alex James when unavailable and Bastin played in an alien position which was inside forward. However, his contribution in helping Arsenal to win the FA Cup against Sheffield United was immense, scoring six times in seven ties.

The 1936-7 season must have seemed strange to Bastin as it was the first time in eight seasons that he was not involved in domestic honours. It was through being switched from position to position, but in the next season he was back to his original position and scored fifteen times in 38 league appearances. On 4 February 1939, he scored his 150th league goal.

During the war, Bastin was exempt from active service owing to his deafness. After the war at the age of 34, he played in a further six league games before a leg injury took its toll and he retired from football in 1947. His club record of 178 first team goals stood for years 50 before Ian Wright broke the record in 1997. Cliff Bastin is not only a legend in Arsenal's history, but will be remembered as a football immortal who never allowed the fact that he was deaf to affect his footballing brilliance. He was never booked, let alone sent off.

He died in 1991 aged 79 at Exeter where he ran the Horse and Groom pub for 20 years before retiring.

Arthur F. Dimmock

*St. Saviour's Church for Deaf people,
London*

Arthur Henry Bather
1829-1892

For a Deaf person to attain both social and occupational positions of high prestige, he would have to face a near-impossible task. In Scotland, the great John Philp Wood achieved the prestigious position of Auditor of Excise in 1809. In England, one Deaf person was to make similar achievement 45 years after Wood. He was Arthur Henry Bather.

Very little is known of the early years of A. H. Bather. The fourth son of John Bather, Recorder of Shrewsbury, and a nephew of Archdeacon Bather of Shropshire, he was born in 1829 in the Shrewsbury area. He had an attack of scarlet fever when only five years old and he became totally deaf and consequently his speech was severely impaired. His father sent him to the Manchester Institution for the Deaf and Dumb at Old Trafford as a private pupil under Henry Brothers Bingham. Bather turned out to be a very sharp and intelligent scholar.

In 1841, Sir William Napier, who had a Deaf son as a private pupil of Bingham, joined with Archdeacon Bather and other wealthy parents to persuade Bingham to retire from being headmaster of the Old Trafford school and open a private school. Bingham accepted after much thought and opened a private school for the Deaf in Rugby. Bather followed his headmaster and stayed there until 1845 when he left school.

Bather's father had contacts in London and he sent his son to a conveyancer's office to read law. However, in 1847, Bather was appointed to a clerkship in the office of the Accountant-General of the Navy and did very well in his role. In fact, Bather's work was so impressive that when the Crimean War broke out in 1854, he was placed in charge of an important branch of that department of the Navy which dealt with claims for transport ships for the service of the war. Bather's selection caused outrage in certain high circles and the Government was attacked in the House of Commons by the chairman of a large shipping company on the supposition that a deaf and partially dumb gentleman was incapable of discharging the duties of such an office.

As reported in Hansard (March 23 1855, Vol. 240, Col. 2028), the First Lord of the Admiralty, Sir James Graham, defended the appointment on the ground of Bather's special fitness for the task. At the next annual meeting of the shipping company, the chairman stated that he wished to make the *amende honorable* to a deaf gentleman whom he had unintentionally injured. The claims of the company, the chairman said, was never before been so expeditiously and satisfactorily discharged as they had been under Bather's administration, and he moved a resolution conveying to Bather the acknowledgement of the company to this effect.

Bather continued in office and in due time attained the position of Assistant Accountant-General of the Navy. Bather had been informed by more than one First Lord of the Admiralty that had it not been for his deafness he would have been selected for the office of Accountant-General of the Navy.

Bather never lost interest in the Deaf community at any time during his life, even though he was more renowned and admired among the hearing than the Deaf! Bather was one of the few Deaf persons who were able to give evidence before the Royal Commission appointed in 1885-86 "to investigate and report on their condition"; Bather gave evidence mainly in writing, and spoke very little. Bather was, however, looked up to by the Deaf community in London as one who had proved himself an unswerving friend. According to an obituary in the *Quarterly Review of Deaf-Mute Education (1892, 3, 123-127)*, Bather was largely instrumental in maintaining and developing the Royal Association in Aid of the Deaf and Dumb (RADD), of which he was honorary secretary for nearly 40 years. During his time with the RADD, Bather played a leading part in the construction of St. Saviour's Church for the Deaf in Oxford Street, London. His brother-in-law, Sir A. W. Blomfield, was the architect.

Arthur Bather married first in 1862 Lucy Elizabeth Blomfield, daughter of the Bishop of London, by whom he had one son, Francis A. Bather, BA., who worked as an assistant in the South Kensington Museum; and secondly, in 1870, Caroline Sophia Bentham, daughter of Colonel Bentham, by whom he had another son, Rowland, a midshipman in the Navy.

Bather retired from his occupation in 1890 with a good pension and he went to live in Meole Brace Hall near Shrewsbury. However, he did not enjoy his retirement for much longer and met his demise in his 63rd year on 25 July 1892.

Raymond Lee

George Beale
1849-1928

George Beale was born on 4 April 1849 at Croxteth Park, the seat of the Earl of Sefton, under whom his father held an important position of trust for many years. He became deaf at the early age of two years, having caught fever whilst staying at a hotel in Scotland, so that, though not a congenital deaf-mute, he was practically a mute, never having enjoyed the faculty of speech. When eight years old, he was sent to the School for the Deaf and Dumb in Oxford Street, Liverpool, where he was taught wholly under the manual method.

On leaving school, he was apprenticed to a well-known firm of Liverpool artists. Whilst serving his term of apprenticeship he could not manage to attend any of the meetings, religious or secular, of the Adult Deaf and Dumb Society, as there was no means of transport and he always had to return to his distant home in the evenings. Immediately after finishing his apprenticeship, he joined another local firm of lithographic artists for the special purpose of obtaining greater proficiency in his own line of work. He then set up his own business, which was quite successful, but then the advances made in photographic processes revolutionised the trade to such an extent that he started to seek alternative employment.

When his father retired and settled on the outskirts of Liverpool, George was able to identify himself more closely with the work of the Adult Deaf. His intellectual power and business like capacity soon attracted notice and honour from those with whom he began to associate, and who almost immediately unanimously elected him a member of the committee, and on one occasion to act as the Deaf Society's chairman.

In April 1894, George was appointed Superintendent of the North Staffordshire Adult Deaf and Dumb Society, which was then, and also for some years afterwards, unable to carry on its proper work for want of adequate rooms. These were obtained in June 1917, through his efforts, with the help of A. J. Story who was later to be General Secretary of the National Institute for the Deaf for many years, but who was then Headmaster of the Stoke School for the Deaf and Blind. The use of these premises enabled Deaf people in Stoke to have a fine centre.

However, George Beale was unable to enjoy his new offices for long. He was forced to retire through ill health in September of the same year; he then suffered a breakdown hastened by the shock of the death of his only son, aged 24 years.

George died on 17 January 1928.

Maureen A. Jackson

Henry Blenkarne Beale
1845-1921

Henry B. Beale was born in Bishopsgate, City of London, on 20 September 1845. His father, Miles Beale, was a London surgeon with considerable practice. At seven years of age, Henry went to Merchant Taylors' School, in Charterhouse Square, City of London, and whilst there, he caught scarlet fever, which caused him to become totally deaf. Consequently he stayed at home, and was taught by his elder sister, Dorothy, until he was twelve, after which he was left on his own. To further his education, Henry turned to his father's library where he read literature. He learned to communicate using the manual method. At the age of 13, Henry began engraving and was apprenticed to the well-known engraver Mr. William J. Linton. On completion of his apprenticeship, he continued working for Linton.

When Mr. Linton left for the U.S.A. in 1866, Henry Beale went to Toronto to set up his business and his brother followed him a year later. Frederick Brigden, who became deaf at 11, and who was also one of Linton's apprentices in London for a short time, arrived in 1872, and partnered with Henry Beale in the establishment of the Toronto Engraving Company, which was the first ever wood engraving business in Canada. It was a very successful business. During his leisure time, Henry was a missionary to the deaf and dumb in Toronto. Beale and his family then returned to England after retiring from his engraving business in 1886 and left Brigden to take over the company. Previously, he married Miss Susan Martin, a deaf lady, and had six hearing children.

H. B. Beale was a man of scholarly attainments, a poet and a lover of Nature and this love is reflected in many of his poems. He was a first class chess player of the same calibre as Leigh Hossell whom he beat once in a challenge match. Broad shouldered and over six feet tall, he was a familiar sight at BDDA Congresses. During the 1890s, he was a frequent contributor to *The British Deaf-Mute* and having visited many British oral schools for the deaf, he launched a scathing attack on oralists in his article *Fanatics*. His favourite quote was *There is no good in oralism for born-mutes*.

H. B. Beale died on 1 January 1921 at his home in Minchinampton, near Stroud, Gloucestershire.

Anthony J. Boyce

Alexander Bilibin
1903-1971

Alexander Bilibin was born in Russia in 1903 to Ivan Bilibin, a talented Russian artist, and an English mother. After a double mastoid operation at the age of 9, Alexander was sent to the Ince Jones Oral School for Deaf Boys at Northampton. From the outset Alexander showed a brilliant aptitude for art and when he left school, at which he passed the Oxford Junior Examination, a considerable achievement for a deaf boy in those days, he went to the Central High School for Arts and Crafts in London. After this, he spent four years at the Royal Academy Schools.

It was whilst he was at the Royal Academy that he heard of a struggling deaf artist who had failed to get into the Academy. This was Alfred R. Thomson, who was later to achieve fame as a war-time artist. Alexander went to see him, and despite the fact that he was oral and relied on lipreading, and Thomson preferred to use sign language, they formed a friendship that was to last 53 years until Alexander's death. The friendship survived numerous rows due to Alexander's temperamental nature.

Alexander Bilibin's chief claim to fame was as a scenic artist in the film industry, both in England and in Hollywood. He also did portraits and other mural work, which were frequently exhibited at the Royal Academy. He was, for instance, largely responsible for the mural decorations on the old Cunard ocean liner *Queen Mary*. During the war some of his camouflage work, though little known, was very valuable, showing both originality and versatility.

Alexander Bilibin died in 1971, three weeks after suffering his third heart attack. Few people attended his funeral, but his great friend A. R. Thomson was one of those who attended.

Peter W. Jackson

Alexander Blackwood
1805-1890

Alexander Blackwood was born in Edinburgh on 22 March 1805. He was the eldest child of John Blackwood, a silk mercer and one of the founders of the renowned firm of Messrs. T. and J. Blackwood. Alexander was not born deaf, but he gradually lost his hearing when he was about seven years old, through an attack of scarlet fever.

Alexander later attended the Edinburgh Institution for the Deaf and Dumb under Robert Kinniburgh for his education. Alexander joined some illustrious pupils such as Joseph Turner, John Carmichael and Alexander Atkinson among others who were present at the school. After leaving school, he went to work in the family business and very little is known of him until June 1830 when Alexander teamed up with other notable deaf persons such as Matthew Robert Burns, Joseph Turner and Walter Geikie to form a small meeting group. Alexander was instrumental in obtaining the first premises, Lady Stairs Close, off High Street in Edinburgh, for the group to meet. Matthew Robert Burns preached to a congregation of between thirty and forty deaf people and the group never looked back and the Edinburgh Deaf Centre still survives to the present day.

Alexander converted to Christianity and devoted his time to working with the deaf people of Edinburgh and its surrounds. In particular, Alexander paid more time attending to those suffering from poverty. He was a wealthy person and used his wealth for the group and the people involved for the next sixty years of his life. Alexander's name became famous and honoured, and his influence was felt far and near, and many, even in distant lands, owe more than they can tell to his teaching and example.

Alexander passed away in his sleep on the morning of Saturday 29 November 1890.

Raymond Lee

Frederick Allen Bloomfield, MBE
1903-1982

Frederick A. Bloomfield was one of four children of Albert James Bloomfield, a Miller's Carter, and his wife, Lilian Elizabeth. Frederick was born in Hoxne, near Eye in Suffolk on 14 September 1903, the year the Wright brothers flew their powered lightweight plane for the first time. Frederick had two brothers and one sister. He became deaf at the age of three and the cause of his deafness was unknown. His mother taught him at home in his early years before he was sent to the Royal School for the Deaf, Margate, from 1915 to 1920.

Frederick was a member of St. Bede's, Clapham, in London from 1926 when it opened as a Deaf Club and a Church for the Deaf. He was involved as a Great Britain Athletics Officer for International Games for the Deaf (IGD) in London (1935) and Stockholm (1939). One former colleague of his recalled that he went to Nuremburg (1930) as an athlete and he was a member of Belgrave Harriers in Battersea in the 1920s to 1930s.

Frederick, with the support of both E. W. Stannard, the headmaster and Physical Training Instructor of Anerley Residential School for Elder Deaf Boys, and Mr Pallate, an athletic coach from Herne Hill Harriers, trained promising young deaf competitors on the school grounds. They were prepared for the forthcoming IGD in Brussels (1953) and Milan (1957); as a result two athletes gained gold medals in Men's 100m and 800m in Brussels.

Frederick married Ivy Margaret Trendle in North London in 1930 and the marriage issued two daughters. He was employed at Roehampton Hospital in South London all his working life where he engaged in creating artificial limbs. There were several deaf employees working at the same hospital.

In 1930, along with other Deaf members, he founded the British Deaf Amateur Sports Association's (BDASA) Athletics Section. Frederick did a great deal of work to promote sport and recreational facilities for Deaf people, especially in London. He was Vice-President of the Federation of London Deaf Clubs (FLDC) and was the Chair of Clapham Deaf Social and Sports Club for some time.

During the war he was unable to join the armed services, but he joined the Air Raid Precautions, known as A.R.P., as a warden and gave invaluable service in reserve operations in his locality. In 1946, he became an executive member of the BDASA. He was Honorary Treasurer in 1950, followed by Honorary General Secretary in 1958, Chairman from 1970 to 1974 and Vice-Chairman for two years from 1976. He was with the British Deaf Sports Council (BDSC) for over forty years. He was elected a member of Comité International des Sports Silencieux, known as CISS, in Washington in 1965 and was a President of the International Football Commission for eight years. He was an expert interpreter of Gestuno Sign Language for foreign guests at the BDA Conferences.

24

Frederick was honoured with the Member of the British Empire medal (MBE) for his splendid services to Deaf Sport, but said at the time of his investiture that he accepted it on behalf of Deaf people, to show the world what Deaf people could achieve given the incentive. He was honoured for his lifelong services to Deaf Sport, both at home and abroad as listed below: -

The Bronze Medal and Diploma from CISS in Helsinki in1961.
Pewter Salver from Royale Federation Sportive des Muets de Belgigue.
The Gold Medal from Commune de Saint Josse Noods of Brussels.
The Medal of Honour from the British Deaf Association in 1976.
The Medal of Honour from the British Deaf Sports Council.

Frederick attended twelve IGDs and World Games for the Deaf, both as a participant and as an official from 1931 to 1939 and 1949 to 1977.

Frederick died at his home in Wimbledon Park, London, on 3 September 1982 after a long illness suffering from cancer. He was cremated at Tooting Crematorium.

Geoffrey J. Eagling

Hiram J. Blount
1870-1935

Hiram J. Blount was the son of Monzo Samuel Blount, a lawyer, and his wife, Harriet (née Green). He was born at home in Queen Street in Ilkeston, Derbyshire, on 29 March 1870. The family moved to Nottingham three years later. He attended St. Anne's Church School and during that time he became deaf at the age of five years when he had a fall and fractured his chin bone. He was educated from the age of eleven at the London Asylum for the Deaf and Dumb under the oral system enforced by Dr. Richard Elliott, the headmaster. Hiram later went to a temporary school in Ramsgate, a branch of Margate Institution for the Deaf and Dumb. He became head boy and received no less than 20 school prizes, as well as winning high commendation for conduct. He left school where he was 15 years old and attended a School Board deaf class in Nottingham for a few months in 1885 that was conducted by Mr. C. H. Green. Hiram taught himself Greek and gained two diplomas for shorthand. After the completion of his education, he was apprenticed to a tailor.

After completing his apprenticeship, he set up a small tailoring business in Nottingham on his own account in 1890, but he gave it up eight years later. During his working career, he was involved with the local Mission to the Deaf. He was a lay reader to the Deaf at the age of nineteen and was later elected Honorary Treasurer to Nottingham Deaf Social Club. He conducted classes as assistant teacher at the School Board Evening Continuation School for the Deaf, assisted a missionary superintendent for four years and became missionary superintendent in 1894 after the resignation of his superior.

In February 1898, he relinquished his tailoring business and devoted his time to the Nottingham Adult Deaf and Dumb Institute for which he had been treasurer for eight years. In 1899, he was invited to take up the post of missioner at Plymouth and he accepted it. He worked at home as a part time missioner to the Deaf and Dumb, in Bedford Street, Plymouth, and moved to 11 Holdsworth Street in Plymouth two years later when new premises were secured.

Hiram returned to his native hometown to marry Margaret Emily, the youngest deaf daughter of Thomas Frederick James, at St. Mary's Church in Nottingham on 5 April 1899. They bore three known hearing children of whom two sons, John and Samuel, became teachers of the Deaf. John was a resident master of Royal School for Deaf Children in Margate, and thence at Anerley Residential School for Elder Deaf Boys. He eventually became headmaster of Rayners School for the Deaf in Penn, Buckinghamshire. Samuel joined the teaching staff at Margate and was later appointed headmaster of a new school in 1954, Nutfield Priory Secondary School for the Deaf in Redhill, Surrey. His wife, Margaret James, became deaf at the age of 7 years when she suffered a severe illness.

It is interesting to note that as missioner of the Deaf and Dumb, Hiram cycled over 1000 miles around Devon and across the River Tamar into Cornwall and travelled as far as Truro, St. Austell and

Camborne to visit his clients and hold monthly meetings in 1916. He doubled the distance a year later. He bought a new motorcycle in around 1920 in order to reduce travelling time and overnight expenses and continued his work all over Devon and Cornwall at his own expense. Hiram had an accident in 1928 when the sidecar became unattached from his motorcycle and he received a sustained a fractured skull. He resumed his employment six months later.

Hiram was in charge of the mission at Plymouth for 34 years and was the founder of the Cornish Deaf and Dumb Mission. When he retired on health grounds in 1933, he continued to work for the Church of England organisation. William Archer took over his role.

Hiram and his wife resided at 26 Peverell Terrace, Plymouth, at the time of his death on 23 November 1935 at the Plymouth City Hospital. He was 65 years old. He was buried in Plymouth Old Cemetery four days later.

Geoffrey J. Eagling

Edward Bone
c.1570 -?

It was about 1595, and the scene was the marketplace in the old town of Truro in Cornwall, and the Town Crier was about to give one of his regular announcements. A young man with a sharp instinct for news pushed his way through the crowd and planted himself directly in front of the speaker. The townsfolk were used to his ways and let him through to stand in his usual place. As the Town Crier spoke, the young man watched him intently, taking in all that was said. Once the speeches were over, the young man would leave and hurry to Ladcock, the home of his Master, Peter Courtney (1559-1605), who was the Member of Parliament for the county, and repeat to him in very effective sign language what had been said in the marketplace. In this manner, his Master was kept well informed of the goings-on in his constituency.

When his immediate services were no longer needed, he would walk eight miles across to the nearby village of Merther and meet with another young man. Together, these two young men would communicate with much hearty laughter in a style of sign language different to that which the first young man had used to communicate with his Master.

This young man was named Edward Bone, and he was Courtney's manservant. He had a Deaf brother who had what nowadays would be called 'learning difficulties'. He was unpopular with the rest of the servants because he would report to the Master any lewd behaviour. His Deaf friend was named John Kempe, who was related to the Courtneys by marriage, and their meetings were recorded in a book written by Richard Carew (1555-1620), *A Survey of Cornwall*. His disinterested observation is the first written independent account in Britain of how a deaf person could lip-read, communicate with his hearing employer by signs, and seek out another deaf person and communicate in a sign language not readily understood by most hearing people.

Bone is said by Carew to be *'assisted with so firme a memorie, that hee would not onely know any partie whome hee had once seene, for ever after, but also make him knowne to any other by some speciall observation, and difference'*, and his sign language conversation with Kempe is referred to by Carew as *'strange and often earnest tokenings'* which were not understood by hearing people.

The use of these phrases, and description of communication systems, suggest that Edward Bone, although an ordinary manservant, had language and intelligence enough to adapt his daily lifestyle so that he could lipread as well, use a form of Signed English with his employer, and BSL with other deaf people, and as Deaf people do today, give people signed names for easy reference in conversation with others.

Peter W. Jackson

28

Mika Brojer
1945-1998

Mika Brojer was born deaf in Balham, South London, to a Jewish family who ran a bakery business in the area. At the age of 4 years, he started to attend the Jewish School for the Deaf which was close to his home. He completed his education at Burwood Park Technical Secondary School, which he attended from the age of 12-16. His first serious involvement in the Deaf World was through drama. In 1969, he was recruited into the RNID Mime Group under the management of Pat Keysell. His best achievement was the *Solo Mime* in which he acted after the fashion of Marcel Marceau, the famous French mime artiste. He also starred in John Steinbeck's *The Pearl* which was about a poor fisherman. His large eyes and expressive face and his long, lean and mobile body served him in good stead. He left the company in 1974 when the British Theatre of the Deaf was formed and joined the Scope Deaf Youth Club in Lewisham, South London, doing comedy sketches.

Mika Brojer joined the Advice Service for Deaf People in 1993 that was set up by the Royal Association in Aid of Deaf People. Before being selected for the post, his involvement with Deaf people was already widely known and therefore he was the ideal choice to give help and advice. He was also a voluntary support worker for elderly deafblind people. His main venue for the work was at the Green Lanes Deaf Club in North London and there he founded the Job Club in which his involvement was finding work for Deaf people, giving advice and troubleshooting where problems existed at their employment. He had a lot of patience and, thereby, won much esteem among those who sought his help. He also dealt with benefit claims and succeeded in various cases. With Deaf people he enabled them to have confidence and pride in themselves and to push their desires to be autonomous.

He died on 30 April 1998 from cancer, which also killed his Deaf sister, Oriella, and nephew Ben Steiner, who was a talented interpreter. All died in the prime of their lives. The RAD launched the Mika Brojer Memorial Fund in his memory.

Arthur F. Dimmock

James Burke
1809-1845

The days of Prize Ring fighting were a brutal business, fought under rules which enabled men to inflict terrible injuries on each other, and fights were fought to a finish when a man was downed and had been battered into insensibility. It might therefore be expected that many contests would provide fatalities, but this was not the case. All the more tragic therefore that one of the earliest deaths in boxing, and perhaps the most controversial, resulted from a fight in which a deaf boxer took part.

James 'Deaf' Burke, or the 'Deaf Un' as he was generally known, was born in Westminster, London, on 8 December 1809, and became orphaned in early childhood. He became a gutter urchin who haunted the London waterfront.

One day, to escape heavy rain, he wandered into a tavern called the 'Spotted Dog' which was kept by Joe Parrish, a veteran fighter, who was impressed with the young lad – then aged 16 – and began to teach him the science of the ring. Although he could not read or write, Burke learnt fast, but it was not until he was nearly 19, when Parrish gave him his first fight. This was against an Irish man named Ned Murphy. They fought 50 rounds, only to have the fight stopped because of darkness. However, Burke's outstanding performance had boxing enthusiasts agog with excitement and wanting more. After this, Burke went on to win 3 out of 4 fights in less than a year, and in 1828 was matched with William Fitzmaurice at Harpenden, which went 106 rounds and lasted 3 hours.

Before his fight with Fitzmaurice took place, Burke achieved fame in entirely different circumstances. He became a hero when he rescued a number of people from a blazing house fire. A newspaper described his feat as follows:

He (Burke) dashed into the blazing furnace with reckless abandon, making trip after trip until he had rescued many persons. He carried out a child, then went back and brought out another, and third time carried a woman to safety. Again and again, he returned amongst the debris and succeeded in bringing out two more children, one of whom died in his arms.

In his next fight, he lost to Bill Cousens after 111 rounds, but instead of being discouraged, went on to beat all foes in the next ten years.

When Jem Ward, the champion, announced his retirement in 1833, James Burke claimed the title and this angered an Irishman called Simon Byrne, who had fought and lost to Ward in 1831.

Byrne was not a particularly big man, standing only 5 feet 9 inches and weighing 13 stone, but Deaf Burke was even smaller at 5 feet 8½ inches, and 12 stone 7 lbs., so the Irishman felt he was onto a good thing. It was a hard, bloody fight lasting 3 hours and 16 minutes (this time still stands as a world record for a championship fight) before Burke knocked out Byrne with a tremendous punch, and became recognised champion. Byrne was carried away from the ring unconscious and died three days later without coming out of his coma. The deaf boxer and all those connected with the fight were arrested and charged with manslaughter. However, conflicting opinions of several doctors gained their acquittals.

However, the tragedy upset Burke and he became convinced people regarded him as a murderer, and to get away from the situation, he sailed across to the United States. He was the first person to bring Prize Ring fighting to America, where he had a fight with a man called Connell, and demolished him in 10 minutes. News spread like wildfire, but it brought Burke unexpected trouble in that a man called Samuel O'Rourke claimed to be a friend of the dead Byrne and challenged Burke to a fight, which Burke did not want. Unable to avoid it, however, he faced O'Rourke in New Orleans where it became apparent that the Irishman had no idea of fighting; Burke was able to hit him at will.

This made the local mob angry. Knives were drawn, and Burke's life was threatened as he punched O'Rourke into helplessness. Suddenly the ropes were cut, and the ring was invaded and Burke had to fight for his life. Somehow, he got hold of a Bowie knife and managed to escape. Someone grabbed his arm and led him to a waiting horse on which he galloped away, leaving behind his winnings.

From New Orleans, Burke went to New York where he had several fights before returning to England in 1837 to face William 'Bold Bendigo' Thompson. Burke was not in the best of condition and had lost his fighting spirit because of his troubles with Byrne and O'Rourke. In the 10th round, he was ruled out for a foul, and lost his world championship. He reclaimed it when Bold Bendigo retired, but lost it again to Mike Ward when the crowd broke into the ring to save Ward from further punishment. That was on 22 September 1840 at Lillingstone Level, Oxfordshire.

Burke never fought again, becoming a stage actor advertising his magnificent physique, but excessive drinking, long fasts and many women took their toll and he died penniless of tuberculosis in a lane off Waterloo Road, London, in 1845.

Peter W. Jackson

AN
HISTORICAL
AND
CHRONOLOGICAL
REMEMBRANCER
OF
ALL REMARKABLE OCCURRENCES,
FROM THE
CREATION TO THIS PRESENT YEAR
OF OUR LORD, 1775.

THE
LIVES AND ACTIONS
OF THE GREATEST
PATRIARCHS, PHILOSOPHERS, HEROES,
HEROINES, MONARCHS, &c.

AMONGST THE

JEWS, GREEKS, ROMANS, SAXONS, DANES,
BRITONS, SCOTS AND IRISH.

WITH

AN ALPHABETICAL INDEX.

BY

JOHN BURNS, OF MONAGHAN,
WHO WAS BORN DEAF AND DUMB.

DUBLIN:
PRINTED FOR THE AUTHOR, 1775.

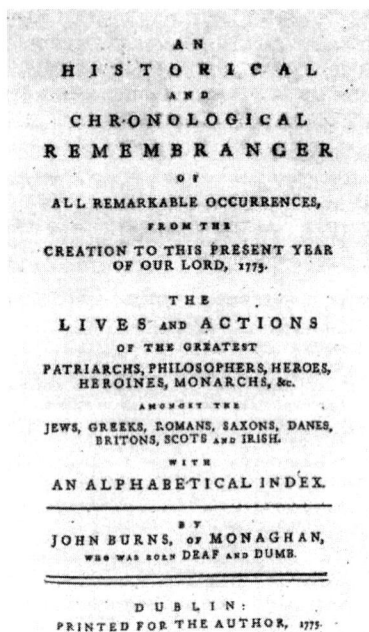

John Burns
c1740-1785

John Burns was born deaf and dumb of humble stock in Monaghan, Ireland, in about the year 1740 and was orphaned before he attained the age of ten, by which time it was discovered that he was highly intelligent. He was taught to read and write and by studiously applying himself to his learning, he acquired a competent knowledge of arithmetic, geography, history and chronology. This brought him to the attention of a learned priest who instructed Burns in the principles of religion so as to qualify him for the Holy Sacrament.

Little is known of John Burns' background, but he had a wife who died young and left him two children to bring up. His first occupation was that of a pedlar and then he became a shopkeeper. He might have led a comfortable life providing for his children had he not been imprisoned for debt.

Released from prison and driven by the need to provide for his children, Burns turned to writing and wrote what is now a classic in Irish literary history, *An Historical and Chronological Remembrancer*. Published in 1775, it had over 1000 subscribers. A rare copy of his book surfaced in the Antiquarian Shop in Dublin in 1998 where it was sold for £65. Another copy is kept in the Gilbert Library in Dublin as a permanent testimony to this remarkable self-taught writer.

John Burns is believed to have died in his native Monaghan in about 1785, and has his place in Deaf History as the earliest known Irish Deaf author.

David Breslin

Matthew Robert Burns
1798-1880

Matthew Robert Burns was born in Dundee, Scotland, on 10 November 1798, a son of a Major in the 84th Regiment of Foot, and his mother was a daughter of a Lombard Street Banker. He was born deaf and acquired severe speech impediments. He was very mischievous as a young boy and delighted in playing practical pranks, which included emptying a bucket of water over the head of a person who was unfortunate enough to walk under a tree.

Matthew was initially educated by his mother at home but later attended a local day school for the hearing where he became well educated. Matthew attributed the fact that he was able to progress educationally to mixing with hearing children and learning the ordinary idioms of society, as well as participating in almost everything at school. After a few years, Matthew was sent by his parents to London to receive an education as a private pupil of Dr. Joseph Watson at The Asylum for the Deaf and Dumb in the Kent Road. Very little is known of Matthew until 13 June 1830, when a new place of worship for the deaf was opened in Edinburgh and Matthew was one of the founders and he managed the place for a few years.

Matthew was reported in the *Edinburgh Long Magazine* (1831) to have endeavoured to establish a Sabbath School for the deaf at Dundee. [The sixth report of *The Edinburgh Deaf and Dumb Benevolent Society* mentioned the Society's regret the Matthew Robert Burns had to part from their company due to his appointment as headmaster at "Dundee".]

In 1832, Matthew opened a day school at Carruber's Close Chapel in Edinburgh, assisted by Charles Buchan and Alexander Campbell, who were both deaf. Matthew left Edinburgh in 1834 for Aberdeen when he was appointed as headmaster of the Aberdeen Institution for the Deaf and Dumb. He stayed in the post for seven years and was assisted by his sister, who was qualified as an assistant and teacher.

Matthew left Aberdeen in 1841 and headed for Bristol to become the first principal of a newly founded Bristol Institution for the Deaf and Dumb in Tyndall's Park. He remained there only for a little over two years, being forced to leave due to hostile circumstances. His reasons for leaving remain a mystery to this day; Bristol people were known to be highly disinterested in the education of the deaf in those days and did not contribute much for the instruction of their deaf children by ignoring truancy, mischief and care of deaf children. When comparing Bristol with Glasgow, Matthew described the former as "heathen Bristol". His resignation was regretted by the committee of the school and this was noted in August 1843 when the secretary of the Bristol Society, Dr. Kay, wrote, accepting Mr. Burns' resignation, about his "zealous and efficient services as the instructor, and regret at their loss". Another theory put forward for Matthew's abrupt decision to resign was that he made numerous enemies in the city, who could not stand his uprightness and determination to impose the same on their deaf children. The event affected Matthew badly and he never taught again.

The following year in March 1844, Matthew was engaged by the committee of the then "Adult Institution for providing Employment for the Deaf and Dumb" for a year until June 1845, when he was obliged to join the old congregation who appointed him as biblical instructor and assistant secretary. At the beginning of his appointment, the Rev. Robert Simson was his superior and spent most of his time preaching to the deaf, therefore rendering Matthew's role as "minimalist with not much public work to do". However, patience paid off when in 1849 Matthew was made exclusively the head, as honorary secretary and paid instructor.

Between 1849 and 1865, Matthew was in the prime of his preaching powers and participated actively with most Deaf Temperance Societies, which preached and attacked the use and abuse of alcohol.

In 1866, owing to increasing old age and infirmity, Mr. Burns' role as honorary secretary was taken over by J. P. Gloyn and he quite suddenly plunged into obscurity. Matthew lived during his twilight years on an income of £30-£40 per annum, a portion of which income was a tardy acknowledgement by the then Association of his just services. There was uproar about his treatment and many deaf people felt that a cruel wrong on the part of the Association was inflicted on Matthew. His friends in London and Scotland alike appeared to forget about him.

The Rev. F. W. Gilby, a son of deaf parents and a Missioner with the Deaf, once reported that Mr. Burns frequently called to see his deaf parents and received as much from them as from any other quarter, in money and comforts, until he died of bronchitis in Barnsbury on 21 January 1880, at the age of 82.

The Deaf erected a tablet to Matthew's memory in St. Saviour's Church in Oxford Street, London. But when the church was demolished and transferred to Acton, the tablet was, like Matthew Robert Burns, lost forever.

Raymond Lee

Helen Marion Burnside
1844-1920

Helen Marion Burnside was born in Bromley Hall, Middlesex. For a large part of her life, she lived and worked with Miss Rosa Nouchette Carey, the novelist, in Surrey.

Up to the time of losing her hearing through scarlet fever at the age of ten, her real interest was towards music as her ambition was to become a composer. This, of course, she had to give up, but when, a few years afterwards, she commenced writing poetry, she had a habit of first picking out song or hymn tunes on a piano, until she had got hold of a rhythm or metre that pleased her. A small volume of these verses was published in 1864, one or two of which were set to music. This suggested the writing of other lyrics and poems for magazines. From then onwards, a great many verses were published, mostly as Christmas Card verses and about 150 of her songs set to music.

Helen also developed a strong love for art, and just before the publication of her first book of verses, she succeeded in getting one of her pictures hung at the Royal Academy. For nine years she also occupied the post of designer to the Royal School of Art (Needlework), occasionally painting vellum-bound books. After leaving the Royal School of Art (Needlework), she spent a period editing for Messrs. Raphael Tuck and Co., a firm of publishers of children's books, and wrote many stories and verses for children in the gift books issued by that enterprising firm. She also wrote for leading juvenile magazines.

A poor lip-reader, she came to use the manual alphabet all her life after becoming deaf and insisted that all her many friends learnt this method to communicate with her. She had neither the time nor the inclination to learn to lipread or to use ear trumpets when those gadgets became fashionable.

Helen Burnside became better known as the "Christmas Card-Laureate", writing Christmas poems for nearly thirty-seven years at the rate of something like 200 a year. In an interview, Miss Burnside confessed that she was extremely proud of the title "Christmas Card-Laureate". She said:-

> *I do not know how I came by it, but even the real Laureate could not wear his official crown more proudly than I do the homely one conferred upon me by the public. I began writing verses when between twelve and thirteen years of age. Previous to this, I had become, and still am, totally deaf from scarlet fever. Up to that time music was my strongest attraction, and it was my childish ambition to become a composer. Having to give up this through deafness was probably the reason why I took to verse writing as another outlet for music. For it was a desire to write words for music which in the first instance induced me to try. When I first began, Christmas verses were of a very elementary character, and I aimed at improving the standard.*

Miss Burnside's verses were famous the world over, one of her best being:-

> *Year after year across the earth*
> *The Christmas story echoes still;*
> *Glad tidings ring to every hearth*
> *Of God's sweet mercy and good-will,*
> *Peace and good-will from heaven above -*
> *Peace and good-will to great and small -*
> *Oh, may "Great Joy" from realms of love*
> *This Christmas Day bless one and all!*

Maureen A. Jackson

Duncan Campbell
1680-1730

The story of Duncan Campbell is both quite bizarre and partly clouded in doubt about its veracity. The question of who wrote the story still remains: Daniel Defoe was accredited as the author of both *The History of the Life and Adventures of Mr Duncan Campbell* (1720) and *Secret Memoirs of the late Mr Duncan Campbell* (1732), but literary historians attribute the authorship to one Grub Street writer, William Bond. The latter work was said to be written by Duncan Campbell himself but published posthumously by others. Whatever the situation, the fact that Duncan Campbell actually existed is not disputed: in 1730, he resided in Exeter Court, beside the Savoy in the Strand (London).

Duncan Campbell was born in Lapland in 1680 to Archibald Campbell and his Lapland wife. Within two years, Duncan's mother died and Duncan was found to be deaf and it was always presumed that he was born deaf and dumb. Archibald returned home to the Shetland Isles with Duncan. In 1683, Archibald married again and the family moved to the Western Isles and Duncan's new stepmother raised him. In 1684, Campbell was still unable to talk and his stepmother sought advice on educating Duncan. This came in the form of John Wallis' book and Duncan was educated under Wallis' method by a doctor undertaking the role of a private tutor when the family moved to Edinburgh in 1685. That year saw Archibald Campbell pass away.

Whilst growing up in Edinburgh, Duncan began to acquire some extraordinary powers in the ability to perceive the future and clairvoyance. People began to note young Duncan's ability and consult him. All of his predictions came true and he became a sort of miniature celebrity in his hometown. The education Duncan received served him well and he excelled in reading, writing and manualism, though Wallis' signs for consonants were somewhat odd. With his high intelligence and sharp mind, it is most likely that Duncan Campbell developed the manual alphabet to a more acceptable form and this was made clear in the manual alphabet chart that was included in the expensive versions of the 1720 book.

In 1692, Duncan's stepmother died and Duncan's uncle took him into his care. Next, Duncan was found in London in 1694, but very little was recorded until 1698 when the author wrote of meeting him again after an absence of three years. Duncan established himself as a "professional predictor" and his fame grew to such an extent that members of the wealthy classes flocked to him for predictions and have their fortunes told. The success rate of Duncan's predictions were high, judging by the satisfaction of his wealthy clients mentioned in the two books on his life and times. Queen Anne summoned Duncan on a number of occasions for consultation and was reported to be impressed with his predictions. Duncan communicated mainly in writing and gestures, but used fingerspelling whenever his clients were able to use it. Moreover, Duncan was making a fortune from his predictions and becoming a wealthy person. He was very popular with the ladies who found him charming and attractive.

Duncan's abilities were not limited to predictions, but to faith healing. There exists an affidavit of Richard Coates, dated 25 January 1725, in which the writer wrote of suffering from 'violent distemper' for four years which doctors were unable to cure. He forked out £500 in trying to find a cure but to no avail until he met Duncan Campbell. Duncan's advice and assistance resulted in the distemper being cured after a few months and the writer of the affidavit had enjoyed uninterrupted good health for 10 years since. (This occurred in 1715). There are numerous other accounts of Duncan's faith healing successes.

Duncan Campbell, in spite of his fame and wealth, had an excessive liking for alcohol that was in abundance in various taverns where he undertook his profession. There was a tale of his visit to Rotterdam where, after an evening of excessive drinking, he took to wandering about the city in "after hours", that is when the town bell tolled and no one was allowed out. This was the law at that time, but Duncan, being deaf, did not hear the bell and was not familiar with the law. He was arrested as a spy and locked in a cell. Fortunately, he was reported missing and some English diplomats were able to obtain his release, but Duncan was immediately ordered back to England. Duncan also had a reputation for fornicating with wives and daughters of his gentlemen friends in his younger days.

Duncan married a wealthy hearing widow who was closely associated with the Digby family (Sir Kenelm?). She was proficient in the manual alphabet. They both went to reside in a house in Monmouth Court for two years before moving to Drury Lane. The marriage issued two children, names as yet unknown.

Women were Duncan's forte and eventually his downfall. Ladies of the wealthy classes were falling over each other for Duncan's company and one Lady M became so jealous that she set out to destroy Duncan Campbell's reputation by calling him a "forgery", "charlatan" and "fake". His fortunes changed for the worse and he spent his last years fighting off accusations and defamations of his character and work, although he still had firm supporters. This caused Duncan to become ill and it led to his demise in 1730.

Raymond Lee

**John Carmichael
1803-1857**

John Carmichael was born on 27 December 1803 in Edinburgh. He was enrolled in the recently-opened Edinburgh Institute for the Deaf and Dumb in 1812, when he was nine years old. There are a number of references to him in school records and memoirs which show that he was known as a skilled signer, who could hold an audience and who was remembered for entertaining his friends with stories about his two passions: cock-fighting and horse-racing. One of his schoolmates, Alexander Atkinson, later wrote:

> *Carmichael had an excellent turn for drawing ... He was a handsome looking lad... a capital "fine chap", with and for us; he had an enthusiastic fancy for cock fights... he was in the habit of fixing our stare on him by gesticulating every incident of the last fight and assuming every air and movement of the combats in all their rounds up to the "Death" with striking fidelity to the "Life" ...*

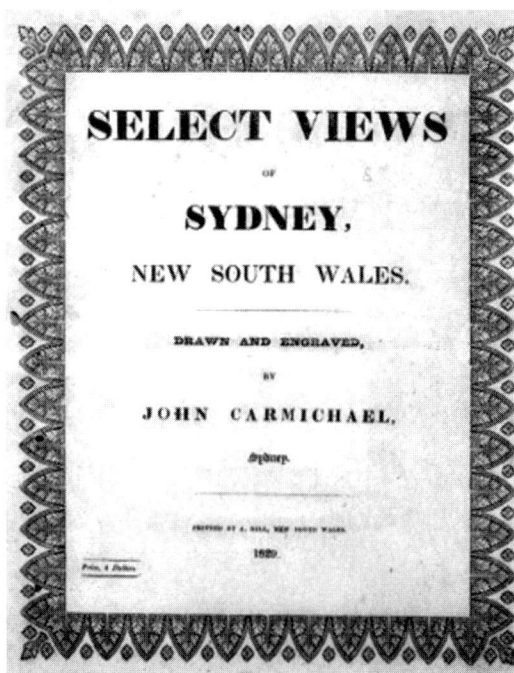

Cover page of Select Views of Sydney, New South Wales – By permission of the National Library of Australia

> *Carmichael had also a mania for horse-racing, to gratify which he was most cheerfully, since he left school, the first and last of the Edinburgh people, trudging five long miles every day in the race week to and from Musselburgh Races. He then came to us, proud of being again great in our eyes, giving rapid, yet distinct gestural pictures of the different races, horses and their riders...*

He also seems to have been an independent person who would follow his interests alone if necessary; a talented artist, and a handsome young man who was well-liked by his Deaf friends, and evidently perceived as part of the group - "with and for us". The quote contains an early statement of what made Deaf people "great in our eyes" - signing skill, the ability to hold a group of Deaf people in thrall to an eloquently signed story.

When Carmichael left school, he was apprenticed to John Horsburgh, a prominent engraver in Edinburgh, where he reached journeyman status. The Edinburgh community in which he lived would have been a stimulating and interesting one for a young Deaf man with his talents. There were other Deaf artists in the city, notably James Howe and Walter Geikie. Other Deaf men worked as engravers too, so Carmichael would have been a member of both an active Deaf community and a wider community, in which Deaf people seem to have had a fair measure of acceptance as artists and tradesmen. It is intriguing to consider what made him leave this environment and embark alone on the voyage to New South Wales, where his prospects were uncertain and Deaf people had nothing like the status and acceptance they had in his native Edinburgh.

By this time, the new colony of New South Wales was encouraging free settlers to move there and set up farms and businesses, including professions such as engraving, drafting and printing. Carmichael arrived in Sydney in October 1825 at the age of 21, on board the *Triton*. It appears he was alone as no other member of his family emigrated with him. By December that year, he was advertising his services in local newspapers, as an engraver in a style superior to any hitherto attempted in the Colony.

Carmichael obtained various commissions, including one for the governor of NSW, William Darling, but his first major work was a self-published series of engravings called *Select Views of Sydney, New South Wales*. Carmichael drew the scenes himself and then engraved them, and advertised them for sale by subscription. While Carmichael was producing the book, local newspapers reported on his progress and it was clear that he was known to be Deaf. One report in the *Australian* newspaper said that the fact that the young artist was not only Deaf, but also dumb, should also interest the public in his favour.

Around this time (1828-29), he also did some painting, mostly watercolours. One was a portrait of a well-known Aboriginal man, Bungaree, King of Port Jackson Tribe. This painting is interesting for us because someone has handwritten in the margin by John Carmichael, he was deaf and dumb. Many other contemporary artists painted Bungaree, but a recent biographer of Bungaree chose Carmichael's portrait of him for the book's cover.

During the next three decades, Carmichael came to be considered one of the most prominent engravers in the colony. He engraved scenes of Sydney and the surrounding area for commercial publications like James Maclehose's *Picture of Sydney*; and *Strangers' Guide in New South Wales*. He engraved some of the first detailed maps of Australia, and was also commissioned to engrave some postage stamps in the early 1850s. While he was completing this job, the Colonial Secretary complained that Carmichael refused to sign a bond which would have committed him to finishing the work by a certain time but in addition to being both deaf and dumb, he appears to have had a will of his own, as he absolutely refused to sign any document.

Some of Carmichael's correspondence with those who commissioned his work still survives, and it is interesting to see early examples of deaf English, which are still very recognisable today, e.g., *it was unfortunate the printing roller was broken last Monday. The printer was blame too hard printing*. Regardless of any problems he had with written English, Carmichael was clearly assertive enough to conduct his business dealings on his own, and his employers seem to have valued his services enough not to be concerned by his imperfect English.

Carmichael married in Sydney in about 1837, to a woman named Margaret. It is not clear if she was deaf too. They had several children, and his wife died in childbirth in 1851. Carmichael himself died in Sydney on 27 July 1857, a week after having been declared bankrupt. Just one year after his death, a former deaf schoolmate of Carmichael from Scotland, Thomas Pattison, arrived in Sydney and in 1860 established the first school for the deaf in Australia.

Carmichael's work can still be found in libraries and galleries in Australia. He has a respectable entry in *The Dictionary of Australian Artists* (Kerr, 1992) and has established a modest place for himself in Australian art history. It is time he now took his place in Deaf history although it is 150 years since he died, it is not too late to make him again great in our eyes.

Breda Carty, Australia

Cyril Carr
1873-1961

Walter Thomas Carr, a steel manager and later a cashier to a local steel manufacturer, and his wife Anne (née Barnsley) lived at 7 Oxford Street in Nether Hallam, about three miles west of Sheffield in Yorkshire. Their youngest son, Cyril, was born at home on 4 January 1873. Cyril's deafness was caused by a fever when he was three years old.

Cyril was educated in three different hearing schools in Sheffield before being sent to High School for Oral Deaf Boys in Northampton, where he was taught under the pure oral system. It was at this school that Cyril developed his skills in science. After leaving school, he attended the Technical School and School of Art, both in Sheffield.

When he was about nine years old, Cyril's father taught him astronomy. He soon bought himself a zinc telescope, which he used to study the map of the moon and sun. However, after two years of being disappointed with the imperfection of the telescope, which he had bought cheaply, he bought a new achromatic telescope. This instrument offered better quality and accuracy. He observed several planets at ten in the evening and was continuously working on his telescope till five in the morning, when he spotted Mercury and Saturn. He was one of the first astronomers to sight Jupiter in broad daylight.

Due to his interest in science, Cyril joined the Sheffield Microscopical Society in 1890. His microscopical research into bacteria present in tap water in his laboratory was a significant scientific development in those days. He gave lectures now and then to hearing audiences about his research. He was not involved with the Deaf community until he was over twenty when George Stephenson, a hearing missioner for the Deaf and Dumb in Sheffield, heard of his work and invited him to deliver lectures at the Sheffield Deaf and Dumb Institute. He was an oralist who did not use sign language, and lectured twice on Astronomy, with Mr. Stephenson acting as his interpreter. Cyril eventually improved his signing skills considerably every time he visited the institute.

Cyril moved to Birmingham sometime after 1898 and married Miss Jessie Saddick on 22 March 1913 at St. Anne's Moseley in Birmingham. She was the daughter of George Saddick, of 13 Sholebottle Terrace, Leeds. In Birmingham, he worked as a dental mechanic and he qualified as a dentist on 27 July 1923. He is the first known deaf person to achieve this distinction, and practised as a dentist until his retirement in 1938.

Cyril Carr died in Birmingham on 27 June 1961.

Geoffrey J. Eagling & David Whiston

William Spencer Cavendish,
6th Duke of Devonshire
1790-1858

William Spencer Cavendish, sixth Duke of Devonshire, was born in Paris on 21 May 1790. Called Hart by his family and always known by his successors as the Bachelor Duke, he inherited Chatsworth together with nearly 200,000 acres of land in England and Ireland, at the age of twenty one, when he succeeded his father in 1811. Though in opposition to the Government of the day, he was immediately appointed Lord-Lieutenant of Derbyshire.

He was educated at Harrow and Cambridge, and became deaf in early childhood, which caused him to become studious. He was said to have had a great sense of humour, which made him both funny and sad, an irresistible combination which led him to be a great host at times. His embassy to the coronation of Tsar Nicholas in Moscow in 1825 (which cost him £50,000 more than the sum allowed by the government) was famous for its splendour, and his entertainments in Derbyshire, London and Ireland were no less magnificent.

Princess Victoria came to stay at Chatsworth in 1832, and later when she was Queen in 1843. He gave many events, taking immense trouble to make his guests enjoy themselves.

The Duke was unusual for a Cavendish in that he was not a politician, although he interested himself in Irish questions, keenly supported the Reform Bill of 1832 and was a willing champion of anyone he thought unjustly treated. Neither, after a short spell as Lord Chamberlain, did he wish to be a courtier. His life, his work and leisure was taken up with Chatsworth and the other houses, and with his friends. He devoted himself to an immense rebuilding and renovation programme at Chatsworth House, Derbyshire, where he loved to spend many hours in the library.

It was he, the 6th Duke, that turned Chatsworth into one of the biggest tourist attractions in the country today. His chief fame rests not on any achievement of his own, but on that of his protégé, Sir Joseph Paxton. Paxton was a young gardener at Chatsworth when, encouraged by the 6th Duke, he built a giant conservatory 300 feet long, 145 feet wide by 60 feet high which soon attracted the world's attention and led to Paxton being commissioned to build the Crystal Palace for the Exhibition of 1851. (The conservatory at Chatsworth was sadly demolished after the first World War, but many of Paxton's improvements still remain to be seen.)

The 6th Duke never married, and died in 1858, a rather disappointed and unhappy man.

The connection of deafness with the Dukes of Devonshire persists to this day: the 11th Duke is Patron of the National Deaf Children's Society, and also of the Royal School for the Deaf, Derby. It is through the generosity of the 11th Duke that the Duke's Barn Countryside Centre, a marvellous study and conference centre on the Chatsworth estate, was presented to the school in 1986.

Peter W. Jackson

Jack Clemo
1916-1994

Jack Clemo was born in 1916 in a stern granite cottage in the hamlet of Goonamarris in Cornwall's remote clay country. By the age of 5, Jack was starting to lose his vision, and by the age of 16, he was also starting to lose his hearing. He was completely deaf at age 19 and totally blind by the time he was 30. The bleak Cornish clay landscape in which he grew up made him a hard and uncompromising man. His deeply religious mother further hardened in him beliefs about religion that were anathema to other people in the local community and this isolated him.

Even before he was totally deaf and blind, Clemo was writing poetry and other philosophical works. His views did not endear himself to his neighbours, especially when they attracted to Goonamarris other writers holding similar views. As a writer, Clemo was always preaching the message that there was a personal God whose will directed the destiny of each individual. He believed that the way to a spiritual experience of God was through the dark communication of two people in sex - a view that was not popular in his small village community.

Jack Clemo married late in life, at the age of 52, to a Ruth Peaty, who was herself 45 years old and another writer. He went to live with her at her home in Weymouth, where he continued to write poetry and had his biography written by Sally Magnusson. He died peacefully in his sleep in the rented cottage that was his home in Weymouth in 1994.

Peter W. Jackson

"West View of Merrion-Square"
by Samuel Close

Samuel Close
c1740-1807

Samuel Close was born deaf in Dublin around 1740, but little is known about his early years or his education. From 1770 to 1780, he carried out a business as an engraver and jeweller at The Ring and Pearl, Upper Blind Quay, Dublin. He did numerous engravings and illustrations for books and magazines, but owing to his intemperate habits, he earned very little.

The *Hibernian Magazine* contained many plates by Samuel Close, such as four small ovals coloured in brown-lint illustration, *Morning, Afternoon, Evening,* and *Night (1794),* which he copied from large coloured pictures. He also did two views of *The Hot House & Green House at Bellevue,* and *Bellevue in the County Wicklow* (both in 1795), besides doing numerous portraits, including an oval of *General Sir Ralph Abercrombie,* a Scotsman who was involved in the peace negotiations with the United Irishmen in the 1798 Rebellion.

At least fifteen other illustration plates by Samuel Close still survive, two of which are held by the National Gallery of Ireland. Others are in private collections. Samuel may have been a contemporary of the Deaf engraver John Duff, as they lived in the same street at around the same time. Walter G. Strickland, who commented favourably on Samuel's engraving talent, mentions him in the 1913 edition of *A Dictionary of Irish Artists.*

Samuel married Elizabeth Barlow in 1765. One of their sons, also named Samuel, worked with his father for a time as an engraver. From 1785 until his death in 1807 at 134 Capel Street in Dublin, Samuel worked as a hatter.

David Breslin

Thomas Cooley
1795-1872

Thomas Cooley was born deaf at his mother's family's home in Sandymount Green near Dublin, Ireland. He was the first son of a barrister, William Cooley, and his wife Emily, the daughter of a woodcarver, Richard Cranfield. When Thomas was a small boy, he used to watch his maternal grandfather at work drawing on woodcarvings. This proved an ideal initiation into the world of drawing and sketching for Thomas, cementing a firm basis for his future as a skilled portrait painter.

Education beckoned and Thomas' parents chose the Braidwood Academy for the Deaf and Dumb in Hackney, London. Thomas attended this famous school in about 1803 and was placed under Isabella Braidwood, who was running the academy separately from that of her father Thomas (1715-1806). One issue of *Gentlemen's Magazine* contains a letter in which the writer wrote of meeting Isabella Braidwood and a group of deaf pupils in Margate and one of the pupils referred to was Thomas Dooley, obviously misspelled by the writer when it should have been Cooley. Thomas stayed at the academy until 1809 after which he attended various courses in art and draughtsmanship in the Royal Academy of Arts schools. During his studies, he resided with Isabella Braidwood as a lodger.

Upon successfully completing his course, Thomas returned home to Dublin in 1810 and set up a studio in his parents' house. He made a series of paintings and exhibited some at the Irish Society of Artists. After a year, Thomas returned to London to attend the Royal Academy and continued to paint there, again residing at Isabella Braidwood's home in Cambridge Heath, Hackney, as a lodger. In 1814, after finding little success, Thomas returned to Dublin.

From 1814 onwards, Thomas painted many portraits of famous Irish characters including John Cash, the Lord Mayor of Dublin (1813-14). His works were exhibited at prestigious venues such as Hibernian Society of Artists and the Artists of Ireland in Dublin. Whatever the reason, the lure of London beckoned again and in 1817 Thomas was working in London, residing at 103 St. Martins Lane. During that time, he produced numerous paintings, mainly of the military, and they were exhibited at the Royal Academy and the British Institution. The death of his father in 1823 forced Thomas to return to Dublin where he was to continue his work, which led to his appointment as an Associate of the Royal Hibernian Academy in July 1826.

In 1828, Thomas was appointed Portrait Painter to His Excellency Lord Lieutenant of Ireland, Henry William Paget. Taking up this appointment, Thomas resigned his associateship of Royal Hibernian Academy in 1829 and went to London. He settled in 19 Manchester Buildings near Baker Street. In the next 13 years from 1829 to 1843, Thomas painted 52 oil paintings for the Royal Academy's exhibitions. Thomas then moved to live with his brother in 8 College Place in Camberwell, London, from 1844 to 1846. In spite of having his paintings regularly exhibited at the Royal Academy, he was never offered membership of the Royal Academy.

In 1846, Thomas returned home to Tritonville, Sandymount, where he continued to paint many more paintings for the exhibitions in Dublin until he appeared to retire in 1856 or 1858. He then went to live at 97 Harcourt Street near St. Stephen's Green and worked for his cousin Thomas Cranfield of 115 Grafton Street, who was an Art and Photographic framer. Thomas also became involved with the Protestant Deaf community and attended religious meetings of the Committee of the Juvenile Deaf and Dumb Association, which was based in 28 Molesworth Street, Dublin.

Thomas Cooley died on 20 June 1872, aged 77, and was buried at the Mount Jerome Cemetery in Harolds Cross, Dublin, in an unmarked grave. His collection of oil paintings, drawings, three sketch-books and personal effects were sent for auction at 9 Upper Ormond Quay on 7 November, raising £600. This was left to his brother William Desborough in London, who never bothered to erect a headstone on Thomas' unmarked grave.

Thomas Cooley's three sketchbooks survived for 98 years and were bought in May 1968 by The Neptune Gallery of Antiquarian Prints, Drawings and Maps at 122a St. Stephen's Street, which was about 300 feet from Harcourt Street where the artist used to live.

In 1972, the centenary of Cooley's death was celebrated by an exhibition of his drawings by Deaf picture framer and art restorer David Breslin Between 26 October and 26 November. This exhibition raised enough funds to erect a headstone on the unmarked grave of Thomas Cooley. The simple limestone headstone inscribed *Thomas Cooley 1795-1872* was unveiled on 22 June 1975 by the Chairman of National Association for the Deaf (Ireland), Anthony Hederman, in a ceremony at Mount Jerome Cemetery attended by Deaf and hearing people.

There are no oil paintings by Thomas Cooley in the National Gallery of Ireland, but in 1994 an oil painting of half-length portrait of the former Lord Mayor, John Cash (1813-14), was bought by Dublin Corporation for display in the committee room in Dublin Castle.

David Breslin and Raymond Lee

**John Creasy
c1774-1855?**

*Site of Britain's first public school for deaf children
at Fort Place, Grange Road, Bermondsey, London.*

There is limited information on John Creasy but he was baptised in Deptford on 18 September 1774. The son of John and Mary Creasy, he was a pupil of Thomas Braidwood at his Academy, first at Edinburgh and then at Hackney for a total of almost ten years.

On Sunday 20 May 1792, John Creasy and his mother were approached by the Reverend John Townsend, the minister of the Jamaica Row Congregation Church in Bermondsey. During her conversation with Townsend, she suggested that a school should be founded for the education of poor deaf children, which had been the dream of Thomas Braidwood in 1769, but he never received public encouragement. In support of this, Mary Creasy presented before him her young deaf son, John, for whom she had paid £1,500 in fees during his ten years of education at Braidwood Academy. Townsend was so fascinated by John's ability and accuracy that he at once agreed with her on the necessity of founding a charitable school for poor deaf children. The new Asylum was founded on 14 November 1792, with the first six poor deaf children admitted and Joseph Watson as head teacher.

The second group of children arrived in January 1793, one of them a boy of 8 years named William Hunter, who later became the first Deaf teacher at the Asylum in 1804. Prior to becoming a full time teacher, William was taught drawing and writing by John Creasy who was hired by the committee for some two and a half years. This was because Joseph Watson had advocated in his book *Instruction of the Deaf and Dumb*, (1809) that a deaf person could be employed to teach deaf children with the *happiest effect*. R. L. Barby explained in *The Teacher of the Deaf* for 1975, that a deaf person should be chosen to teach because:

> *They share the disability of their pupils, because they had first-hand knowledge of the frustrations and difficulties ...*

Creasy employed fingerspelling in his teaching rather than sign language, as evidenced in an extract from *The Quarterly Review of Deaf-Mute Education* for 1887 by David Buxton, a former teacher at the Asylum:

> *... he was communicated with by means of the manual alphabet... although he could speak very well.*

Later Creasy also taught both private and charity pupils under the Asylum's second headmaster, Thomas James Watson, for a fee not exceeding thirty pounds per year sometime between 1829 to 1855. It is known that there is a portrait of John Creasy with others painted by Thomas Arrowsmith, but it is now presumed lost, or perhaps still in a private collection somewhere. It is not known where or when Creasy died but it is said that he *lived on to a cheerful and active old age*.

Peter R. Brown

Richard Crosse
1742-1810

The last three decades of the eighteenth century were a golden age in the history of British miniature portrait painting. Some of the best miniature painters flourished at this time, and deaf art produced three such painters - Shirreff, Roche and Crosse. Of these three, Richard Crosse was regarded as one of the best of the second rank of British miniature portrait painters.

He was the second son of John Crosse and his wife Mary and was born in Knowle, near Cullompton, Devon, on 24 April 1742. He had a Deaf sister, Alice, and it is evident that both of them were fairly well educated although neither could speak. It is not known who educated them as a large part of the family records perished when the ancestral manor home of the Crosse family was destroyed by fire in the 1870s when a servant set alight some straw in the kennels where the Crosse hounds were kept. One of the manuscripts, which survived the fire, however, was a well-written letter by Alice to her brother James complaining about a portrait that Richard Crosse had painted of her husband on wood instead of on canvas!

Bearing in mind some of the family members were lawyers, it would appear that the deaf siblings shared the same tutor(s) as the other children at the family home. When aged 16, Richard Crosse won a premium at the Society of Arts in 1758 and went to study in London at Sibley's Drawing School and the Duke of Richmond's Gallery.

Richard Crosse was a prolific painter, painting hundreds of miniatures between 1½ inches and 6 inches high. He kept a ledger in which he meticulously recorded every painting done and sold. In the space between 13 September 1776 and 30 January 1777, he painted and sold 56 small miniatures for eight guineas each, two of a medium size for ten and twelve guineas, a half-size portrait for fifteen guineas, and two large size portraits for thirty guineas each – total of 61 works for £572, an excellent income for those days. This ledger can be seen in the Victoria and Albert Museum, London.

Many of his paintings and miniatures were unsigned which resulted in his not getting the credit he deserved in latter years. Those, which he did sign, were either with his initials R. C. or in four different ways in full in careful handwriting.

In 1789, he was appointed Court Painter in Enamel to King George III. He fell in love with his cousin, Miss Sarah Cobley, who refused his offer of marriage and instead married a Mr. Haydon, the father of B. R. Haydon, the painter. This left him embittered and turned him into a recluse in his later years, causing him to retire from painting in 1798, already a wealthy man. He lived for a time with Miss Cobley's brother, the Prebendary Cobley, at Wells, Somerset, before ending his final years in Knowle where he died in May 1810.

Peter W. Jackson

48

Thomas Davidson
1842-1910

Thomas Davidson was born in Hyde Park Corner in 1842 of Scottish parents who originated from Kelso, and became deaf at the age of four due to illness. He was educated as a private pupil of Dr. Thomas Watson of the Asylum for the Deaf and Dumb in the Kent Road, Bermondsey. Upon the latter's death, Thomas was educated at a hearing school in Clapham and thence at the Marlborough School of Art and Design until 1861.

From the very first, Thomas painted professionally for a living and first exhibited at the Royal Academy in 1863. For a year in 1868, he shared a studio in Paris with another artist studying there.

Thomas Davidson was famous primarily for his paintings of incidents associated with Horatio Nelson, a subject on which he was an acknowledged authority. Several paintings were of battles or incidents, which had never before been seen on canvas. Most of his paintings were elaborate, detailed, large-scale battle-pieces, some of which found their way to city municipalities in Canada and Australia.

Occasionally, Thomas also painted religious or Roman events. One of his paintings, *Ephphatha,* can be found hanging in the school canteen at the Royal School for Deaf Children, Margate. Other paintings can be seen in the Imperial War Museum, London.

He married his hearing wife, Charlotte, in 1865 and had two sons and two daughters by her. One of his sons, Allan, was also to achieve fame as a painter.

Thomas was a regular attendant at services for Deaf people held at St. Saviour's Church, London, and was on the committee of the Royal Association for the Deaf and Dumb. He was also one of the first members of the British Deaf and Dumb Association when that was formed in 1890, although he was reputed to be a strong supporter of the Oral Method that was all the rage at that time.

Thomas was also keen on debate and he was the first President of the Deaf and Dumb Debating Society that held regular debates and lectures in St. Saviour's Church Lecture Hall.

After living and painting for many years at his studio in Hampstead, he retired to Walberswick, Suffolk, where he died on 15 November 1910. He was buried in St. Andrew's Church in the same plot of ground as his hearing wife Charlotte, and painter son Allan Douglas Davidson (1873–1932).

Jack Hart

Rupert Arthur Dent
1853-1910

Rupert Dent was born deaf in Wolverhampton. The third son of a solicitor, William Dent, Rupert was sent to the Manchester Institution for the Deaf and Dumb, Old Trafford, when aged 8 after receiving an education at home from Miss Jane Besemeres, the founder of the Wolverhampton Mission for the Deaf. Unfortunately a serious illness cut short his schooldays at Old Trafford and he returned home once more to be educated by Miss Besemeres. By then, however, Rupert had developed an interest in art, particularly of animals. As soon as his health was restored, Rupert was sent to the Wolverhampton School of Art where he remained until he was aged 23. He was then sent to the Royal Academy for further study, but was instead advised to begin exhibiting his work immediately.

His speciality was animal painting, generally of dogs, and he frequently exhibited at the Royal Academy. Like many other artists of his era, Rupert Dent also had work accepted by magazines such as *Punch* and *Graphic.*

Rupert never married and always lived with his father (who lived well into his nineties). When his father retired from his solicitor's practice and moved to Cheltenham, Rupert moved with him. At Cheltenham, he conducted a Sunday afternoon class for local deaf people.

Rupert died on 2 January 1910 after a short, sudden attack of pneumonia.

Martin Binysh

James Docharty
1868-1928
&
Edwin Docharty
1869-1931

Glasgow in the 1890s was fortunate in having many Deaf people who maintained a high profile in the local community. In maintaining this profile, the Deaf community in this Scottish city was helped by the fact that a number of these Deaf people found work in journalism, which resulted in a local evening paper, the *Glasgow Evening Times*, having a weekly column called *Deaf Notes* that kept readers abreast of deaf events. Two such Deaf people were James L.C. and Edwin Docharty, the sons of a well-known Scottish painter, James L. Docharty, of Arsa, Glasgow. Born in 1868 and 1869 respectively, both brothers were educated at the Glasgow Institution for the Deaf and Dumb and both were later employed as artists with the *Glasgow Weekly Mail*.

Edwin Docharty

James L. C. Docharty was the more talented painter of the two brothers and exhibited regularly at exhibitions in Glasgow and throughout Scotland. His younger brother Edwin was more inclined to become involved in voluntary work with Deaf people, and was for some years a vice president of the British Deaf and Dumb Association as well as representative of Scotland on that body. When the post of missioner to the East Lancashire Deaf and Dumb became vacant at Blackburn due to the death of James Muir in 1906, Edwin was successful in his application for the position. He resigned as vice president of the BDDA in order to devote his full attention to his new duties.

James stayed in Scotland, devoting more time to his painting until he died in 1928. Edwin died after a brief illness in 1931, still missioner to the East Lancashire Deaf and Dumb Society.

James L. C. Docharty

Peter W. Jackson

51

Dudhope Castle, Dundee
Site of the Dundee School of the Deaf and Dumb

Alexander Drysdale
1812-1880

Little is known of the early years of Alexander Drysdale. He was either born deaf or became so at a very early age, receiving his education at the Deaf and Dumb Institution in Edinburgh. After finishing school, he assisted the Principal, Mr. Kinniburgh for some years. Another teacher was a Miss McKay, whom Alexander later married. She seems to have died after a few years of married life.

They were not yet married in 1841 when Alexander, then 29 years of age, started to apply for a new position. He wrote from "Edinburgh Deaf and Dumb School", 18 St. John Street, to the Directors of the Aberdeen Institution and stated *"I am Deaf and Dumb ... have been a Teacher of a Deaf and Dumb Day-School here for upwards of five years ... I am led to believe that my system of teaching has been approved of."*

He accompanied his application with 13 testimonials from various clergymen, directors, and others. All spoke most highly of his *"steadiness, diligence, ability, good conduct and success in teaching." "His quickness in communicating knowledge to his pupils"* was remarked on by several, and his "admirable discipline" noted by others.

The day-school seems to have been almost totally in his care and the numbers had risen from six to forty-one. From parents came nine more testimonials all of equally approving sentiments. Some of these came from Dundee as nine or ten of his pupils attended from Dundee. Both sets of testimonials suggest that Alexander is worthy of a wider sphere.

Alexander also sent cuttings from local newspapers and these show that he often gave exhibitions and examinations of his pupils, as was customary at that time. He seems to have used an interpreter, a Mr. McLaurin. The perfection of the pupils' finger-language was noted, but signs were also used. This was seen to be very expressive, and the pupils' knowledge of all their lessons excellent. As one report said Alexander was *"one of their own"* as far as the children were concerned.

It seems, however, that he did not get the post in Aberdeen, but on 9 March 1846 he and the then Mrs. Drysdale, whom he married in the previous year, opened the Dundee Institution, in Meadow Street. They remained in charge for the next thirty-five years. The school rapidly grew and after two years moved to a leased building. Here blind and deaf children were taught together, but, after ten years, a new building was opened for Deaf children only in Dudhope Bank, Logie Den.

Soon his niece, Miss Pattison, joined him and his wife, although she died before Alexander. It appears that Alexander was not much interested in the many educational meetings and discussions that went on, but concentrated on his pupils and on the needs of the local Adult deaf people. He was voluntarily the missionary for some years and then had a formal appointment with salary. He took two services each Sunday, gave lectures in the week, visited the sick and helped in troubles. He encouraged them to *"visit him for conversation".* All this at the same time as maintaining his

52

high educational standards. Alexander continued with his public displays and his pupils continued to impress all who saw them.

In 1880 Mr. and Mrs. Drysdale were thinking of retiring. They had a house in mind and the school was thinking of a successor. (It would be another Deaf man). The thirty-fifth anniversary of the opening was celebrated at a gathering of about 100 deaf people and 50 hearing people. One month later, in April 1880, Alexander died suddenly, sitting in a chair in his bedroom, from what appeared to be a heart-attack.

Alexander Drysdale is notable as a Deaf man who, after getting experience, opened a school for the Deaf and who dedicated the whole of his life to providing high-quality education to Deaf children, as well as helping his adult fellows.

Doreen E. Woodford

John Duff
c. 1730/40-1788

The engraver, John I. Duff, was presumed to have been born deaf in Dublin between 1730 and 1740. There is some uncertainty about the date and place of birth and very little is known of his background. His name appears in *A Dictionary of Irish Artists* (1913) by Walter George Strickland. In recent years, John Duff's works began to surface little by little.

"South View of the Cathedral Church of Limerick"
by John Duff

John was living at 13 Smock Alley near Dublin Castle in about 1770, but between 1777 and 1782, he lived firstly at 44 Essex Street and latterly at 17 Exchange Street, where he ran his business as an engraver. His first known work was an engraved plate entitled *A Plan of Dublin (1777)*. The inscription, *John Duff Sculpt. No. 44 Essex Street* is shown on the bottom right of this 16½ by 12½ inch plate.

John contributed a number of etchings, quite poor in execution, to some magazines between 1779 and 1781. John also engraved numerous plates and two other different town plans of Dublin, executed in 1777 and 1783 respectively. Irish scenes engraved by John and featured in a number of different magazines were *Round Tower at Kildare, Abbey of St. John's Kilkenny* and *Irishtown and Kilkenny*. John also did portraits of Irishmen and a Trinity College Prize plate dated 1770.

A book entitled *The History of Limerick,* published in 1787, contains illustrations of 13 plates of Limerick engraved by John Duff in 1786, which includes ruins of castles and abbeys. This book came into the possession of the writer of this article. A fold-out, *This Plan of the City of Limerick, 1 December 1786,* with *"John Duff Sculpfit"* inscribed on the bottom of the 21 by 13 inch plate is in perfect condition.

John died suddenly from a fit of apoplexy while riding from Dublin to Dallispellane in Co. Wicklow on 22 July 1787. The engraving business in Exchange Street was continued by his hearing wife, Catherine Duff, until 1789 when she sold it to Charles Henecy.

Many magazines and books containing illustrations by John Duff are kept in the National Library of Ireland. Other books are known to be in private collections.

David Breslin

John Dyott
1606-1664

John Dyott was born deaf into a military family in Lichfield, to Sir John Dyott. Although treated rather shabbily by his family and known by the nickname of Dumb Dyott, there is no doubt that he acquired military skills from other members of the family, who were staunch Royalists.

The gun used by John Dyott at the Siege of Lichfield

Three of Dumb Dyott's brothers held officer commissions in King Charles I's Royalist armies. His elder brother, Sir Charles Dyott, commanded the Lichfield Volunteers and was in charge of the local garrison when the Civil War arrived in Lichfield in March 1643.

When Oliver Cromwell's Parliamentarians laid siege to Lichfield, the Royalist garrison was small and weak, but they were determined to dent access to the Commanding Officer of the Parliamentary Army, General Robert Greville, the Lord Brooke, who had vowed to reduce Lichfield Cathedral to rubble.

John Dyott, aged 37 at the time, was one of only three men who were up on the castle battlements when the Parliamentarians began their assault on the morning of 2 March 1643. Those three men caused such havoc to the Parliamentarians that the assault was held up. During a lull, a horseman expensively clad in ermine rode into view. It was Lord Brooke, who had come to see for himself what was holding up what should have been an easy assault. Almost immediately, John Dyott fired his gun, and the bullet went straight through Lord Brooke's right eye into the brain and the General fell dead from his horse. The assault died away with the death of Lord Brooke and John "Dumb" Dyott was led down from the battlements to a hero's reception from the townsfolk of Lichfield.

Despite this setback, however, the Parliamentary forces captured Lichfield three days later on 5 March 1643 with a renewed assault, but the Cathedral was spared destruction.

Very little is known of John Dyott after this incident that earned him fame, as he seems to have been ignored by the rest of his wealthy family. He is not mentioned in his father's Will, or in any other family Wills. He is not buried in the family vault in the Dyott Chapel in Lichfield, but is stated to have been buried in Temple Church, London, in 1664. What we do know, however, is that he married a deaf and dumb girl called Katherine after the Civil War who bore him four daughters and a son. This must be one of the earliest ever-recorded marriages between two born-deaf people.

The gun with which John "Dumb" Dyott felled Lord Brooke is still in possession of the family at the ancestral home, Freeford Manor in Lichfield. It occupies pride of place on the mantelpiece in a room adorned by family portraits of long-dead soldiers, including some who fought at Waterloo and in many of Britain's foreign battles.

Peter W. Jackson

Arthur Edmond
1914-1982

Arthur Edmond was educated at the Royal School for Deaf Children, Margate; in his final year, he was Head boy. At school, he received training in printing, which enabled him to make a successful career in that trade. Showing great courage and dedication, he started his own printing business in a small garden shed, which grew into several shops.

He was always active in the affairs of his local community and he became Mayor of Wembley in 1954.

Arthur Edmond always had a deep love for his old school, and in 1964 accepted an appointment to become a Governor of the School, and was elected to the Committee of Management.

In 1973, he received what was probably his highest honour, his appointment as High Sheriff of Greater London by H.M. the Queen and it was during his year as High Sheriff that he personally raised £100,000 towards his old school's costly rebuilding programme, a most remarkable achievement.

Besides these fund-raising activities, he found time to organise special tickets for the schoolchildren to attend the Lord Mayor's Show and encouraged the Variety Club of Great Britain to donate video equipment to the school, besides doing a host of other things for his Alma Mater.

Arthur Edmond is the only known born-deaf person ever to be elected a mayor and appointed a High Sheriff of Britain's capital city.

Peter W. Jackson

George Edward
1867-1929

George Edward was born with partial hearing loss in Glasgow where he was partly educated at the Glasgow Institution before spending three years in Mr. Van Asch's Oral School. The son of a wealthy Glasgow jeweller, he originally wanted to be an artist and for some time was a student at the Glasgow School of Art. However, he found that artists could not always make a living, so he entered the business established by his grandfather in 1838.

After working through every department, he became a partner in it, and then a prominent Glasgow businessman in his own right. His firm, Messrs. G. Edward and Sons, was sometimes called "The Tiffany of Glasgow", such was the quality of its work.

George Edward, although an accomplished speech-reader, was also an expert user of the manual alphabet, but he transacted almost all his business by oral speech. He was skilled enough to be able to design and produce a number of ornate trophies, some of which were presented by Queen Victoria to the Royal Clyde, the Royal Northern and the Royal Forth Yacht Clubs. He also designed and presented to St. Saviour's Church, London, two magnificent trophies.

Yachting was his first love, and his wealth enabled him to run two racing yachts on the Clyde with which he won a number of trophies.

George Edward also travelled widely, visiting India, China, Japan, Canada and America, where he met Edwin Miner Gallaudet, a short time before the latter died.

He was also a director of the Glasgow Institute for the Deaf and Dumb, and was associated with that Institute for many years up to his death in 1929.

George Edward was a rare example of a successful deaf businessman who was a successful Oralist, but who also nonetheless associated with the signing Deaf.

Peter W. Jackson

Leslie Edwards, OBE
1885-1951

One of the greatest of Deaf Englishmen that strode the first half of the 20th century was Leslie Edwards. A very private man who rarely mentioned his family background and upbringing, little is known about his early years. However, it is known that he became deaf through meningitis at the age of seven. From the age of nine until he was fourteen, he attended a small private school for the deaf where there were ten to twelve children whose ages ranged from seven to eighteen. He has described this time as being the most unhappy and unprofitable period of his life. After this, he attended a London County Council day school for one and half years, and a further three years at an art school in London. Whilst in London, he joined the congregation of the Mission Church (for the Deaf) of All Saints at West Ham and became one of the first to be baptised there. He also attended a course for the Lay-Readers' licence at King's College, London, with other deaf candidates and passed his examination. After being granted his licence, he helped in the West Ham and Hackney district as a voluntary Lay-Reader.

His first occupation was that of a lithographer and a designer. At the age of 27, he was offered a position as Art Teacher at the East Anglian School for the Deaf at Gorleston where he was to remain for three years. During that time, he obtained his National College of Teachers of the Deaf diploma and met his future wife, Marion F. Thorpe, who was also a teacher at the school.

In 1915, Leslie Edwards was elected to the post of Missioner to the Deaf to the Diocese of Peterborough. He worked in Leicester, Loughborough, Northampton, Irthlingborough, Peterborough and Rutlandshire, travelling around this very large diocese on a motor-cycle in all weathers. In 1926, the diocese of Peterborough was split into two, Peterborough and Leicester. He remained in Leicester and served Deaf people in that diocese, which included Loughborough, right up to his death at the age of 65 in October 1951.

He was responsible for helping to complete the Leicester centre and was a bit of a disciplinarian. For instance, he decreed that no women were to be allowed into the Billiards Room, and that any Deaf person who left the club to go to the public house three or four doors down the road were not to be allowed back into the club after their drink. He was also a noted cricketer and helped Leicester Deaf Cricket Club achieve their first district championship trophy in 1929.

His wife Marion became a Lady Worker for the Leicester Mission, helping her husband to support various local groups. These included the Hard-of-Hearing Club, the Rangers, Mothers Union, Youth Club and Lipreading classes. Whilst Leslie worked at the Leicester Mission, he was allowed to get involved in various outside organisations. These included being a committee member of the National Institute for the Deaf (later the RNID), the Midland Regional Association for the Deaf, the Central Advisory Council for the Spiritual Care of the Deaf and Dumb and the Post-War Reconstruction Committee for the Deaf. He was Honorary Registrar of the Joint Examination Board of Training and Qualification of Missioners and Welfare Workers to the Deaf, and Honorary Treasurer to the Council of Church Missioners to the Deaf.

58

Perhaps his greatest contribution to the British Deaf community was as Honorary Secretary/Treasurer of the British Deaf and Dumb Association, a position which he held for 16 years from 1935 onwards. Under his leadership, the BDDA built upon the foundations set down by his predecessor, William McDougall, and gained considerably in reputation and strength. He had the reputation of being a great speaker and was in demand at national and international conferences where he gave eloquent and thought-provoking speeches. His ability to use masterly command of sign and gesture could thrill and hold Deaf and hearing alike in a manner that excited admiration.

Outside his work with Deaf people, Leslie Edwards was a talented artist and cartoonist and a devout family man with one son and one daughter. Towards the end of his career, he was subjected to ill-health but continued working with Deaf people until he died in harness on 3 October 1951. He was buried in Leicester's Saffron Lane Cemetery after a funeral that attracted many friends and colleagues throughout the country.

Peter W. Jackson, Philip Kilgour & Winnie Gilbert

Magdalene Tower, Drogheda
By Lawrence Fagan

Lawrence Fagan
1825-1898

Lawrence Fagan was born in Drogheda, Co Louth, in 1825. His parents, Silvester, a poor labourer, and May Fagan, had seven children, and besides Lawrence, there was also a deaf daughter. Nothing is known about her. Lawrence was admitted on 28 July 1836, aged 11, to the National Institution for the Deaf and Dumb Children of the Poor, Claremont, Glasnevin, Dublin. According to the admission book, he was pupil number 543. It states that he was born deaf, was quite intelligent and knew some signs. He was taught at Claremont for over six years through the manual alphabet and sign language introduced from the Edinburgh Deaf and Dumb Institution, as well from the Birmingham Institution.

Lawrence, like other pupils, was instructed in art, geography, English, religion, arithmetic and industrious habits under the direction of Mr Joseph Humphreys, the schoolmaster who had previously worked in Edinburgh and Birmingham. When Lawrence completed his education and was able to look after himself, he left Claremont in 1842 and settled down in Trinity Street, Drogheda, with his family. He began looking for work there while he developed his skills as a draughtsman and sketcher.

Lawrence liked to travel all over Ireland by horse-drawn carriage, occasionally stopping to bring out his satchel with pens, ink, papers and equipment with stool and easel to draw his scenes. It was said that he had red hair and a massive red beard to match. He was an artist of considerable skill and produced pen and ink drawings of local ruins. He was very industrious and some of his works are now in the National Library of Ireland. Two woodcut prints are in the Municipal Gallery, Parnell Square, Dublin.

Lawrence Fagan was remarkable for the accuracy and detail of his work. He usually signed his work as "*drawn by L. F. deaf-mute*", or "*sketched with pen... L. F. *", sometimes "*L. Fagan*". He also did portraits. One of "*an Arab Boy in his costume*", inscribed with "*Copied in the Royal Dublin Society by L. Fagan Deaf Mute*" was presented to the Committee of the Juvenile Deaf and Dumb Association at 28 Molesworth Street, which provided facilities for meetings and worship services for Deaf Protestant ex-pupils of Claremont.

Lawrence sent seven pictures of sketched local scenes in Co. Meath and Co. Louth to the Exhibition of Manufacturers Machinery & Fine Arts held at the Royal Dublin Society in 1864. Two pictures by him, "*St. Lawrence Gate, Drogheda*" and "*Magdalene Tower, Drogheda*" are now owned by the author of this article.

Lawrence died a bachelor in 1898 and he is believed to be buried in Drogheda.

David Breslin

Robert Fagan
1761-1816

Robert Fagan was born deaf on 5 March 1761 in Cork, Ireland, the only son of Michael Fagan, a prosperous banker. Robert moved to London in 1775 with his parents who settled in Long Acre. Robert's education background is not known, but he attended the Royal Academy School of Arts on 21 June 1781, as a pupil of Bartolozzi. Robert specialised in painting portraits of the British aristocracy who passed through Rome.

After the death of his widower father in 1783, Robert, then aged 22, inherited a sizeable fortune, which enabled him to travel around Europe with a hearing friend. They visited Paris in 1783 before going on to Italy in 1784 where Robert lived with an English painter, Hugh Robinson (1756-1790), in Rome.

Fagan was a proficient artist, his portraits reflecting contemporary neo-classical taste and his knowledge of antique sculpture. He had a number of British patrons in Italy. Later, Robert took up an interest in archaeology and he worked as a dealer in antiquities and pictures, acting for patrons such as the 4th Earl of Bristol and Bishop of Derry. Robert became the most successful archaeological excavator of the period and reaped rich gains by repeated searches in the ancient Roman ruins at Ostia and Laurentum. In 1794, he moved to Palermo in Sicily where he continued his interest in archaeology until 1800. Some fragments of sculpture in the Palermo Museum today are said to have been acquired from Robert Fagan.

Robert was supported financially during his early years in Rome through an allowance of £100 a year. He married twice into wealthy Italian families. His first marriage on 12 April 1790 was to Ann Maria Ferri, aged 17, the daughter of Pietro Ferri, an employee of Cardinal Rezzonico. They had one daughter, Estiria, born on 15 November 1792. However, Robert appears to have neglected his wife and within six weeks of her death in 1800, Robert married Maria Ludovica Flajani, who appears semi-naked in his self-portrait of 1803. He had two children by her, Emile (1806) and George (1812). In 1809, through the recommendation of Lord Nelson and Sir William Hamilton, Robert was appointed British Consul-General for Sicily and Malta. In that year, Sir John Acton, Prime Minister to Queen Caroline of Naples, commissioned him to paint a portrait of his wife, Mary Ann with her children. This painting bears an inscription, *Painted by Robert Fagan His Britannic Majesty's Consul Governor for Sicily 1809.*

In 1815, Robert spent a few months in England following the death of his daughter Estina's husband, William Baker of Bayfordbury, Hertfordshire. When he returned to Rome in January 1816, he began to suffer from financial difficulties and health problems. On 26 August 1816, he flung himself out of his apartment window to his death.

David Breslin

Sir Arthur Henderson Fairbairn
1852-1915

The landed gentry in Britain which appears threatened with extinction today can look back with equanimity to a past with special glories in which there was the only Deaf and Dumb baronet then living in the world. Arthur Fairbairn was born on 11 April 1852 in Lancashire as the eldest child of Sir Thomas Fairbairn. The family wealth came from the first baronet, Sir William Fairbairn, an engineer who invented riveting machines and other useful gadgets, and built great bridges and dockyards, which rewarded him with large fortunes and a title from Queen Victoria. There is power in riches and regalia; but that power does not govern the laws of nature, and the family was helpless when deafness made its appearance in Arthur of the third generation and also in his sister, Constance. Their brother, Thomas Andrew, was hearing.

The family wealth enabled Arthur and his sister to have an excellent private education a private academy for the Deaf in Rugby run by the great Henry Brothers Bingham, a former teacher at the Edgbaston Institution for the Deaf and Dumb, Birmingham. Bingham had taught under Thomas Braidwood, the grandson of the founder of British Deaf education, Thomas Braidwood (1715-1806) and had also been a former principal of two other schools for the Deaf at Exeter and Manchester.

There were some unconfirmed reports that he went to Cambridge and acquired a degree but there were not any literary works of distinction from his pen to record his academic standing. At the age of thirty after years in typical aristocratic pursuits like hunting and collecting curios, Arthur married Florence Frideswyde Long on 5 July 1882, the daughter of the Honourable Richard Penruddock Long, a member of Parliament. The marriage brought him the valuable association of his wife's brother, William Long, a power in British politics and a useful contact in the uplift of the Deaf.

Arthur and his Deaf sister, the Hon. Constance, mingled with the Deaf freely and did their best to improve their conditions. His father died in 1891 and the title passed to Arthur who became the third Baronet of Ardwick, Manchester, with the right to bear arms of the house. As a baronet, Sir Arthur was an excellent philanthropist especially with charities connected with deaf people. He was the treasurer of the Royal Association in Aid of the Deaf and Dumb and his residence at Wren's House in Chichester, Sussex, was the focal point where so many charitable occasions were held. He took care in his appearance and was always smartly dressed with a finely trimmed beard and waxed moustache.

He died on 2 June 1915 in Tunbridge Wells, Kent, and was greatly mourned. He had no children and the title passed to his hearing brother, Thomas Andrew. The Deaf Centre at Southampton which bears his name stands out as a example of the good he had done and it appears to be the only memorial left to remind people of the existence of a Deaf and Dumb Baronet.

Arthur F. Dimmock

62

Abraham Farrar, F.G.S.
1861 - 1944

Abraham Farrar was born in Leeds on 26 January 1861, the son of Abraham Farrar, a small landed proprietor, and Sarah Shaw. His father's family lived in Bramley, Leeds, for several generations and was well known there. He had a younger sister, Blanche. At the age of 3 years, Abraham became totally deaf through scarlet fever, a very common cause of deafness and lost his speech. His father took him to Doncaster to seek advice from the celebrated headmaster, Charles Baker, who recommended him to the Reverend Thomas Arnold, a former teacher of the deaf who had become a Northampton minister.

In late January 1868, the Rev. Thomas Arnold, who was minister of Doddridge Church, took Abraham as a private pupil at his home in Northampton. This began a special one-to-one pure oral tutorial, which lasted just under thirteen years. In those days, most deaf pupils received only four or five years of education in crowded classrooms using either the manual or combined systems. By taking on Farrar as a private pupil, Arnold laid the foundation not only for the boy's success, but for his own as well. Arnold's reputation as an authority on deaf education began with Farrar's achievements.

In the winter of 1876, Abraham was entered for the Cambridge University Local Examinations, which he passed just before his 16th birthday. The five obligatory subjects included Latin and mathematics. That summer, Arnold took Farrar on a tour of Europe including a visit to the battlefield of Waterloo. On return, Arnold prepared Farrar for the matriculation examinations in scientific subjects, which, if passed, would ensure an automatic entry in any university. Farrar passed the South Kensington Science and Art examinations in Chemistry and Geology in 1880 and finally the following year saw his passing the London University Matriculation examinations. It was a wonderful achievement for young Farrar.

Arnold suggested that Abraham should try for a degree course at the London University but Abraham's father preferred him to have a professional career. Abraham was apprenticed with Messrs. E. F. Law and Sons, a firm of architects and surveyors, and resided as a paying guest at Arnold's home in Northampton. From Arnold, Farrar developed a passion for scholarly research, especially in the field of deafness, which was to sustain him for the remainder of his life. After four years of training in architecture and surveying, he left Northampton and never practised the profession again. Instead, Abraham concentrated on geology as a hobby and visited many quarries and coastal cliffs. At Cromer, he studied the different strata of the cliffs. He researched the remnants from the marine deposit found in one of the strata and examined the plant remains found in the deposit. His observations supported the work of the previous geologists and led to the submission of a paper to the Geological Society for which he received the Society's Fellowship in 1887. Moving to Harrogate, he joined the Leeds Geological Society and contributed some articles during meetings. He also joined the committee of the Leeds Adult Deaf and Dumb Society.

During the two decades before the turn of the 20th century, an emotive and fierce controversy between the oral and manual systems was the subject of many articles in all magazines related to the Deaf and Farrar found himself in the centre of it and wrote articles defending the oral system. He preferred the pure oral method because it brought him success. However, Farrar was always fair to those who used the manual system and even preached tolerance in the education of those who would benefit more from manualism than oralism. He acknowledged that oralism would not suit everybody. In the *Teacher of the Deaf* in 1934, his reply to the questionnaire set by Mr. G. S. Haycock, who wrote *The Deaf Child and the Written Word,* read :-

> *All the time I was at school I knew fingerspelling, but it was never used in school by teacher and pupils. I often used it out of school with my fellow-pupils, some of whom had acquired it at other schools before coming to Arnold's. We were strictly told to use finger-spelling, not signs, if we could not always lipread one another's speech - or had the patience to do so - but, as might be expected, it inevitably involved some signing as well ... My experience, however, is that very few hearing people know finger-spelling, and I usually ask them to write when I am not always able to read their lips.*

It was known in Deaf circles that Abraham Farrar was a proficient finger-speller. Francis Maginn commented once at a BDDA congress that *".. even Mr. Farrar spells on his fingers very well indeed."*

From his strict discipline and experience in his geological studies, he was induced to another area of research - the field of Deaf History. Out of his many valuable contributions was the writing of an historical introduction to Hugh Neville Dixon's 1890 translation from the original Spanish of Bonet's *Simplification of the letters of the Alphabet and Method of teaching deaf-mutes to speak.* It was the result of many weeks of careful research carried out at the British Museum and other libraries. At the request of the National College of Teachers of the Deaf, he compiled an edition of *Arnold's Manual for Teachers.* The book came out in 1901 and was the standard reference book for the education of the deaf until 1923.

He spent forty years collecting books relating to the deaf, some of them rare. He wrote articles about education of the deaf in Middle Ages quoting Ponce and Bonet, the 16th century pioneers of deaf education in Spain. Using Dixon's translation of the Spanish version on the two educators and the pupils they tutored, he produced 58 pages of a book which was real meat of this particular intellectual feast. He also went to Madrid to further his studies about the early days of deaf education. There, he discovered the existence of Emmanuel Philbert, the born deaf son of the Prince of Carignano, who rose to become an ambassador and military genius in command of a Spanish army before the turn of the 18th century. Another discovery was Don Luis de Velasco, a descendant of the Constable of Castile, born deaf in 1604, who was able to speak and write well in several languages and gain the admiration of King Philip IV. Farrar's revelations of the deaf characters stand out as a valuable contribution to Deaf History. Farrar's additions to the Arnold Library were transferred to the Rylands Library in the University of Manchester as the Dixon collection during the 1930s. For his services to Deaf History, he was elected the Vice-President of the National College of Teachers of the Deaf and was the only Deaf person to have been honoured by the NCTD.

In 1912, Farrar married Miss Hardy, a hearing lady whose ancestor was the famous Thomas Hardy, the man who was involved in the Battle of Trafalgar in 1815. They did not have any children. Farrar was fond of the open-air life of an English countryman and travelling around Europe. Abraham Farrar died on 14 May 1944, his wife having died in 1937.

Arthur F. Dimmock, Anthony J. Boyce & Peter W. Jackson

Oliver Fenning
1834-1861

Oliver Fenning was the last child of Richard and Lydia Fenning (née Vincent) from the remote village of Gosbeck in Suffolk and was christened on 13 July 1834. He became deaf during his childhood and the cause of his deafness was not known. The Census Return of 1841 listed Richard Fenning as a road surveyor as well as a census enumerator, and his address was known as 'The Parsonage House' in Gosbeck. Around 1851, he was a land and road surveyor who surveyed and drew tithe maps for a number of local villages including Gosbeck, Hemingstone and Coddenham.

The Brighton Institution for the Deaf and Dumb

Oliver Fenning was sent to the Brighton Institution for the Deaf and Dumb Children at 12 Egremont Place, Kemp Town. He was admitted in August 1843 and was taught under the care of William Sleight, the headmaster. In 1848, the school building became overcrowded and moved to 134/136 Eastern Road in the same town. On completion of his education, Oliver went on to become the first Deaf assistant master at the Brighton Institution at the age of 17 years in 1851. In 1852, he was earning £10 per year and it rose to £15 after two years.

Oliver became ill with inflammation of the brain whilst at the Institution and was sent to Sussex County Hospital in Kemp Town, a short walking distance along Eastern Road from the Institution. He died ten days later on 11 December 1861, at the age of 27. William Sleight was the sole executor of his Will.

Oliver was buried on 14 December 1861 in Brighton parochial cemetery, known today as Woodvale Crematorium. One former pupil and a Matron were interred into his grave in 1869 and 1885 respectively. A kerb slab laid over the grave contained an inscription that read:

In memory of
Oliver Fenning
Who died 11 Dec 1861
Aged 27 years
He was for seven years – a pupil and
For eleven years – Assistant Master
In the Deaf and Dumb Institution
In this town.
Also of
Mary Baker
Who died April 20 1885
Aged 77 years

Geoffrey J. Eagling

Sir John Ambrose Fleming
1849-1945

The son of a Congregational minister, John Ambrose Fleming was born in Lancaster on 29 November 1849. At school Fleming showed great interest in science and mechanics but fared poorly in other subjects such as Latin. It was during his schooldays that his hearing deficiency was noticed and it became gradually worse as he grew up. Fleming attended and graduated from University College London in 1870 and from there he entered Cambridge University where he worked for James Clerk Maxwell repeating the experiments of Henry Cavendish.

Fleming became a consultant to the Edison Electric Light Company in London and during that time Edison's company combined with the Bell Telephone interests. Fleming's attention was turned to photometry after Edison and Joseph Swan improved the carbon filament lamp; and this eventually led to employment with the Marconi Wireless Telegraph Company. Fleming was engaged as an advisor on electrical generation and distribution networks, and his work with the generating plant for the Atlantic transmission from Cornwall to Newfoundland found much success in Marconi's successful reception of Morse telegraph signals in December 1901. From this work, Fleming took interest in developing further the potentiometer, an adjustable resistance device, which was later marketed by R.E.B. Crompton.

Fleming's deafness increased as the years advanced and he would employ an assistant as a note-taker in any scientific discussions in which he participated. The Physical Society was founded in 1874 and Fleming read the first paper, a discussion of a form of voltaic cell. By a strange turn of fate, Fleming would read his last professional paper to the same organisation sixty-five years later. Fleming's work covered a wide variety of the electrical spectrum; he worked on transmitters, receivers, wireless telegraphy and lighting systems. He served as president of the Television Society until his death at ninety-five years of age.

As a teacher at the University College, London, between 1885 and 1926, Fleming had a sterling reputation as an efficient organiser and a motivating speaker. Despite his deafness, he remained an excellent lecturer. It was not, however, easy to get Fleming to understand questions in class, and as years went on he became less involved with the actual supervision of students in their laboratory work. It has been said that Fleming's deafness may have caused him to be impatient and hindered his work at times, but it also enabled him to isolate himself from outside disturbances and concentrate on the work in hand in a way that would have been more difficult for a person with normal hearing. Fleming worked at home virtually every evening on writing and scientific problems, whilst during normal working hours at University College his daily life tested his limited communication and bothered him more. Fleming was the first to hold the title of professor of electrical engineering at the university.

Fleming worked with high voltage alternating currents and designed some of the first electric lighting for ships. However, he is best remembered as the inventor of the two-electrode radio rectifier, which he called the thermionic valve. This device, patented in 1904, was also known as the vacuum diode, kenotron, thermionic tube and Fleming valve. It was the first electronic rectifier of radio waves, converting alternating-current (AC) radio signals into weak direct currents (DC) detectable by a telephone receiver. Augmented by the amplifier grid invented in 1906 by Lee De Forest (USA), Fleming's invention was the ancestor of the triode and other multi-electrode vacuum tubes. From these inventions of Fleming and De Forest came the television, radar and computer industries.

Fleming received many honours. In 1892, he was elected Fellow of the Royal Society; and in 1910 he was awarded the Hughes Medal. The Institution of Electrical Engineers (IEE) presented him with the Faraday Medal in 1928. In 1929, he was knighted. In 1933, he was given the Gold Medal of Honour of the Institute of Radio Engineers for his pioneering work and making great advance in the science or art of radio communication.

Fleming passed away on 18 April 1945 in Sidmouth, Devon.

Peter W. Jackson and Raymond Lee

David Fyfe
1883-1967

Born deaf in Kilmarnock, David Fyfe was educated at the Langside School for the Deaf, Glasgow, and on leaving school, served his apprenticeship as a brass finisher, remaining with the same firm for 24 years.

During this period he did much work on a voluntary basis for the Ayrshire Mission to the Deaf and Dumb, where James Paul was missioner. Inspired by Paul, it was already clear in his own mind that it would be in this direction that he would find his real calling.

The opportunity presented itself when a vacancy occurred in Warrington in 1921, and David secured the appointment of missioner at the Warrington Deaf and Dumb Society. Almost every day for thirty years he welcomed visitors to his home and Institute. If the visitor happened to be an "outsider" with no knowledge of sign language, David Fyfe conversed with them happily through hastily scribbled notes and no one ever felt embarrassed.

It was in the Wilson Patten Street building at Warrington that he founded the Society's Chapel and so enabled members to enjoy sermons by the town's best preachers through an interpreter using sign language. During the 1939-45 War, he took on extra duties as cover for absent missioners in Cheshire and encouraged rural Deaf communities in Northwich, Winsford and Crewe to meet and hold services.

On his retirement in 1951, he hoped to devote just a little more time to the only hobby he had ever found time for - photography. But this was not to be so. He was in demand as a preacher and visited many Deaf centres up and down the country. In 1958 his wife, who had been ill for some years, died. This came as a great shock, but like all professionals he continued giving his help when needed. And in 1960, when the Liverpool Adult Deaf and Dumb Benevolent Society decided to open a branch in the Wirral, David Fyfe, although 77 years old, came forward and offered his continued help and experience. As the Social Club grew, the members looked to him as their leader, and he assumed the mantle of responsibility. It was through his efforts the Club is now as successful as it is.

All through his time as a Missioner at Warrington and afterwards, David Fyfe was an active member of the BDDA and he was awarded the Medal of Honour by the British Deaf and Dumb Association for services to Deaf people.

David died on 19 July 1967, aged 84, at his home in Bromsborough.

Maureen A. Jackson

Sir John Gaudy
1639-1708
Framlingham Gaudy
1642-1673

The deaf brothers Sir John and Framlingham Gaudy came from a wealthy family residing in Norfolk with ancestors who were at times Members of Parliament or High Sheriffs of Norfolk. They were the second and fourth of four sons of Sir William Gaudy, 2nd Baronet, and his wife Elizabeth, who also had a daughter Mary.

All four brothers, and their sister, received an excellent education at home, and the two hearing brothers also went to Bury St. Edmunds Grammar School. After this, the two hearing brothers went on to university and the deaf brothers went to study art in the school run by Sir Peter Lely intending to become professional artists. However, when the eldest brother, Bassingbourne, died of smallpox, John (as the second son) became the heir to the baronetcy. On the death of his father in 1669, Sir John painted for amusement only whilst Framlingham Gaudy got such a severe attack of smallpox at the height of his excellent academic progress that he retired to the family home, and after a long illness, died unmarried, aged only 31 years.

Sir John Gaudy

The Gaudy brothers' place in Deaf History lies in the wealth of correspondence that they left for historians to discover. These two brothers are the earliest known (and proven) born-deaf sign language users who were inveterate correspondents. They give credence to the writings of John Bulwer in his *Philocophus* where he mentions a number of Deaf people who were able to write as a means of communication.

Framlingham, who was probably the more academic of the two deaf brothers, wrote regularly to his father, brothers and his sister while he was studying at Sir Peter Lely's school in London. Some of these letters are preserved and wait to be discovered in the museums of Norfolk and the British Library. In one of these letters, he wrote to his elder brother William in 1660 making reference to his invalid sister Mary (who was disfigured with goitre), *"The swellinge in here face is more swelled than evere, it was quite down and is lately increased verye much. I would have you ask the King's Surgeon what hee would advise you"*. In another, to his father dated 2 October 1667, he refers to his sister again and tells his father that there had been no medical benefit to Mary from the consultation by a Dr. Bokenham.

Framlingham Gaudy also left a remarkable legacy. His Will, which was proved at Norwich on 5 September 1673, is interesting in that it is the first **known** Will to have been written by a deaf person. It contains a certificate to validate this, which says:

> *These instructions for a Will were written with the proper handwriting of the said Framlingham Gaudy, who is a person both deafe and dumbe and soe not able otherwise to express his minde and this was written of his proper motion, the second day of May 1672, in the presence of William Smyth, Preb. Norv. B. Gibson.*

The Will shows the excellent quality of Framlingham's handwriting and use of English grammar. The British Library holds several letters written by Sir John Gaudy, many of them in poor and ink-splattered handwriting, which makes them difficult to read.

As the Gaudy brothers lived long before the start of Deaf Education in 1760 and were so academically gifted, the person who taught them to read and write is probably the first true teacher of the Deaf in Britain. This person was most certainly John Cressener, the rector of West Harling, who is mentioned several times in correspondence.

Although both were painters, no paintings done by Framlingham can be traced but there are three paintings still in existence in Bury St. Edmunds by Sir John, a self-portrait of himself and two of his wife.

Sir John Gaudy married a Anne de Grey and had by her four children. In a visit to Bury St. Edmunds in 1677, the diarist John Evelyn wrote:

> *There dined this day at my Lord's one Sir John Gaudy, a very handsome person but quite dumb, yet very intelligent by signs and a very fine painter; he was so civil and well-bred, as it was not possible to discern any imperfection in him. His lady and children were also there, and he was at church in the morning with us.*

By this, we see that Sir John, and presumably his deceased brother as well, used sign language.

Sir John's use of sign language is also mentioned in the family papers particularly with regard to Sir John's grandson, Jacky, who was "retarded" (as the correspondence calls him) and brought up by his grandfather. Jacky was taught by his grandfather to communicate in ***sign language*** and apparently used sign language until he died at an early age.

As for Framlingham, there is mention in his father's correspondence that whilst Framlingham was seriously ill with smallpox, the family were looking for a nurse able to sign to take care of him during his illness.

Peter W. Jackson

Joseph Gawen
1825-1901

Joseph Gawen was born in Brighton, Sussex, on 31 October 1825 to a distinguished cabinetmaker. Joseph was deaf but there is no evidence to show how his deafness was caused. He also had a deaf brother Charles.

In 1839, Joseph and his brother were sent to the Kent Road Asylum for their education. After five years at the Asylum, Joseph found employment as an apprentice with England's most eminent sculptor, Edward Hodges Bailey. Charles found employment with William Linton, a London engraver, and later worked on the magazine *London Illustrated News*. As time went on and communication became more reliant on ears and mouth, Charles lost his occupation and found it difficult to break into the world of media art. Depression gradually took over Charles, who displayed bouts of suicidal tendencies. He was later admitted as an inmate at the notorious Middlesex Asylum where he eventually died.

Gawen's Statute of the Good Shepherd before removal and renovation by the British Deaf History Society.

There have been rumours for years as to who actually sculpted the statute of Nelson, which is mounted on top of the column in Trafalgar Square. Gawen's employer, Bailey, is stated in all historical documents to be responsible for the design and sculpture and although the credit was given to Bailey, there is some question as to whether this was accurate. Accounts of Gawen's family history recorded a well-known fact that Gawen did all the 'donkey work' on Nelson's statue. A distant relation of Gawen wrote during the time when the V1 bombs were dropped on London in 1944, that she had to hide under table, and whilst there doing some homework, she overheard her mother and aunt talking. She vividly remembered her aunt saying: *Yes he (Gawen) did all the work but got none of the credit.* Her mother added: *And there it is in Trafalgar Square.*

After leaving Bailey, Gawen became an assistant to the distinguished sculptor, John Henry Foley, with whom he worked on an outline of the Albert Memorial but the contract was unfortunately awarded to someone else. Gawen sculpted two busts in marble of King Edward VIII, then Prince of Wales, one of which can be seen today at the Royal School for Deaf Children in Margate and the other at St. Saviour's Centre in Acton. As Gawen was making the bust from a photograph, he decided to ask the Prince for a sitting to finish off his work. Impatiently the Prince asked him: *Shall not you want to measure me? I am sure you have made me too fat!* (There is evidence that Gawen was himself a fat man and rather jolly one too!)

Joseph Gawen died in 1901 after a fall from a hansom cab in Holborn, London.

In 1996, Gawen's sculptural masterpiece *The Good Shepherd* was discovered in a terrible state outside St. Saviour's Centre for the Deaf in Acton, London. Nearly three years later in 1998, his masterpiece was recovered and renovated by the British Deaf History Society and the Royal Association in Aid of Deaf People (RAD) before being placed inside the church at the Centre.

Peter R. Brown

Walter Geikie
1795–1837

Show Jamie
one of Geikie's famous etchings

Walter Geikie was born on 9 November 1795 in Charles Street, off George Square, in Edinburgh. The second child of Archibald and Helen Geikie, he appeared to be a healthy and normal baby until at the age of two years when he was struck down with a nervous fever and violent convulsions, after which Walter became deaf. His father sent him to various physicians in an endeavour to cure his deafness, but to no avail. Archibald Geikie finally accepted his son's deafness. Growing up during his formative years, Walter took to drawing and it became a passion for him. He would be drawing all over the place – on walls, floors, doors, pavements, etc. His father bought him pencils and sketchpads to keep him away from drawing on buildings!

The question of Walter's education had to be faced and Archibald could not afford to send him to Thomas Braidwood's Academy for the Deaf in Hackney and the London Asylum for the Deaf and Dumb was considered too far from home for Walter. Archibald had the luck to come across Joseph Watson's *The Instruction of the Deaf and Dumb* (pub: 1809) and used this book as a guidance to educate Walter himself. To the surprise of many people, Archibald's attempt at teaching turned out to be successful and he was approached to become a teacher at a new school for the deaf in Edinburgh, but he declined the offer. However, when the new school opened under John Braidwood at 8 Union Street, Edinburgh, Walter was sent there as a pupil. Braidwood, however, became aware of his abilities and quickly made Walter a monitor. Braidwood was an alcoholic and tended to desert the school in the afternoons, leaving everything in the hands of Walter, who was effectively the school's teacher until Robert Kinniburgh was engaged as a trainee assistant to Braidwood who left his post after a year and departed for America and the school had to close. Walter never returned to it when it later reopened under Robert Kinniburgh.

Walter pursued his love of drawing and honed his skills to perfection with near-endless practice and he concentrated his interest solely on the city of Edinburgh, its people and characters, its buildings and environs and he created a series of sketches that many regarded as "photo-drawings", long before the invention of photography. During his lifetime, Walter drew more than 1100 sketches that are priceless images of Edinburgh at the very beginning of the 19th century. Walter developed an interest in etching and took it up with great vigour.

Walter's work gained respect and the Scottish Academy recognised his talents by making him an Associate in 1831. In 1834, he was honoured by the Scottish Academy who made him an Academician.

Walter was a manualist and communicated with fellow deaf people via that method. His association with the local Deaf of Edinburgh resulted in the foundation of the Edinburgh Deaf and Dumb Benevolent Society, which was founded by Alexander Blackwood and Matthew Robert Burns. This society first met at Lady Stairs Close, off High Street. Walter took active part in the work of the society, but this did not mean he lived a segregated life among the deaf. Walter was in fact an outgoing and robust character who was never shy of people. He was very well known and the inhabitants of Edinburgh, from the poor beggar in the street all the way up to the aristocrats of the city and its surrounds, knew and loved him.

On 26 July 1837, Walter became ill and took to his bed in his house at 11 Charles Street. Not long later in the same day, he sank into a state of deep unconsciousness from which he was never to recover. On 1 August, he was pronounced dead.

Walter was buried in Greyfriars Churchyard on 3 August. Scandalously, no one dedicated a memorial to this artist whose works contributed enormously to the history of the city of Edinburgh and it was considered to be typical of the hearing society's negative attitudes towards the Deaf that Walter's name was allowed to fade into oblivion. It was not until 6 April 1996 that a memorial plaque dedicated to Walter Geikie was unveiled in Greyfriars Churchyard. The Deaf old pupils of Donaldson's College funded the costs.

Raymond Lee

William "Bill" Gilbert, BEM
1910-1998

Leicester's Deaf community has been well served by Deaf stalwarts. One of these was Bill Gilbert who was associated with the community for over 80 years. Profoundly deaf, he was educated at Leicester's Churchgate School for the Deaf, leaving at the age of 15 to become an apprentice shoemaker with a local company called J. F. Palfreyman's, a well-known Leicester firm. He remained with this company all his working life, retiring at the age of 68 after an incredible 52 years' service.

His long service in his paid employment was matched with his voluntary service with the BDA, both locally and nationally. He was the Leicester branch Secretary/Treasurer for 40 years, the Midland Regional Council Secretary and Treasurer for over 25 years, and was an Executive Councillor on the BDA National Executive Council for 18 years. In addition, he was also a member of the Leicester & County Mission's Management Committee for over 40 years. For this long dedicated service to the Deaf community, he was awarded several honours, including the British Empire Medal in 1990, the National Council of Social Workers for the Deaf's Oloman-Ellis Award in 1981, and the BDA's Medal of Honour in 1984.

It is perhaps on the sporting front that Bill was renowned throughout Leicester. He was regarded as a demon spin bowler, highly regarded and feared throughout the local cricket leagues. He had the unique distinction of playing league cricket from the age of 16 until bad eyesight forced his retirement at the age of 70, a playing career spanning 54 years. During that time, he also had the distinction of taking 10 wickets in a match twice, the first at the age of 44 in 1954 when he took all 10 wickets for 21 runs, and the second at the grand old age of 65. On this occasion, he took all 10 wickets for 18 runs! For this latter feat, he was awarded a special top-grade cricket bat by the national *Sun* newspaper. His local league also elected him their Sportsman of the Year twice, the first in 1959, and the second two years later.

Bill Gilbert passed away peacefully in hospital on his birthday, 29 March 1998, and was survived by his wife, Winnie, with whom he celebrated his Diamond Wedding Anniversary in 1996, for which they received a telegram from the Queen.

Peter W. Jackson

John Goodricke, F.R.S.
1764-1786

John Goodricke was born on 17 September 1764 at Groningen, Holland, the eldest child of Sir Henry Goodricke, a diplomat who had married Levina Benjamina Sessler on 31 January 1761 in Weldbuynen, East Friedland, Holland. They had three sons and four daughters of whom five were born in Groningen and two in York. John was baptised two days later at the register office of the civilians at the town of Groningen. Their residence at that time was Oude Ebbingestraat. In 1769, John contracted a fever and consequently lost his hearing.

In 1773, John Goodricke was sent to the Braidwood Academy for the Deaf and Dumb in Edinburgh by his father in order to receive a good education. Goodricke's achievements in Braidwood Academy was satisfactory and he later attended Warrington Academy in Cheshire in 1778. At Warrington Academy, he became reasonably proficient in Greek and Latin and acquired an excellent knowledge of mathematics from a teacher named William Enfield whose hobby was astronomy. It was through Enfield that John Goodricke developed his interest and love of astronomy.

After his education at Warrington Academy, Goodricke rejoined his family who were by then residing at Lendal in York where they had become acquainted with Nathaniel Pigott, a surveyor and an astronomer, whose family lived at 33 Bootham Place, York. John's sister, Mary, married one of Nathaniel's sons in 1794. There was another son named Edward (1753-1825) who, like his father, became a keen astronomer. The elder Pigott had constructed a well-equipped observatory in the garden at the rear of his house, modelled on the Greenwich Observatory. This was a godsend to John, who was to form an astronomical alliance with Edward Pigott and they began to study the variable stars.

By 1781, the Goodricke family had moved to the Treasurer's House in York, a stone's throw from York Minster. This was where John Goodricke made his historic observations of the star, *Algol*, using a Dollond achromatic telescope. In November 1781, he made the first entry in his *Journal of astronomical observations*:

Mr E Pigott told me that at 9 o'clock pm yesterday he discovered a Comet.

In November 1782, he found that *Algol*, usually a second magnitude object, had dropped to fourth magnitude. On 12 November, he recorded in his Journal:

This night I looked at β Persei (the scientific name for Algol), and was much amazed to find its brightness altered – it now appears to be of about the 4th magnitude. I observed it diligently for about one hour. I hardly believed that it changed its brightness, because I never heard of any star varying so quickly...

Both John Goodricke and Edward Pigott began to note that the changes were regular and concluded that a large body must be orbiting *Algol*, causing an eclipse between the star and the Earth. It was not the first time that the variability of *Algol* had been noted. The Italian astronomer, Montanari, had observed this more than a century before. Goodricke, however, was the first to establish that these light changes were periodic. He and Pigott continued their observations for some time until the end of the season when *Algol* could no longer be seen over the horizon at York, then communicated his findings to the Royal Society on 12 May 1783. This communication caused considerable interest in astronomical circles.

With the remaining short life vouchsafed to him, Goodricke discovered, besides that of *Algol,* the variability of two other naked-eye stars β Lyrae and δ Cephei. He presented four known *Algol* papers to the Royal Society in London: -

'A series of observations on, and a discovery of, the period of the variation of the light of the bright star in the Head of Medusa, called Algol' (written in 1783).

'On the period of the changes of light in the star Algol' (written in 1784).

'A series of observations on, and a discovery of, the period of the variation of the light of the star by Bayer, near the Head of Cepheus' (written in 1784).

'Observations of the new variable star' (written in 1785).

On 30 March 1786, he observed the star, *Lyrae*, for the last time and he died tragically on 20 April 1786 at the age of 22 years old and was later buried in a family vault at Hunsingore, Yorkshire. His death was caused by pneumonia contracted from long exposure to the night air during his astronomical observations of the stars.

Goodricke's discoveries laid the foundations of an important branch of stellar astronomy. For this work, he was posthumously awarded the prestigious Copley Medal two weeks after his death. The award cited that "the discovery was made by a deaf and dumb man". He was not aware of the award. Two weeks before his death, he was elected a Fellow of the Royal Society. There is a commemorative plaque on the wall marking the house where he discovered *Algol.*

Geoffrey J Eagling & David R Kettle

Charles Gorham
1861-1922

Charles Gorham was a well known Deaf missioner in the Midlands, more especially in Derby and its district. He was born deaf in Walkeringham, Nottingham, on 19 October 1861, the son of a country clergyman and educated by Mr. J. Barber at a private school in West Brompton. He never acquired speech at this school. He was a high-spirited and mischievous boy, devoted to games and very sociable. After leaving school, he took up draughtsmanship and resided at Derby around 1880. He appears to have been an exceptionally clever man and talented sportsman, helping to found both Derby and Nottingham Deaf football and cricket clubs. He introduced cricket to the Deaf world. He was a good opening bat and was instrumental in organising cricket matches between the deaf clubs. He gave reports on Deaf cricket as well as articles explaining the principles of cricket. Gorham was also the captain of the first Deaf English football team, playing full-back in the international against Scotland at Queen's Park on 28 March 1891, which ended in a 3-3 draw.

Gorham was never in favour of the exclusive use of oralism for the deaf and was a strong advocate of the combined system. He was the editor of *The Deaf and Dumb Times*, which he published for two years from 1889-1891 until it was taken over by *The Deaf Chronicle*. Gorham helped to make *The Deaf and Dumb Times* an influential monthly magazine for which he wrote a number of characteristically spirited articles. It was as Editor of *The Deaf and Dumb Times* that Gorham made his greatest contribution to the Deaf community. He was a great motivator and took up the issue of a need for a national Deaf organisation. He used the pages of his magazine to support Maginn's proposal to form a National Deaf association, reporting on international conferences such as the Paris Congress in 1889 that showed what strengths Deaf people could gain as a collective body.

He used his magazine to help with the arrangements that led to the first British National Deaf Conference held at St. Saviour's Church in Oxford Street, London, in January 1890 and the congress that was staged at the Church Institute, 5 Albion Place, Leeds, during summer 1890. This led to the formation of the BDDA. He was one of the founding members of the British Deaf and Dumb Association. It was Gorham who was largely responsible for the first draft constitution of the newly formed BDDA, paying out of his own pocket for the services of a solicitor to help with the draft. Although this draft constitution was subjected to a few amendments at the inaugural Congress of the BDDA, it remained as the framework of the organisation until 1970. One of the amendments that Gorham disagreed with (like Maginn) was the use of the word 'Dumb' in the title. Although he was appointed the first Honorary Secretary, he resigned after one year.

In 1893, Gorham did his best to promote the interests of the BDDA. He brought in the proposal to allow the BDDA a free hand and should not be bound down to the obligations to any existing societies" and succeeded.

After his retirement from work on *The Deaf and Dumb Times* and national Deaf politics, he devoted most of his leisure time to the welfare of the deaf. He was closely connected with the Derby Association for the Deaf, canvassing widely for subscriptions and conducting or helping in Sunday Mission Services in Derby.

He moved to Nottingham and spent his last twenty years of his life there, but still retained his deep interest in the Derby Mission, visiting there on a regular basis.

Gorham fell ill and spent his convalescence in his old Yorkshire home, Leeds. He passed away at the age of 60 on 26 August 1922.

Anthony J. Boyce & Peter W. Jackson

Sir Edward Gostwicke
1620-1671

Sir Edward Gostwicke was the sixth child of Sir William Gostwicke, second Baronet of Willington, Bedfordshire, and his wife, Anne Wentworth. Edward became the heir to the baronetcy when his elder brother William died as a child. Born deaf, he succeeded to the baronetcy when aged 10 on the death of his father a few months before the birth of his youngest brother - also named William, who was also born deaf. Sir Edward was described by John Hacket, Archdeacon of Bedford between 1631 and 1637, as: -

a sweet creature of rare perspicuity of nature whose behaviour, gestures and zealous signs have procured and allowed him admittance to sermons, prayers, the Lords Supper and to the marriage of a lady of a great and prudent family, his understanding speaking as much in all his motions as if his tongue could articulately deliver his mind.

Sir Edward and his brother William (1630-1696) were both given to pursuing women of their fancy, even after marriages (Sir Edward to a Mary Lytton, and William to a Joanna Wharton). Sir Edward for many years pursued the affections of Dorothy Osborne who was later to complain:-

just now, I was called away to entertain two dumb gentlemen… They have made such a tedious visit and I am tired of making signs and tokens for everything I had to say! Good God! How do those that always live with them? They are brothers; and the eldest is a baronet, has a good estate, a wife and three or four children. He was my servant (suitor) heretofore and comes to see me still for old love's sake but if he could have made me mistress of the world I could not have had him. And yet I'll swear he has nothing to be disliked in him except for his want of tongue.

It is a pity, perhaps, that Dorothy Osborne rejected Sir Edward - her family was ruined by the Civil War whereas Sir Edward's deafness prevented his being involved and his estate came through unscathed, and he was quite a rich man.

Bulwer dedicated *Philocophus; Or the Deafe and Dumbe Man's Friende* to the Gostwicke brothers for their lip reading abilities, yet we can see from Hacket's and Dorothy Osborne's letters that they used sign language. Because Sir Edward was rich and could travel, he undoubtly met many other deaf people, and gave their names to Bulwer.

Peter W. Jackson

**Sir James Graham,
Sixth Duke of Montrose
1878-1954**

Born into one of one of Scotland's most aristocratic families, James Graham went deaf when he was a boy of 15 while at school at Eton. He blamed a rifle going off close to his ear during a Volunteer field day. However, the great floods of 1894 that affected Eton badly caused many septic throats amongst the boys when he was at school, and it is more probable that his deafness (and his fixed vocal cords) were post-diphtheritic. His deafness put paid to a planned military and political career but did not stop him from going to India with a Royal Astronomical Society party in 1899 where he became the first man ever to cine-film a total eclipse of the sun in 1899.

From India, he went to fight in the South African (Boer) War of 1900 where he was awarded a medal. After that war, he tried to stand for the South African Parliament but was unsuccessful and he returned home and stood as the Conservative candidate for Stirlingshire, where he was again unsuccessful. He also fought two unsuccessful by-elections for the Eye constituency in Suffolk.

Always active in naval affairs, he resuscitated the Royal Naval Volunteer Reserve at the start of the 1914-8 War and became its Commodore. He also designed the first-ever aircraft carrier, the *Argus*, and was the designer and owner of the world's first heavy seagoing oil-fired motor ship. For this work, he was elected president of the Institute of Marine Engineers. For his wartime service as Commodore, he was awarded two medals.

After the death of his father, the fifth Duke, Sir James Graham finally got the political career he desired, but in the House of Lords. In a successful career as well, his most noteworthy moment came when he persuaded the Labour Government that to provide *free* artificial limbs, *free* dentures and *free* spectacles under the new National Health Service but to *actually charge* for the provision of hearing aids to deaf people was blatant discrimination. The Government was shamed into amending their Bill so that it could pass through the House of Lords. This allowed for the free provision of hearing aids as well as batteries under the National Health Service.

He became President of the National Institute for the Deaf (later the RNID) in 1944 and served in this capacity until his death on 20 January 1954 at his home near Loch Lomond. He left a widow, Lady Mary Douglas Hamilton, whom he had married in 1906, two sons and two daughters.

Note: the 2nd Duke of Montrose (1712-1790) was also deaf, unable to speak, and for the last thirty years of his life from 1760 onwards, totally blind as well and needed an interpreter for even everyday communication with his wife.

Peter W. Jackson

80

William Gray
1806-1881

William Gray was born in the Scottish village of Scone, near Perth, in 1806. Being deaf, he was admitted at the age of 13 to the Edinburgh Institution for the Education of Deaf and Dumb Children on 26 March 1819 where he remained until 1824. Little is known about Gray's movements between 1824 and 1855, although it is known that he attended religious services organised by Edinburgh Deaf Church, established in 1830 by Matthew Robert Burns and also he married a Deaf Aberdonian woman named Isabella. Gray earned his living as a tailor. In August 1855, Gray, his wife and daughter emigrated to Canada to seek his fortune. Upon their arrival in Halifax, the provincial capital of Nova Scotia, William Gray set up his tailoring shop but it lasted only one year due to lack of business.

During the summer of 1856, a momentous event in Gray's life occurred when a fellow Deaf Scotsman, George Tait, espied him sign-conversing with his wife and daughter in the street. Tait, already having a Deaf girl under his private tuition, suggested that Gray join him to establish a school for deaf children in the province with Gray as a teacher and Tait doing promotional work and soliciting funds. Gray warmed to the idea. The school was opened in the back of a house *destitute of common comforts and even necessities of life* in Argyle Street in Halifax on 4 August 1856 with two pupils.

The existence of the new school attracted the attention of a local Anglican minister, the Rev. James C Cochrane, who had subsequently visited it because of his interest in deaf people sparked by a chance meeting on board of a ship with the celebrated Laurent Clerc. Cochrane started his 23-year association with the school, commencing with raising funds.

Upon the successful petition for financial support prepared by Cochrane, in February 1857 the provincial government took over the administration of the school. That made Nova Scotia the first among the British Canadian provinces to recognise through governmental support for the need for the appropriate education for its deaf children. William Gray was re-designated as assistant teacher when Cochrane successfully prised James Scott Hutton, a hearing teacher from the Edinburgh Deaf and Dumb Institution, to become its first Principal in August 1857.

There are, however, records that Gray had neither the abilities nor the qualities to work with deaf children. Tait reported in 1877 that *Gray was not capable of supplying the place of a first class teacher.* Nevertheless, the Institution had a consistently growing school roll and it moved to several locations, into a bigger building every time.

On 12 March 1870, Gray was summoned to a special meeting of the Directors of the Nova Scotia Institution to hear complaints against him for intemperance and maltreatment of pupils and he was summarily dismissed from his teaching post after 13 years' service.

Gray resumed his tailoring trade for about two years. In 1873, he and his wife departed Halifax for the Boston suburb of Cambridge in the United States to be with their daughter and her husband. Between 1880 and 1881, Gray was admitted to an almshouse at the Middlesex County Hospital in the Massachusetts town of Tewkesbury, where he met his end through paraplegia on 30 June 1881, at the age of 74. His wife eventually returned to Nova Scotia with her daughter and son-in-law around 1884. In 1893 Isabella Gray died and was interred in a pauper's grave.

In September 1907, at its 3rd Annual Convention, the Maritime Deaf-Mute Association, by committee vote, decreed that William Gray be considered as the founder of the Institution for the Deaf and Dumb in Halifax. They also voted to erect a monument on school grounds in his memory. This, however, was never carried out.

In 1976, the recognition of William Gray's founding of the Halifax Institution and his contribution to deaf education of Nova Scotians during its early days was honoured by the Canadian Cultural Society of the Deaf by including his name on its Deaf Hall of Fame roll.

John A. Hay

William A. Griffiths
1842-1927

The Deaf community in Birmingham owes its development to the tenacity and determination of one man, William A. Griffiths. Born in 1842, he became deaf due to "brain fever" (probably meningitis) at the age of 3½ and was educated at the Institution for the Deaf and Dumb at Edgbaston, leaving at the age of 15 to become an apprentice brass-chaser.

Soon after his marriage in 1860, he observed that Deaf people in Birmingham had no place for religious and social intercourse and began to campaign on their behalf for special services. At the same time, he studied late into the night to improve his command of language so that he could write letters to local newspapers describing the needs of local Deaf people. All his efforts were ignored until a local Baptist minister, the Reverend Scrivon, approached the Institution of the Deaf and Dumb to learn the manual alphabet so that he could converse with his local Deaf parishioners and was put in touch with Griffiths. Learning of Griffiths' abortive efforts to start up services for local Deaf people, the minister offered the use of a room at the Lodge Road Baptist Chapel.

The first meeting of adult Deaf people in Birmingham took place in 1867. Meetings were later moved to the Highbury Chapel and Griffiths continued to hold prayer meetings until 1870 when, through his efforts and a growing band of sympathisers, the Birmingham Town Mission established a special branch for the deaf and a room at the Highbury Hall was made available for his use. The Town Mission also offered William Griffiths the post of missioner to the local Deaf at a small salary. Accepting this post was a financial sacrifice for the young missioner as he already had a full time job that was much better paid.

In 1906, the Birmingham Town Mission decided to give up its Deaf branch and a separate society, the Birmingham and Midland Adult Deaf and Dumb Association, was formed, with William Griffiths still as its missioner. This Association was later to become the present day Birmingham Institute for the Deaf.

In 1917, W. A. Griffiths retired after 50 years faithful service with the Deaf people of Birmingham, and was replaced by a hearing missioner, the Reverend F. W. Gilby, who was able to build on the energy and perseverance of the former missioner and to take the Adult Deaf and Dumb mission to greater heights. Even in his retirement, Griffiths continued to serve the Deaf community of Birmingham after being persuaded by the Reverend Gilby to become a lay-preacher.

William A. Griffiths died peacefully in his sleep at his home in Handsworth, Birmingham, in 1927.

Peter W. Jackson

Jane Elizabeth Groom
1839 -1908

Jane Groom was genetically born deaf on 18 December 1839 at Woodgate, near Wem in the county of Salop. Her father was a land surveyor and estate agent. Her unhappy early years led to her placement with her uncles who showed kindness to her, as well as to her sister who was also deaf. In 1850, at the age of 10, she went to the Manchester Institution for the Deaf and Dumb at Old Trafford and was educated under Mr. Patterson for four years. Her progress was so rapid that she eventually became an assistant teacher at the same school. Whilst there, she knew William Stainer as a colleague and was impressed with his skills in teaching young deaf children.

Jane moved out of Manchester to gain further practical training in different institutions and settled in London. During the early 1870s, she showed much interest in the newly established London School Board. When the Board did not include any plans for deaf children living in London and areas round it, she thought it was not right that deaf children should not be admitted to Board schools in the same way as hearing children. So she presented her petition to the Board in that day classes for deaf children should be established. She also recommended the Board to appoint her old colleague from Manchester, the Rev. William Stainer. Stainer duly took charge of all day classes for deaf children in London. At the same time in 1875, the Board appointed Jane Groom as a teacher of deaf children at Wilmot Green School in Bethnal Green, East End of London. Her day class for deaf children was formed as a department of the school, which had 1,500 hearing children on its roll. It was a challenge which succeeded and Jane's reputation grew during her seven years of teaching there.

After the Milan Conference in 1880, the Rev. William Stainer dismissed three deaf teachers of the deaf, including Jane Groom, from Board schools. When the oral system was increasingly put into practice throughout the Board schools containing classes for deaf children by trained hearing teachers using the system, Jane felt unhappy and felt that she was almost at a standstill, uncertain of where she was going. She thought the oral system was good for one-to-one basis for private conversations but not for deaf children assembled together. She favoured a combination of the sign language and oral teaching in the classroom situation. However she insisted that *"in many instances the sign language is the best, and is likely to remain so while the world lasts."* Jane left her teaching career for good and took up deaf missionary work in 1882.

In her spare time during her teaching spell in London, she ran her Bible classes twice on Sundays for about 100 deaf adults who came from the densely populated suburb of Hackney and extended her work there after she left the Board school. It was in this deprived area she experienced much sadness in witnessing distress, poverty, starvation and unemployment amongst the young deaf adults. She appealed to the London Royal Association in Aid of the Deaf and Dumb for help and also suggested the setting up of a Ladies' Committee to look into the working conditions of deaf women in London. Having received little or no hope from that quarter, she decided to take a year's break by visiting Canada in 1883. Whilst there, she thought it would be a splendid locality for British deaf people to settle in and resolved to set up a party of deaf people and their families for emigration to Canada.

Returning to England, Jane Groom wasted no time in drawing up her famous petition, which included the detailed explanations as to how the scheme regarding the emigration of a party of deaf people was to be operated. Her application was signed by many influential people from Shropshire and others. The Prime Minister of the day, W. E. Gladstone, favoured the scheme by giving £100 out of the Royal Bounty Fund, not because of the scheme itself but to acknowledge Jane Groom's services amongst the deaf. She presented her petition to the Canadian Government and whilst waiting for their reply, Jane continued her campaign by presenting herself during public lectures, which were addressed to by her hearing supporters, and solicited for her growing funds which would support her scheme. Drama performances in public theatres were given by deaf actors to support the scheme. Mr. Cronshey, a gentleman, wrote:-

> … I am truly amazed at her (Miss Groom), seeing she is the only lady doing good among the deaf and dumb in London….

In April 1884, Jane Groom received the news that the Canadian Government approved her scheme and duly started for Canada in charge of a party of deaf emigrants in the following month. The party included 10 men and two boys, all deaf. They went to Manitoba and were employed according to their skills, which ranged from farming and harness-making to cabinet-making, bricklaying and shoe-making. Jane was naturally pleased but was dismayed at the criticism and abuse, which she read in local Manitoba papers. Yet she returned to England and brought in her second party of 24 deaf settlers and families to the same area. It was reported in 1886 by a Francis George Jefferson, a deaf man from the first party, that all deaf settlers obtained their employment. Groom continued her work with deaf settlers but her petition for further funding was stopped in 1892 when she was compelled to return to England with her deaf sister.

On 3 March 1908, Jane Elizabeth Groom died in London, finishing her days as spinster and dressmaker. Summarising, Jane Groom was a hard-working Deaf lady who gave her all to the Deaf community and was forced out of her 30 years' teaching career. Then she turned, at a considerable loss to herself, to preaching evangelism amongst the Deaf and was the first Deaf lady to petition at governmental level with great success. Here she gave opportunities to parties of British deaf emigrants for employment, settlement and better living conditions.

Doreen E. Woodford & Anthony J. Boyce

Painting by Beatrice Gubbins

Beatrice Gubbins
1878-1944

Dunkathel House stands about three miles outside Cork City, Ireland. A charming and elegant 18th-century Georgian house, it was purchased by Thomas Wise Gubbins who had five deaf daughters. It now houses an exhibition room open to the public where more than 50 paintings by one of these daughters may be viewed.

Beatrice Gubbins was born in 1878 in Limerick. It is not known where she was formally educated, but she attended the Crawford School of Art near the King's University (now the University College of Cork), where her sister Frances Gertrude also attended in 1885. A very talented water-colourist, Beatrice lived nearly all her life in Dunkathel although she was also a determined traveller in search of scenery for her water-colours. In her travels all over Europe and North Africa (and also the West Indies in 1930), Beatrice recorded her journeys in the form of a visual diary. She did the same during World War I whilst serving as a nurse, cycling all over Devon sketching and painting.

Beatrice Gubbins is regarded as one of the best of the highly talented amateur water-colourists of the early 20th century. Her subjects were very varied; intimate genre and domestic scenes, still life and landscapes. For many years she was secretary to the Queenstown Sketching Club, an enthusiastic amateur group whose rules and papers are still preserved at Dunkathel. Beatrice exhibited a number of water-colours at the Royal Hibernan Academy in Dublin in 1910 and 1911, where for the purpose of anonymity amongst highly critical Sketching Club members, she signed her works either as 'Greyhound', 'Jessamine' or 'Benjamin'.

Most of her 60 pictures are still at Dunkathel, where she died in 1944.

David Breslin

**Joseph Hague
1844-1879**

By the time Joseph Hague was born in Newton Heath, Manchester, in 1844, the education of Deaf children was well established in the United Kingdom. Joseph's mother, Charlotte, who was Deaf, had been educated at the Manchester Institution for the Deaf and Dumb and his Deaf brother was being educated as well. It is not clear whether Joseph's father, a shoemaker, was also Deaf.

The Manchester Institution for the Deaf and Dumb (later the Royal Schools for the Deaf) where Joseph Hague was educated.

However, the education of deaf children who were blind was only just beginning. There was much speculation, investigation and discussion about the possibilities and practicalities of such education. Joseph became blind at the age of two and was fortunate that one of the most experienced and successful practitioners of this new skill of bringing education to children who were both deaf and blind was the then headmaster at the Manchester Institution for the Deaf and Dumb – Andrew Patterson.

Andrew Patterson already had some experience in this field by the time Joseph Hague joined his school at the age of 8 in 1852. The fee was two shillings per week. Joseph had the advantage of coming from a home with Deaf people in it. As soon as her little boy became blind, Charlotte Hague had started to use touch to communicate with him and he already had acquaintance with signs and was a "communicating" child. Joseph also used touch to feel objects, work out their use and identify them and there position. He had developed the use of his tongue to add to that knowledge. This obviously intelligent and very determined child was ready for all that the Institution had to offer. Joseph learned from a more advanced fellow pupil (Mary Bradley who died young), from his deaf fellow pupils and above all, from Andrew Patterson and his staff.

Joseph learned rapidly, being greatly interested in words and their meanings. He mastered reading in the specially embossed books purchased for him, showing a particular interest in the Bible and religious matters. A very independent boy, Joseph insisted on doing the normal dormitory and other tasks for himself. At the same time, Joseph showed himself as humorous and capable of teasing others. His awareness of the approach of another person, and the identity of that person, was acute. He also knew the exact clothing of each pupil and used this knowledge to help identify each one. He had both likes and dislikes amongst other pupils.

It was fortunate that the Henshaw's Blind Asylum was adjacent to the Deaf Institution. Joseph went there for a few hours daily to learn basket-making and showed sufficient skill to be considered capable of earning his own living. This was what he wanted to do and, appreciating his parents' ability and willingness to converse with him, went home. Home was now in Sheffield where he did begin to earn a living. However, trouble came to the family and Joseph ended up in the workhouse. This was not a disaster, for he was treated well and was able to continue attending all local activities and religious services. These were a great source of pleasure to him and the local Deaf community took good care of him. At services, one friend would sit by him and, holding

Joseph's left hand, would spell everything for him. Others would take him to their homes for a meal between services and then, after the last service, walk him back to the workhouse.

Joseph kept in continuous touch (by "perforated writing") with Andrew Patterson. Learning portions of the Bible, reading especially biographies and making baskets filled his days. Joseph's exceptional memory for people and events amazed those who knew him; his carefully reasoned questions were proof of a very alert mind.

In 1878, Joseph was, to his great grief, absent for the first time in 13 years, from the annual Christmas treat provided for the Deaf by the treasurer of the Sheffield Association. He had become seriously ill and was thinking even more of the religious faith and hope he had. He looked forward to meeting Deaf friends in heaven. Much of his conversation in the weeks before he died was about his faith.

While in the workhouse hospital, Joseph received visits and gifts from his many friends, both Deaf and hearing. He died on 28 February 1879, a fine example of the possibilities of education and development for those Deaf persons who were also blind. Much that was written about him encouraged others to try this new branch of education of the Deaf. At the same time, Joseph Hague is notable because he learned from his Deaf family, from other Deaf pupils and was fully integrated into, and helped by, his local Deaf community. He was buried in the Sheffield General Cemetery, and was later joined there with his mother Charlotte, who passed away on 21 November 1880.

A friend who had received what may well have been Joseph's last letter, wrote a poem about him after his death. The poem included these lines:-

> *Walled in by Deafness, Dumbness, Blindness, all!*
> *Could life exist beneath that dreadful pall?*
> *It did.*

Doreen E. Woodford

Felicia "Kate" Catherine Harvey
1862-1946

The baby girl, born in 1862 to a Frederick Glanville, a clerk working in the London Investment Company, and his wife Felicia was destined to become famous in ways that they can never have imagined. Deafness would mean that she made no speeches and entered into no discussions, yet her actions influenced many areas of the next seventy or so years.

Brackenhill Open-Air School about 1928. Kate Harvey is the middle person in the middle row wearing her head-dress.

When and how that loss of hearing came about is not clear, but well before the new century began the word "deaf" was often included in accounts of her doings. Her early interests were in medical care, particularly physiotherapy. Having married Frank Harvey, a member of a very well known firm of cotton merchants, she went with him to India, using her knowledge to help the local people.

On their return to England they settled in Kent. Frank died in 1905, leaving Kate and their three daughters, very comfortably provided for. By now Kate had become active in the local Suffrage movement. (Being always non-militant, she was a "suffragist" rather than a "suffragette", but the more common term is usually used in accounts of her activities).

These activities increased and she became prominent in national suffragette doings. She was closely linked with the famous Charlotte Despard, travelling as secretary to national and international gatherings, selling suffragette publications, organising protest marches and, like many other women, withholding her taxes and refusing to complete census forms. Neither would she pay the insurance for her gardener.

The house was repeatedly barricaded to keep out the bailiffs who attempted to seize her possessions so that they could be sold to pay the money and the outstanding fines. During one sale, her "pocket-electrophone" was taken by a bystander, and it was reported that this meant she could hear nothing.

Eventually she was put in prison in Holloway, being discharged as a very sick woman, and this sparked local and national protests that a deaf lady should be so treated. She returned to her home in Bromley, and to her activities there. This was a house named "Brackenhill" and as well as being the base for her political activities, it was the setting for another of her major interests. There she ran a home for handicapped children, mostly from the East End of London, where she was already deeply engaged in welfare work. She used her therapy skills and also spent her own money on equipping the house and employing people to look after the children.

The outbreak of the First World War changed Kate's life entirely. Like many other suffragettes, she ceased all political activities and devoted herself to aiding the war efforts. The children at "Brackenhill" were sent home and the whole house given over to caring for poor women and children who could not enter the regular hospitals, where the beds were all occupied by the wounded of the fighting forces. Again, all the expenses were borne by Kate herself. Others she housed included French and Belgian refugees. The care given in the 31 beds received praise from all who knew about it.

Kate's other interests included Irish Affairs and the teachings of "Theosophy". In everything she depended on Charlotte Despard, travelling with her, doing a great deal of administrative work for her and staying with her, often including her three children in the holidays. This led to the joint purchase by the two women of a property, in the second year of the War, in Hartfield, Sussex. It was a house in large grounds and a pleasant setting. The two ladies gave the name "Kurundai" to this house. The fact that Kate seemed to have few other friends may be explained by two factors; the first was the intensity of the affection Kate had for Charlotte who in some ways made use of her and the second was the effect of her deafness, which made the cultivation of other friendships less easy as the years passed.

However, there came a great lessening in the closeness between the two and in 1921 Kate became the sole owner of "Kurundai". She changed its name to "Brackenhill", opened a school there and based the day-to-day running on Greek and Roman practices of education that had been developed in Germany and attracted her attention during one of her earlier visits. Life, including sleeping, was open-air, there was a religious in-put according to her beliefs, and service to the community was important. The diet was vegetarian. Meanwhile the community supported fund-raising activities for the school.

Kate, (called "Godmother" by the pupils) wearing simple clothes and sandals, and always a headscarf, was fully involved in the running, joined by her unmarried daughter, until the school was taken over by "The Invalid Children's Aid Society". (It was moved elsewhere in 1928). Everyone communicated with Kate by fingerspelling, and had done so far many years. She added international organisations to her many interests, especially those to do with women.

When Kate entered her seventies, and slowly withdrew to her own house in Hartfield, cared for by a succession of paid and faithful persons, some of whom she remembered in her will. When she died at the age of 83, few outside the village and her family remembered this indomitable deaf activist. It seems fitting that it was "The Women's Bulletin", the paper of "The Women's Freedom League" that mentioned the death of the "pioneer member, Mrs. Kate Harvey".

Doreen E. Woodford

**George Frederick Healey
1843-1927**

George Healey was born in Gateacre, near Liverpool, and was found to be deaf sometime before the age of two. (It was attributed to a fall from the arms of his nurse at the age of 3 months). He was sent first to the private school at Rugby to be educated under Henry Brothers Bingham and then to the Liverpool School under Dr. Buxton. On leaving school, he was apprenticed to his father's coach-building business, rising to work in the office where he stayed till his father's death in 1890. Every year he visited London and, while there, went to the services conducted by Samuel Smith and Charles Rhind. He found these so helpful for deaf people that he determined that the deaf of Liverpool should have similar services. He started these in 1864 and they became the start of the Liverpool Adult Deaf and Dumb Benevolent Society. Healey became Hon. Missioner and Hon. Secretary of the Society and stayed its Secretary until he died.

The very first report of the Institute in 1864 lists many activities. The sick were visited; employment was found for 21 deaf people and many other unemployed deaf people received financial help. There had been free Christmas breakfasts for 34 deaf people and 158 religious services, together with 20 public lectures, had been held. The services and other activities moved from one place to another until 1887 when a new purpose-built institute was opened in Princes Avenue, Liverpool. Healey conducted services regularly, but was now licensed as a lay-reader.

It was Healey, said to be "a leader in activity and example", who attended the first convention of the short-lived National Deaf and Dumb Society, and was involved in the founding of the NDDS, which lasted for seven years. Following the collapse of the NDDS, Healey then became involved in initial discussions, held in Liverpool in 1886, of the desirability of having a national association for deaf people. This was eventually to lead to the founding of the British Deaf and Dumb Association in 1890. One of the reasons for the foundation was the refusal of the Royal Commission on the Blind and the Deaf in 1886 to accept the views of deaf people: but the Commissioners had thought well enough of Healey's own submission to include it in the published evidence. George Healey was to be Honorary Treasurer of the BDDA for an incredible quarter of a century almost up to his death, earning himself the affectionate title of 'the Grand Old Man'.

Healey then became involved with the newly founded Institute of Missionaries for the Deaf in 1893 and was instrumental in setting up a very much-needed Pension Fund. There was little happening at that time that did not have the help and encouragement of George Healey. He received many honours including a Testimonial at the BDDA Congress in 1925.

Healey never married but was cared for by his devoted sister. In 1927 at the age of 84, he had a stroke and died. He was buried in Anfield with a private ceremony. At a public memorial service the next day attended by many deaf and hearing people, tribute was paid to one of the most remarkable and respected deaf persons that graced the Deaf community.

Doreen E. Woodford

Oliver Heaviside
1850 - 1925

Oliver, the youngest son of Thomas Heaviside, a wood engraver, and Rachael Elizabeth West, was born at 55 King Street (since re-named Plender Street), Camden Town, London, on 18 May 1850. His father was a strict disciplinarian and often used the strap when called for. Oliver had three brothers Herbert, Arthur and Charles. At the age of eight, he had scarlet fever from which he recovered slowly but was rendered permanently deaf. He received his education at the Camden House School, St. Pancras, and by the time he was fifteen, being the youngest candidate, he was awarded a special prize for the highest marks in natural science and passed examinations in many academic subjects with flying colours.

Oliver's uncle was a well-known physicist, Sir Charles Wheatstone, who was a pioneer in telegraphy. He saw how talented both Oliver and his brother Arthur were, and interested them in telegraphy. Oliver continued to study science, French, Danish and German. He was proficient in the use of Morse code. In 1868, he was employed as a telegraphic operator in Denmark and after the amalgamation of the Danish and Newcastle telegraphic firms, he found himself appointed as the chief operator at Newcastle and worked there for four years. His brother was also at Newcastle, employed as a Post Office engineer. In 1874, Oliver left and at his parents' home, locking himself in his room, he concentrated on mathematics and applied it to the field of telegraphy. At the same time, his brother at Newcastle was able to up-date him the latest practical progress being made in the field of telegraphy. Oliver's greatest contribution in telegraphy was the elimination of signal distortions in telecommunication. His brilliant scientific achievements are well documented. He was elected a Fellow of the Royal Society in 1891. Although he never did any practical work on radios, he was made famous by his suggestion that there was a conducting layer in the upper atmosphere of the earth which would allow radio signals to go round the earth. This layer was eventually called the Heaviside Layer, now known as the ionosphere.

As a result of Oliver's self-study, he developed his own style of mathematical reasoning. This led to much confusion amongst the conventional scientists of the day who wished to learn something from him. Editors of the Society of Telegraphic Engineers repeatedly rejected his early articles for publication as the standards set by the Post Office had to be conformed to. He was very bitter about this rejection. Eventually his articles were published and news spread round the world. He became famous. A well-known scientist, who often visited Oliver, wrote of him:

His habit was to retire to his room about 10 o'clock at night and to work there until the early hours of the morning. He closed his door and window, lit his oil lamp, and allowed the air to become hot and stifling. He worked also during that day, in seclusion. In order that he might not be disturbed, his food was placed outside his door, and there it remained until he was disposed to take it.

For many reasons, he was a neglected person but he was an extraordinary eccentric character with a mischievous sense of humour.

Tired of praises and of being showered with honours which he rejected, he fled to Devon and never left that place, living the life of a virtual recluse to the end of his days.

Living alone in his bachelor quarters, he found company in Mary Way who got on well with him. Oliver did not pay much attention to her at that time, but once when Mary was out and did not return by the time Oliver expected, she eventually returned and found Oliver in the garden with a lit candle *"looking for her dead body"*. Oliver was really fond of her. Later Mary had a stroke and had to leave. Oliver was devastated. Then he was on his own. As he made no money out of his amazing inventions and discoveries, he lived in relative poverty. Oliver's friends helped him out with his unpaid bills, and brought some candles. One of his very few friends was the village bobby who did the shopping for him and when he came to his house, he blew his whistle through the letter box to attract attention. Oliver corresponded with many famous scientists and in one such letter, he titled himself as O. Heaviside, W.O.R.M. His neighbours gave him the nickname Worm. Such was his eccentricity.

It is interesting to note that he provided, in theory, the basic foundation of the telephone transmission. At the same time, Alexander Graham Bell whose wife was deaf, and Thomas Edison, the deaf inventor of the electric light, were experimenting with and improvising the telephone system. One thing led to another throughout the 20th century until the fax machine, the minicom and the internet came into being which are used extensively by the Deaf community today. One can say that Oliver Heaviside, himself deaf, is the father of all telecommunication devices used by the Deaf.

Oliver Heaviside moved to a nursing home, proved himself to be very popular with the elderly residents. He dyed his hair black and wore a tea-pot cover as a hat. He died on 3 February 1925. *"He was such a dear old man"* was echoed by all at the nursing home.

World-wide tributes were paid to Oliver Heaviside at the Heaviside Centenary meeting on 18 May 1950.

Anthony J. Boyce

Joseph Hepworth
1865-1921

When it comes to appreciating Deaf people who did a lot to preserve the history and writings of their own people, Abraham Farrar tends to spring to mind. However, Farrar's contribution, admirable as it is, was mainly in the area of preservation of published works on the Deaf and their related issues. There is one other person whose contribution is immeasurable and in no small way priceless. This person is none other than Joseph Hepworth, the proprietor and editor of *British Deaf Times*. His publication is now a rich source of information for researchers in the history of the British Deaf and its community.

Joseph Hepworth was born in 1865 at Wakefield, Yorkshire, of parents who worked in factories associated with boiler and engineering works. He was hearing until the age of eight years when he went deaf. The cause of deafness was unknown and for some years since becoming deaf, Joseph suffered from the additional trouble of being almost blind. Fortunately, the blindness went and Joseph retained his speech, but never went to a school for the deaf. Joseph took an apprenticeship in the factory where his parents worked; Joseph worked through all departments, gaining experience that would sufficiently equip him with a bright future in engineering.

When Joseph was 22 years old, he bumped into a Deaf house painter by chance and a conversation ensued. Joseph, like many hearing people of his time, was familiar with the manual alphabet and was able to hold a conversation. The Deaf man asked him which deaf school he went and this surprised Joseph, as he was unaware that there were many other deaf persons around; he often assumed there were no more than a dozen deaf people in the whole of Britain! His meeting with the Deaf painter was the turning point of his career – Joseph proceeded to Leeds and started to mix with the Deaf in that city, participating in the daily life of the community. During his early period mixing with the Deaf of Leeds, Joseph learnt for the first time that the Deaf required special treatment; that they possessed their own peculiarities, which could be understood only by those who devoted their whole undivided energies to the task. Joseph applied and succeeded in becoming an assistant missioner under Joseph Moreton and he studied not only sign language, but also other elements such as the psychology of the Deaf. After his association with Moreton, Joseph became an assistant missioner to the Bolton and District Deaf and Dumb Society.

In 1896, he was appointed a missioner to the Glamorgan and Monmouth Mission to the Deaf and Dumb, a position that he held up to the time of his death. This mission in Cardiff was then in an unsatisfactory condition, but Joseph in quite a short period of time turned it into a very popular place, where many local deaf persons freely came for help.

Side by side with his mission work, Joseph was deeply involved with journalistic work. For nearly 30 years he was connected with Deaf journalism. First, it was the *Deaf Chronicle*, in which he was associated with A.M. Cuttell, Charles Gorham, H.B. Beale and Edward Alfred Kirk. Then the *British Deaf Mute* was started, this again to become the *British Deaf Monthly*. In 1902, the *British Deaf Times* appeared. The *British Deaf Times* was a successful journal, rich in information on Deaf people, its community, its aspirations and views, not only of Britain, but worldwide. This particular journal was the flagship of the British Deaf, promoting all that was good within the Deaf community of Britain. As an editor, Joseph Hepworth churned out editorials after editorials in which he continually pleaded for unity and co-operation amongst the various workers and associations concerned in the welfare of the Deaf. Joseph fought hard against oppression, prejudice, bigotry and tyranny in every shape and form. And he never sought payment for all his work as editor of the *British Deaf Times*.

As a Yorkshireman, Joseph was tough and would not stand for any nonsense, preferring not to beat about the bush. He could not suffer fools gladly; he had no use for both the timewaster and the man who changed his opinion as he changed his coat. However, those who knew him mentioned that he was a man who possessed tenderness and pity for fellows less fortunate than himself. He possessed many qualities that endeared himself to Deaf people – amongst those charisma, humility and generosity. Joseph married a deaf lady, but little is known of her.

Joseph passed away on 15 July 1921, aged only 56 years. His funeral was on 19 July at Cardiff Cemetery and a very large crowd of deaf and hearing mourners attended to pay their last respects.

Raymond Lee

James Herriot
1815-1880

James Herriot was a deaf Scotsman who founded the Manchester and Salford Deaf and Dumb Benevolent Association, the first of its kind established in the North of England. He encouraged other deaf people across the north of England to start deaf associations based on the model of self-help society which he had first seen in action in Edinburgh.

James Herriot was born in Leith, a seaport near Edinburgh, on 1 September 1815. In September 1821, he was admitted to the Edinburgh Institution for the Deaf and Dumb. After five years' schooling under Mr. Kinniburgh the well-known headmaster, he was apprenticed to be a tailor and worked at Stockbridge, Edinburgh.

In 1831, he married Isabella Shannon, a school friend. During this time, they were amongst the first members of the Deaf and Dumb Congregation of Edinburgh. This congregation was an early deaf-run self-help organisation and it included several Deaf celebrities such as Walter Geikie and Alexander Blackwood. James Herriot forged his identity in this group and throughout his life, he constantly referred to the expertise of Deaf people, rather than that of hearing.

James' tailor business started off well but somehow it did not do well during the recession of 1838. There followed five years' hardship for James and his family in Edinburgh. In 1843, they moved to Salford, Manchester, in search of new prospects. James set up his own tailor's shop and within the next twelve years, his shop moved twice and in each case, it was nearer to the centre of the town. He was a very successful tailor and in 1851 he employed 12 men in business, six of whom were deaf. He was well known and respected by many who frequented his shop.

When James arrived in Manchester, there was no social or religious meeting place for Deaf people in Manchester. He met many local Deaf people who sought for his advice and where his shop was, it was also a meeting place for Deaf people. In 1846, James approached the Rev. Alexander Munro and asked for the use of a library-room next to his Presbyterian Church on St. Peter's Square and thus followed the first ever Deaf Association in Manchester. It was called The Manchester and Salford Adult Deaf and Dumb Benevolent Association. Herriot acted as a lay preacher. After two years' steady progress, the new group was forced to leave the premises due to litigation in the Church. Herriot wasted no time and turned to the Bishop of Manchester for help. The Bishop was not able to help out because of the non-denominational character of Herriot's Deaf congregation.

Herriot did not want to let his Deaf group down and decided to give up the cutting-room of his tailoring premises and had it renovated at his own expense as a chapel for them. Regular church services were then continued for three years. During that time, many unemployed Deaf people resorted to this room and their presence took up much of Herriot's time in attending to their needs. His appeal to the public for financial support was successful and this led to the renting of larger rooms located in the centre of the city. The Deaf Association secured continuity. Releasing himself from his tailoring business, Herriot spent all his time in helping the Deaf.

James Herriot had radical ideas and was a strong believer in self-help. He thought Deaf people should run their own organisations and use money from charity to pay for them. His group was successful. The money raised was used to find work for members of the Deaf community who were unemployed, and to pay for education, welfare benefits and religious teaching. His organisation was managed by the all-Deaf committee. This was very unusual because at that time charities wanted to help disabled people, but did not want them to be involved in their management committees.

In 1850, the Manchester School for the Deaf officials were alarmed at the successful fund-raising campaigns by Herriot as the school relied heavily on local subscribers and donors for its running costs. They set up a rival Church of England deaf organisation operated by a hearing management committee. There followed a long controversy between Herriot and Mr. William Stainer who represented the rival deaf organisation over the local sponsors. The local newspaper published correspondence between them. In the end, Herriot succeeded in securing the full backing from his original sponsors and in ensuring the continuity of his own deaf association. The club moved to a more central site in Quay Street.

Herriot also promoted and helped to establish the Adult Deaf and Dumb associations at Leeds and Liverpool. He visited Huddersfield, Halifax and Bradford Deaf clubs and encouraged the Deaf community to take interest in the Gospel. He continued his work until he was 65 when he had been ill for two years and died in 1880. His hearing son, Henry Herriot, took his place.

On 15 October 1998, the James Herriot Plaque ceremony was performed on the site of the original meeting place in 1846 and the plaque, unveiled by the British Deaf History Society, can be seen on the Elizabeth House on St. Peter's Square, Manchester.

Rachel O'Neill & Anthony J. Boyce

Edwin Allan Hodgson
1854-1933

Edwin Allan Hodgson was born hearing in Manchester, England, on 28 February 1854 and he never achieved fame in Britain, for his parents emigrated to Canada while he was a young child, settling in Peterborough. However, Hodgson was to create history in the USA: he is regarded as the one person who deserves honour as the founder of the American National Association of the Deaf (NAD).

Hodgson's father was a wealthy man and was able to put his son in the best schools. Hodgson studied for two years at Collegiate Institute setting his sights on becoming a lawyer. He became fairly proficient in French, Greek and Latin. However, when his father died suddenly, in the same year, 1872, Hodgson became deaf following an attack of cerebro-spinal meningitis. This caused Hodgson to drop out of his studies and he began to pursue a professional career because he needed immediate means of support. His condition altered his outlook to life and he chose printing and typography as his vocation. Hodgson became a rapid and accurate typesetter and began to master all branches of the printing business.

He moved to America, settling first in Cleveland and later in New York. In September 1876, he obtained employment as instructor of printing at the New York School for the Deaf (also known as Fanwood). Hodgson quickly settled in, enlarged the premises to take in new printing equipments and turned the place into a fine school for teaching printing.

The New York School for the Deaf purchased *The Deaf Mutes' Journal* and Hodgson became not only its editor, but managed its business. The journal quickly grew in circulation, containing both influence and information on everything relating to the Deaf. More importantly, Hodgson became a proficient tutor in printing and this resulted in a large number of Deaf printers graduating from his department, many of whom have established their own printing business and several others gained reputation as instructors of printing in other schools for the Deaf across America. Hodgson eventually purchased *The Deaf Mutes Journal* from Henry C. Rider and became the proprietor of this famous journal. It was in this position, that Hodgson continually publicised the idea of a national organisation for the deaf, and this eventually led to the founding of the NAD.

Hodgson's interest in the Deaf community was profound; he was always involved in almost every aspect of social life of the Deaf community. For over 30 years, he had been a trustee of the Gallaudet Home for the Aged and Infirm Deaf-Mutes, charter member of the Gallaudet Club, member of the League of Elect Surds and President of the Empire State Association of the Deaf, besides being the founder and first Corresponding Secretary of the NAD which was established in Cincinnati in August 1880.

In 1883, the National Deaf-Mute Institute, now known as Gallaudet University, conferred upon Hodgson the honorary degree of Master of Arts in recognition of his scholarly attainments and of the services rendered by him in raising the standards of literary taste and performance among the Deaf. Later in 1913, he was decorated with the Legion of Honour insignia by the French Government in recognition of his work along the same line. In 1883 and again in 1912, Hodgson was a US delegate to the World Congress of the Deaf in Paris.

Hodgson had been married twice; the first to Mary Whitehead, who was a former pupil of the New York School for the Deaf. However, she died just only a year after the marriage. Hodgson's second wife was Lillian Jones, the daughter of a wealthy merchant of New York. She gave Hodgson two daughters. Lillian passed away around 1916.

Hodgson found joy with the two grandchildren of his first daughter and was able to overcome the sadness of loneliness since his wife's demise. He took to enjoy touring New England and it was during one of these tours in August 1933 that he fell ill en route to his New York home at 97 Fort Washington Avenue. Hodgson died on 14 August from cerebral haemorrhage.

Raymond Lee

George Edwin Hartnoll Hogg
1819-1906

George E. Hogg was a brilliant arithmetician, a long serving Deaf teacher of the deaf and Deaf missioner in Lancashire. George E. Hogg was probably born deaf in Bideford, a small seaport in North Devon, on 13 February 1819. His father, Mr. John Hogg, was a chemist and druggist and a classical Latin scholar, whilst his mother was an energetic Nonconformist. George derived his name from his grandfather, a merchant and ship owner of Northam. In 1827, he and his deaf brother, John Jewell Hogg, were educated at the Exeter Institution for the Deaf and Dumb under the famed Henry Brothers Bingham. The combined system was in use at this school. George remained there for seven years and he excelled himself in arithmetic and performed complex numerical calculations mentally in an amazingly short time. He was used in public exhibitions for this purpose.

In 1834, Mr. Bingham left Exeter to become the headmaster of the Manchester Institution for the Deaf and Dumb in Salford, and two years later Hogg joined his teaching staff. In 1837, the school moved to new buildings at Old Trafford. Hogg remained at this same residential school for forty-three years as its longest serving Deaf teacher of the Deaf. He carried out his duties much to the satisfaction of both headmasters Mr. Bingham and Mr. Andrew Patterson.

In 1879, Hogg resigned his post when the school decided to adopt the oral policy and became a lay-missionary, preaching to the Deaf in Bolton, Oldham, Rochdale, Ashton and Stockport. On 16 May 1892, he married Miss Louisa Williams in Stockport and very soon afterwards they moved to Macclesfield, before finally settling in Leicester. George died on 22 April 1906.

George Hogg was a quiet and unostentatious Deaf teacher. He carried out a life full of good work accomplished under difficult conditions, which could only be appreciated by his fellow colleagues in those days.

Anthony J. Boyce

Leigh Hossell
1867-1906

Born in 1867, Leigh Hossell was the son of Mr. J. J. Hossell of Cheddleton, Droitwich. It was thought that that he was either congenitally deaf or became deaf at the age of four through an attack of sunstroke. At the age of seven, he went to the Edgbaston Institution for the Deaf and Dumb as a private pupil under Mr. Hopper, the headmaster, using the manual and fingerspelling system up to the age of 15. It was whilst at the Birmingham school that Leigh first took a liking to chess, and developed a passion for this game that was to last until his death.

After the death of Mr. Hopper, Leigh's parents transferred him to the Old Trafford Schools for the Deaf as a private pupil under Mr. W. S. Bessant, the headmaster who taught orally. On the completion of his education, Leigh received training as a pupil teacher and eventually became a resident teacher there. In his leisure time, he was one of the lay helpers of the Grosvenor Street Institute for the Deaf, Manchester.

Leigh showed an aptitude for all games, both indoor and outdoor. He played for England as a goalkeeper in the second international game against Scotland. He was a skilful player in both croquet and lawn tennis. He was a remarkably fine chess player who played local hearing chess club matches. He defeated the champion of Manchester YMCA Chess club in five straight games to win the silver cup in 1896 and also won against the famous English chess champion, Mr. Blackburn, in a simultaneous chess match. He initiated great interest in chess amongst the Deaf by writing regular articles on chess and problems in *The British Deaf Times* and by arranging chess matches between Deaf clubs.

Leigh Hossell left Manchester to take up the post of Missionary to the Deaf and Dumb at Oxford. Before he left, he was presented with an illuminated testimonial to show appreciation on his 13 years' association with the school. After a year at Oxford, he relinquished the post. He continued playing in the Midlands chess league competitions as a representative of the Droitwich Workmen's Chess Club. Leigh died on 26 October 1906 at his sister's home in Handsworth after an illness, which lasted seven weeks.

Anthony J. Boyce & Phillip K. Gardner

James Howe
1780-1836

James Howe was Scotland's first, and is arguably its greatest animal painter. His drawings and paintings offer a richly detailed, often humorous, view of Scotland in the early nineteenth-century - of social custom, of transport, of life and town and country. He was fascinated by horses and came to be called 'The Man who Loved to Draw Horses'.

Born on 31 August 1780 in the village of Skirling in Peebleshire, James Howe attended the village school in Skirling but left still young and incompletely educated on account of his deafness. It has been suggested that despite his lack of education, James was considerably influenced by the schoolmaster Robert Davidson who had such neat handwriting that he was often asked to write people's names in their bibles and would do so, adorning them with little drawings of flowers and animals. James was always making drawings on every piece of paper he could lay his hands on - even his father's sermons were not safe. He would sometimes open his notes in the pulpit when ready to preach and find that they had been decorated with James' latest drawings of animals.

When he was 14, he was appointed to the Edinburgh firm of Smiton and Chancellor, coach painters – hardly an ideal apprenticeship for what he wanted to be. When this ended, James set himself up first as a portrait painter. He did paint a number of portraits, but a painting of a piebald pony in the window of his studio was so lifelike that people started to ask him to paint animals.

Howe's reputation as animal painter was made when Sir John Sinclair of the Board of Agriculture commissioned him to draw details of various breeds of cattle, and he went on to paint hundreds more pictures, mostly of horses.

After the battle of Waterloo, Howe visited the battlefield and on his return produced a panorama covering many feet of canvas that depicted incidents in the fight. This was exhibited in various places with great financial success.

Flushed with success, however, Howe was turning into an alcoholic owing to his frequenting many alehouses around Edinburgh and this, coupled with his deafness, meant he was preyed upon by unscrupulous acquaintances so that when he died in 1836, he was almost a pauper. Prior to his death, he had returned to Skirling, where he was born, in an attempt to have the country air restore his health but constant coughing made him weak, and he died of a burst blood vessel on 11 July 1836. He was interred in Skirling churchyard quite close to the house where he was born. Relatives and admirers erected to his memory a tombstone, which contains a carved palette and brushes.

Peter W. Jackson.

William Hunter
1785-1861

William Hunter has the unique distinction of being Britain's first Deaf public school teacher of the Deaf. He was born deaf and dumb in Southwark, Surrey, on 6 February 1785, one of two children of a London wharfinger's clerk and was baptised at the church of St. Olave in Tooley Street on 27 February.

The Asylum for the Deaf and Dumb in Kent Road, London, in the mid 19th century.

His father died when he was young and his widowed mother raised William in poverty. With her help, William developed a form of communication using gestures. In January 1793, William was admitted to the London Asylum for the Deaf and Dumb in Fort Place on Grange Road in Bermondsey. Under the headship of Joseph Watson, William began to learn spoken and written English through the use of manualism. From humble beginnings when he communicated using gestures, William acquired a full grasp and command of the English language.

After completing five years as a pupil at the Asylum in 1798, he was allowed to stay on to further his education. In 1801, Joseph Watson recommended to the Board of Governors that William be considered for a post of a teacher. Watson felt that certain Deaf pupils would benefit by having a Deaf teacher who would get information through to deaf people in their own manner of communication. The Board accepted Watson's recommendation and a Deaf Braidwoodian, John Creasy, was engaged to train William to become a teacher of the Deaf. After completing his training in 1804, William was engaged as a writing assistant at a salary of £15. 15s per annum, plus an allowance of £7.10s for his board. In a teaching career that was to span 57 years until 1861, he taught and served as a role model for approximately three thousand deaf pupils and worked alongside three headmasters. Evidence in the archives of Royal School for the Deaf, Margate, reveals that William Hunter taught mainly through manualism and signs.

On 21 December 1822, William married a hearing lady named Sarah Whitmore at the church of St. George the Martyr, Southwark. They raised four hearing children. William survived two epidemics that hit the Asylum, a cholera epidemic in 1832, which affected many pupils, killing one, and the influenza epidemic of 1833 in which two teachers died. He also survived a most amazing and terrifying incident. In one report in the school archives, a headmaster wrote: -

> *There was a Press Gang roaming about looking for seamen as the Napoleonic War was in full swing. Among those they seized was William Hunter. He was carried off to a warship, which was being readied for the sea. William's captors did not believe that he was profoundly deaf and as his speech was quite good, this presented a difficulty. So William lied to them that he was 'deafened'. In this way, he managed to persuade them to release him and succeeded!*

In 1861, William was struck down by apoplexy and he died on Tuesday 9 April 1861 at his family home in Peckham, Surrey.

Peter R. Brown

103

Ambrose Isted
1797-1881

Ambrose Isted was born deaf and dumb and was baptised on 22 February 1797 in Ecton, a village east of Northampton. His parents were Samuel Isted (1750-1827) and Barbara, the eldest daughter of Thomas Percy, Bishop of Dromore. The wealthy Isted family originated from Framfield, Sussex, and during the early eighteenth century settled at the Manor of Ecton (later Ecton Hall).

At the age of eight, Ambrose Isted was sent to Dromore, Ireland, and received his early tuition from his grandfather. Afterwards, Ambrose attended the London Asylum for the Deaf and Dumb as a private fee-paying pupil under Dr. Joseph Watson, the celebrated headmaster. He received a good all round education using fingerspelling and sign language; he was also taught in articulation. His efforts at articulation were apparently painful to himself and not pleasant to hear but to some extent were intelligible to his close hearing friends. In general, whoever he addressed, not one word would be understood, and during conversations in high society gatherings, he often gave *a vacant smile and a nod of apparent comprehension.* However, Ambrose's main means of communication with hearing people was via pencil and paper.

Ambrose's coming of age in February 1818 was celebrated by a ball at Ecton and on each consecutive day of the week, all the fashionable families in Northamptonshire attended. For the villagers, an ox was slaughtered and roasted whole. Being the son and heir, Ambrose succeeded his father on 12 August 1827. Assuming his father's role, he inherited his love of horses and the Pytchley Hunt. His one-eyed grey horse, 'Rosebud', was his favourite and was the mother of three horses 'Reindeer', 'Rejoicer' and 'Reformer' which he later rode. He thoroughly enjoyed hunting and all kinds of sports. Every year for sixty years, Ambrose rode ten miles north to Pytchley for the Meet of the famous Pytchley Hunt. He wore the traditional red coat with the white collar, the Pytchley trademark, and was always well mounted. He had *a striking presence and peculiarly pleasing and aristocratic features*, and was *all over a sportsman* and *every inch a gentleman,* besides *a first-class man to hounds.*

Around 1828, an extract from a poem by Matthew Fortescue written on the Pytchley Hunt read: -

> *Then Isted prepar'd for the chase has no doubt,*
> *To get his first place when he's mounted on Gout;*
> *But he had been wrong to have back'd his good luck,*
> *As Gout and his rider fell slap in a brook;*

This was Ambrose and his chestnut horse, Gout. He was reputed to be a difficult man to beat across the country. Ambrose was an avid reader of sporting journals but rarely read the rare books collected by his father. Nevertheless, he took great care of the valuable library.

Ambrose was a keen artist and drew many sketches of hunting scenes, some of which were very humorous and he contributed some to the sporting journals. He painted the Pytchley scenes of circa 1850 on the screen. An example of his sketch drawing of Jack Musters, the famous master of the Pytchley Hunt, shows his economic use of lines and his meticulous and well-practised line drawings of horses are evident in many of his sketches.

> *Though quite unable to catch a note of the music, he had few greater enjoyments than that of dancing...*

Ambrose was a brilliant dancer.

On 26 July 1832, Ambrose married Eleanor-Elizabeth Stopford, eldest daughter of the Hon. and Rev. Richard-Bruce Stopford, Canon of Windsor, and had a happy marriage. Two years after his wife's death in 1851, he married the Hon. Frances Elizabeth, daughter of Viscount Anson, and had another happy marriage, but his two marriages did not bear him any children. He had eleven servants on his estate and he was able to manage his day-to-day business but he *naturally had some difficulty in finding servants able and willing to adapt themselves to his condition.* Three servants had been with him for forty years and often accompanied Ambrose during the hunt to help with the interpreting. They also had the privilege of hearing stories about hunting from Ambrose, either from his *mouth* or from his *mysterious language of the fingers.*

As he advanced in years, Ambrose ceased riding to distant meets. Instead, he gathered a new pack of harriers and assumed the horn for his local hunt as the master of the Pytchley Harriers. Before each meet, he provided free *capital hunting breakfasts.* He also started a new business making currant jelly from his kitchen garden produce. He always took pride in his landscaped park planned by his ancestors and improvised it. He allowed villagers to enter during Easter when the daffodils were in full bloom. He was very popular with the villagers, was generous and allowed his Hall grounds for garden fetes where large sums of money were raised for good causes. He was the Deputy Lieutenant of Northamptonshire. He also showed a lifetime interest in both the affairs of his old school and the London Association in Aid of the Deaf and Dumb, often attending its meetings and was a ready donor for its funds.

Ambrose died on 13 May 1881 and was buried in the family vault within the church next to his first wife. He was the last of the Isted line.

Ambrose Isted was able to establish for himself a distinguished position in Northamptonshire, earning the nickname *The Deaf Squire of Ecton.* He excelled foxhunting and in view of today's decline of foxhunting, Ambrose Isted is unique as the only Deaf Master of this traditional English hunting.

Anthony J. Boyce

John Jennings
1833-1884

John Jennings was born in Southwark in 1833 and lost his hearing when he was around the age of three years old. When John was ten years old, he went to the London Asylum for the Deaf and Dumb in the Kent Road for his education and remained there for only four years before he left school to commence an apprenticeship to a deaf woodcarver. John hated the job, as he had to commence work at dawn and did not finish until around ten o'clock in the night. However, he struggled on until the completion of his period of apprenticeship.

During his adolescent years, he became a regular attendant at the Shaftesbury Hall in Aldersgate Street, where Matthew Robert Burns was a biblical instructor. This began his association with Burns, which was to last seventeen years, and they were prominent in maintaining the Society for the Propagation of the Gospel among the Deaf and Dumb. During all that time, Jennings was working full-time as a carver and his voluntary religious work was done in his spare time. For a good number of years, Jennings witnessed Deaf people suffering from poverty and loneliness, often intoxicated and drunkened, due to the lack of close community and interaction amongst themselves. This led him to decide that drastic action had to be taken to eradicate such a situation. He felt that religion was the key and the way.

Jennings, despite being a poor man, eventually packed in his trade as a carver and devoted his whole time to "the Lord's cause". He took a room at Christ Church, Westminster Road, for Monday evening lectures and a room at Shaftesbury Hall for Sabbath Day services. Needing funds, Jennings solicited subscriptions from several gentlemen who took an interest in both his mission and his endeavours to rehabilitate the poor and lonely Deaf people, and he was able to receive donations towards the rent and other expenses. After Jennings taught for three years, Shaftesbury Hall was demolished. Jennings then rented the Memorial Lecture Hall in New Kent Road, where he held two services on Sundays, a debate fortnightly and lectures every other Monday. Not only that, Jennings re-organised the Deaf and Dumb Teetotal Society in 1879 under the title of "Anchor of Hope", of which he was President and Samuel Bright Lucas was vice-President.

In 1882, Jennings succeeded in erecting a new mission in Ossery Road, off Old Kent Road, and he continued his Sunday services and weekly lectures. With this new mission, he founded the South London Mission to the Deaf and Dumb, which attracted more than 200 deaf people, not counting its hearing friends and supporters. However, in the same year, he contracted cancer of the liver and he suffered the next two years until his death on Monday 3 November 1884, aged 51.

Jennings' funeral on 10 November 1884 was attended by upwards of 100 deaf people and Ernest Abraham, Jennings' step-son, led the funeral cortege. Abraham carried a large cross of white flowers and was followed behind by notable religious Deaf persons such as Ebenezer South. Jennings left a widow and eight children; the youngest was only five weeks old when he died.

Raymond Lee

106

Charles Joseph Kickham
1828-1882

Charles Joseph Kickham was born on 9 May 1828 in Mallinahone, Tipperary, Ireland, the son of Joseph Kickham, a wealthy draper, and Ann O'Mahoney, a kinswoman of the Fenian chief, John O'Mahony. Charles's early education was received from a private tutor Mr James Fox.

His parents were determined to get him to study for the medical profession but a tragic accident put an end to their hopes. When he was fifteen years old, his sight and hearing were permanently damaged by the explosion of a flask of damp gunpowder which he was drying. Deaf, partly blind and also permanently disfigured, Charles studied hard and became better informed than any of his relatives and friends. The accident may be seen as a blessing in disguise as it enabled him to pursue his love of literature and of Ireland.

In his prime, Charles stood about five-foot eleven inches tall and was strongly built. He wore his black hair in long ringlets on his neck. In 1848, he took part in the "Young Ireland" movement and helped to form the Confederate Club at Mullinahone. After the failure of the Young Ireland uprising near his home at Ballingarry, he was forced to hide for a time. He then joined the Tenant Right League and when it failed, he lost all faith in legal agitation. He joined the Fenians in 1860. Charles was the finest intellectual of the Fenian Movement either in Ireland or America. In 1860s, he visited America where he attended the first-ever Convention of the Fenian Brotherhood in Chicago. Returning to Ireland, he was appointed one of the editors of *The Irish People*, the organ of the Fenian Party, along with other famous Irish nationalists such as John O'Leary.

Among the arrests made in Ireland on 15 September 1865 was that of the entire staff of *The Irish People*. Kickham was arrested at Fairfield House, Sandymount, Dublin, on 11 March 1865 along with James O'Connor, a member of Parliament, and James Stephans, founder of the Irish Republican Brotherhood. At his indictment on Tuesday 14 November, Kickham's poor hearing posed an obstacle to the proper conduct of proceeding and the magistrate decided to pass on to him copies of all the information as they were sworn and give him time to read them. He undertook to provide Kickham with a commentary as the proceedings by means of an ear trunpet and this allowed him to repeat very loudly and with humorous effect many of the statements of the magistrates and the witnesses. He was tried for treasonable felony at Dublin on 5 January 1866. He was sentenced to fourteen years imprisonment for being a member of an outlawed organisation.

On account of his very delicate health, he was released after serving three years and four months in Mountjoy in Dublin, Pentonville, Portland and Woking prisons. Kickham's life in Woking prison had been miserable and he was admitted to hospital on 5 January 1859 for the fourth time and he liked to get to the hospital, where the food was better. It was probably in Woking that he learned the "finger" or "manual" alphabet. He came out in broken health in March 1869, practically blind. He was returned as member of Parliament for Tipperary later the same year, but was defeated upon a scrutiny in February 1870. Thenceforth, he confined himself to literary work.

Kickham lived for a time at his home, Mullinahone, and then moved to Dublin where he stayed first with his brother, Alexander, and then at Montpelier Place, Blackrock, with his fellow prisoner, James O'Connor.

Charles was a devout Catholic but he was not allowed receive the sacraments on account of his being a Fenian. However, in 1877 following a meeting with Dr. Croke, Archbishop of Cashel, which was undertaken with Thomas P. O'Connor of Laffana, Cashel, acting as his interpreter, the privilege of receiving the sacraments was returned to him.

Kickham died on 22 August 1882 at Montpelier Place as a result of a stroke. He wish was that his grave should be where his cradle had been, beside the Anner at the foot of Shievenamon. He was buried on 25 August with his own people in Mullinahone.

Charles Kickham had wonderful powers of observation and delicate analysis of character and he contributed largely to Irish national periodicals. Whilst imprisoned, he wrote his first novel *Sally Cavanagh, or the Untenanted Graves* in which he lovingly described his mother. His second novel, *Knocknagow or the Homes of Tipperary* (1879), is considered by many to be the greatest of Irish novels. No other writer is said to have produced more faithful pictures of Irish country life.

David Breslin

Edward Alfred Kirk
1855-1924

Edward Alfred Kirk was born on 22 February 1855 in his father's drapery shop directly opposite the Mansion House in Doncaster. At the age of seven he became deaf through scarlet fever. Four years later, he was admitted as a private pupil to the Yorkshire Institution for the Deaf and Dumb and educated under the celebrated Charles Baker, using the silent method of communication. Kirk was given special tuition in advanced studies, besides articulation training because he had imperfect speech.

After five years in 1871, Kirk was employed as a resident assistant teacher. After Baker's death in 1874, James Howard became the new head and Kirk continued teaching under him. Howard immediately introduced the oral method and put up posters of "NO SIGNING!" in the school. He emphasised the importance of speaking to deaf children. Kirk had a very trying time and had to go along with the new changes being enforced, witnessing the gradual conversion from the silent method to the oral method. He had never advocated either method for a class of deaf children, although he was a bit alarmed to find the oral method gradually taking over completely. He felt strongly that the silent method was necessary for some deaf children and said:

> *I maintain that the most imperfect speech is better than none at all and therefore speech should receive every possible encouragement. Those who cannot or will not recognise the benefit of the manual alphabet should change places with a deaf person.*

After the Milan Conference of 1880, Kirk was faced with decreasing number of deaf children in his class using the silent method. A vacancy for a teacher of deaf children in Leeds was advertised. After a successful interview, in 1883 he took charge of a small class of deaf children in an out-dated large hearing school in Leeds. The Leeds School Board's planning policy was to spend large sums of money on the building of new hearing schools in the forthcoming years and did not consider the future developments for deaf children. Kirk was unhappy about this policy, as he wanted new buildings for the deaf.

Since then, Kirk had to deal by himself the whole organisation, staffing and establishment of the curriculum starting from scratch. The problems of running the day school were very different from those of the residential school for the deaf in Doncaster. It was a formidable challenge and the future of the school for the deaf in Leeds rested entirely on young Kirk. The roll of deaf children averaged 30 up to 1888. Meanwhile, he married a lady from Sheffield, Fanny Crookes, in January 1884 and had a son, George Edward. During weekends, he voluntarily visited local deaf clubs and other schools for the deaf, and entertained them with his popular limelight shows.

Kirk's persistence, patience, goodwill and co-operation with the Leeds School Board paid off when in 1888 he was asked to work with them on plans for a new school for deaf children. After moving round his school to four different sites, a new residential school for the deaf and blind children at Blenheim Walk, Leeds, was completed at the turn of 20th century. With a staff of twelve teachers and one hundred deaf children, Kirk had achieved his objective.

Kirk was aware of the controversy over the issues on deaf teachers, the number having declined dramatically since 1880, and he took the stance of one who showed that action spoke louder than words and encouraged headmasters and teachers from schools for the Deaf to visit his school. A comprehensive survey for all schools for the Deaf in the United Kingdom in 1895 was carried out and it was found that Kirk's school was the only day school for the Deaf that was a real success.

Kirk was a very active member of the National Association of Teachers of the Deaf (NATOD) and encouraged practising teachers of the Deaf to interchange their ideas and views. His frequent appearances at many meetings reminded many oral teachers of the Deaf that he still relied on the services of his fingerspelling interpreter in order to follow what was said at the meeting. "*Fingerspelling is here to stay and stay it will,*" was Kirk's cry. His reputation for his skills in teaching deaf children and also for his wide and updated knowledge on Deaf issues earned him a place on the executive committee. In committee meetings, he felt isolated as the only deaf teacher of the Deaf and his deafness was a constant reminder to those present who pressed for greater improvement in methods of oral teaching. Facing committee members who were avid supporters of the oral method of teaching and seeing their resolutions being passed by majority votes presented many problems for Kirk. He often used his dry humour to put across his points and beliefs.

Kirk made sure that the Deaf community was aware of what was going on by writing about such issues in *The British Deaf Times* up to 1918. He also wrote and edited the "Chat with Our Readers" column and from his articles he was able to keep abreast the importance of co-operation between parents and teachers. Much of what Kirk advocated is still as relevant as ever to the needs of the Deaf today; for example, the need to have skilled interpreters at law courts. In 1918, he voluntarily joined the editorial board of *The Teacher of the Deaf* and continued to write articles aimed at teachers of the Deaf to present an alternative viewpoint from that of oralism at all costs.

Kirk continued to run his school successfully until January 1924 when he fell ill. On 18 March 1924, he died of exhaustion.

Throughout his career as a brilliant deaf teacher of the Deaf, having taught Deaf children for 53 years, and as an outstanding headmaster, the fact that Edward Alfred Kirk kept the "light of Deaf education burning" for so long during the dark age of oralism is a testament to his courage and skills of persuasion and a great achievement in itself. The British Deaf History Society recognised his immense contribution to the field of Deaf education by erecting a memorial stone over his gravesite at St. Mary's Church, Whitkirk, just outside Leeds in February 1996.

Anthony J. Boyce

John Kitto
1804-1854

John Kitto, the son of John and Elizabeth Kitto, was born on 4 December 1804 in a house at the corner of Seven Stars Lane (now Sullivan Street) in the parish of Charles, Plymouth. At his birth, he was a puny and sickly infant, and hardly expected to live. However, his home life changed for the worse by the time he was four years old, his father having developed excessive fondness for fine ales of the alcoholic variety, and consequently the family plunged into abject poverty. His paternal grandmother, Cecilia, took little John Kitto from his alcoholic family and in due time raised him to become a studious boy, showing interest in both books and the Holy Scriptures.

As John grew up his grandmother lost her independent income and had to live with her younger daughter and John had to return to his parents, to whom he began to slowly get closer and he often assisted his father on menial work, like repairing parts of buildings. Although his father never shook off his liking for alcohol, he in a little way cut down his intake and started to work for a living. It was when helping his father that John slipped off the top of the ladder whilst carrying roofing slates, causing him to crash to the ground. This accident, which occurred on 13 February 1817, was near fatal but John recovered. However, he suffered a total loss of the sense of hearing - in other words, he became deaf. Afterwards John struggled to survive as his father showed little interest in him; John tried a variety of means to raise money to help him to buy books and to eat, but to very little avail. He eventually became so poor that he entered a workhouse in Plymouth in 1819. This workhouse was known as "The Hospital of the Poor's Portion". From there, he was apprenticed to a shoemaker named Bowden. This man turned out to be a ruffian and he was so harsh that the authorities cancelled John Kitto's indentures, even though he did well in the trade. John continued to read and write and his *Workhouse Journal* was eventually published.

The Governors in charge of the workhouse were impressed by his good conduct and they loaned him books, mainly religious ones, and asked him to write a course of lectures to read to the other boys. At the same time, he was forwarding articles to the weekly local paper and people were impressed. Local wealthy people made an appeal to raise money for John to board outside the workhouse, to work in the local library and eventually to go to university. John used the time to study Latin, followed by Greek, but the employment in the library came to an abrupt end. John had a particular yearning to become a missionary, but in 1824 took up an offer of training in dentistry on a salary from one Mr. Groves, a dentist in Exeter, who had read John's published articles.

In 1825, John published his first book, *Essays and Letters,* and it was very successful. Almost immediately after this publication, Mr. Groves made a decision to devote himself to missionary work and paid for John to study at the Islington College which was a place of training for missionaries belonging to The Church Missionary Society. John is listed as no.128 in the Society's list of missionaries and in 1827 was sent to their Malta Press where literature for Moslem and other countries were written, or translated, and printed for wide distribution. When John went out to Malta, he was engaged to a lady at the college who was to follow him out. However, she married someone else and the news so upset John that he stayed in his room for two days. This lady died two years later and it was said she expressed her regret at what she had done to him.

John Kitto left the Society in 1828 in slightly acrimonious circumstances, and he was ill at that time. On leaving, John stayed on in Malta for at least a month to regain his strength. On recovering, he found himself unemployed, penniless and with no employment prospects. John eventually returned to England but he found that he was out of favour with many of his previous supporters and colleagues, except for Mr Groves, who was still his friend and about to embark on his own private missionary enterprise in 1829. He asked John to accompany him as a tutor to his sons. John made new friends during the journey via St. Petersburg to Baghdad, where he encountered frightening experiences of flood, siege and an outbreak of the plague, which killed Mrs Groves. John left the missionary and returned to England, visiting many places on the way and learning a great deal about the antiquities.

On his arrival in England, he resumed writing, becoming a paid and regular contributor to various magazines. In 1833, he married a Miss Fenwick and from then onwards had a very happy home life. His mother lived with him and was help with the children, one of whom later became the rector of St. Martin's-in-the-Fields in Trafalgar Square, London.

John went on writing and studying for the rest of his life and the list of books he wrote, illustrated and published is very long, starting with *Essays and Letters* (1825), *The Deaf Traveller* (1833-35), *The Pictorial Bible* (1835-38) through to *Cyclopædia of Biblical Literature* (1845), *The Lost Senses* (Deafness & Blindness –1845), *Daily Bible Illustrations* (1849-51) and continuing via various publications to his very last work, *Daily Bible Illustrations – Evening Series* (1851-1853). John's health never improved but he was honoured with a Doctorate in Divinity from the University of Giessen and a Fellowship of the Society of Antiquaries. He was given a pension of £100 a year from the Royal Fund in 1850. In 1853 John was so ill that a subscription was raised for him and brought in £1800. His eldest and youngest children died, but the other two survived him. In 1854, John and his family left for Germany in the hope of improving his health and they settled in the town of Cannstätt, but in less than three months, John died. He was buried there and his publisher, who was also a good friend, placed a tombstone over his grave.

It was written of him - *"In whatever aspect we view him, he is a wonder."* In addition, the name of John Kitto is now immortally associated with biblical study and literature.

Raymond Lee & Doreen E. Woodford

Thomas Landseer
1798-1880

Thomas Landseer was one of the most outstanding Victorian engravers, an Associate of the Royal Academy and the brother of the famous painter, Edwin Landseer. Tom was born in 1798, the eldest son of John and Jane Landseer who had seven children. His deafness was hereditary, although there was no mention of his being born deaf. Charles was the second son who was slightly deaf and became progressively deafer and Edwin, the third son, had normal hearing. They received early education at the parental home in Upper Conway Street (later Southampton Street), London. Their father, John, who was a well known deaf engraver, trained his three sons as artists. Thomas was Tom to his family and close friends.

The three Landseer brothers were destined for careers in art and began studying earnestly under the celebrated painter B. R. Hayden in 1815. By 1822, Edwin was already on the path to fame and he eventually became Queen Victoria's commissioned Royal Painter. By 1827, Tom showed originality and skill as a draughtsman and produced a series of 24 etchings from his own drawings called *Monkeyana, or Men in Miniature*, showing monkeys in a variety of human roles as dandies, drinkers, gossipers and so on. The pictures showed a feeling for satire, indicating his keen observations on people in the street and his love for animals.

However, his father had a very strong personality and knew that Tom had natural aptitude for engraving. With that in mind, he had Tom apprenticed to wood engraving at a very early age. As Edwin, Tom's hearing brother, showed flair for art, he needed money and to make prints for his illustrations and paintings, he brought in Tom to engrave them for printing and thus Tom began a lifelong career as an engraver of Edwin's works and therefore did not have much chance with the pencil and brush artwork. Charles, however, took a different direction, becoming the Keeper of the Royal Academy School of Art and owed much to Edwin for achieving that prestigious position.

While Edwin was enjoying himself in high society, Tom's down-to-earth character, deafness and eccentricity prevented him from mixing with such company as Edwin's. The partnership of painter Edwin and engraver Tom worked extremely well in terms of success. The wonderful achievements of Thomas Landseer in artwork are well documented. In 1842 he engraved Edwin's drawing for Queen Victoria's private note-paper and also gave her some lessons on engraving.

Generally, Tom used an ear trumpet and shouting through his trumpet was required to make him understand what was said. He loved music and would stand very near any musical instrument in order to hear sounds. If Tom was excluded from many of the world's pleasures, he certainly did not let it embitter him. His habitual expression was a beaming smile – almost as though he was basking in endless tributes to his benignity. *"Dear old Tom"* was the expression most applied to him.

113

Dickens wrote, *"Everyone quite loves (Tom) for his sweet nature under a most deplorable infirmity."* Algernon Graves, a famous art critic, regularly visited Tom and spent some whole evenings writing out art news on pieces of paper for Tom. Tom spoke in a loud staccato, booming voice during one-sided conversations with his friends. It was his practice to sign proofs of his engravings. Algernon used to give him a box of 100 cigars for every hundred signatures.

Tom was short and stout in appearance, built like a barrel and with curly reddish-brown hair. He was the only one of the Landseer brothers who ever married. The marriage, however, was a disaster. His wife, Mary, was unfaithful to him, presenting him with a son, George, in 1834 by another man. However, Tom always supported his own family.

Tom's studio was at 14 Cunningham Place at the corner of St. John's Wood Road, London. Tom excelled as a picture doctor. Artists who could not get their pictures right would call in Tom who would seat himself silently in front of the canvas, peering intently for up to an hour, before announcing the steps necessary to achieve the missing balance.

In 1868, Thomas was elected an Associate Engraver of the New Class of the Royal Academy and later became an Associate Engraver and finally A.R.A. in 1876. He produced a volume of work that was highly professional and often distinguished. His engravings of Edwin's works, particularly the deer studies, were of the highest order. Tom's specialities were snow scenes and storms and the depiction in black-and-white of atmosphere and the elements.

In 1873, after the death of Edwin, Tom moved to 11 Grove End Road where he lived till his death. In all, Tom engraved 108 of Edwin's pictures before his considerable powers as an engraver went into a steady decline after that. Later he suffered a crashing fall down a river bank, sustaining head injuries and he died on 20 January 1880.

Thomas Landseer's deafness throughout his life did nothing to cloud his sunny disposition. He sat and smiled in life-long silence, quite regardless of what might be said of him or his doings. His legacy was his printed engravings.

Anthony J. Boyce

John William Lowe
1804-1876

John William Lowe was born on 24 September 1804 in Russell Square, London. His parents, Eliza and William Lowe were very wealthy, William being an eminent solicitor of the Inner Temple. A few months after his birth, Eliza discovered that her son was deaf when he did not respond to sounds and it may be possible that John was born deaf.

When John was five years old, his father decided it was time for an education and he attended the London Asylum for the Deaf and Dumb as a private pupil of Joseph Watson. In March 1810, young John William Lowe began his education and commenced an association with Watson that was to become famous in British Deaf history along the same lines as that of Thomas Gallaudet and Laurent Clerc in the US and Abbé Sicard and Jean Massieu in France. The only difference was that Lowe did not take up teaching the Deaf, but made history in a different profession. Lowe excelled as Watson's pupil and upon leaving Watson in 1822 he was in fact educationally advanced and his knowledge ranged from the classics, French, mathematics and other attainments within the usual scope of school education to other branches of science and languages seldom attempted except at a more advanced period of life.

William Lowe had already mapped out his son's future and he was determined that John William enter the legal profession, a formidable challenge for a young Deaf person in these days. Lowe had on his mind certain occupations within either teaching or mission work with the Deaf, but succumbed to his father's persuasions and took up the challenge. In the early months of 1822, Lowe became a member of the Society of Middle Temple, and began his legal training initially as a clerk to practising solicitors and then as a pupil to a notable judge. When the judge, Tindal, was promoted to Lord Chief Justice of England and Wales, Lowe became a pupil of Mr. Justice Patterson and continued his legal studies in all branches of law. However, Lowe developed a great interest in conveyancing and chose that branch as his speciality.

During his training, Lowe maintained close contact with his former school by making weekly visits and Joseph Watson employed him as his personal solicitor. Lowe received news that he had triumphed in his training and would be accepted to the Bar of the Society of Middle Temple, an initiation that would take place on Saturday 28 November 1829. Joseph Watson was heartened by the news of the achievement of his pupil but would never live to see that historical day when Lowe would become the first Deaf person to be accepted as a barrister. Watson died on 23 November 1829 and this hit Lowe badly, for he always looked up to Watson not only as a friend, but also as a second father.

Lowe's legal career was an illustrious one and many eminent judges and lawyers commented on Lowe's skill and professionalism in the branch of conveyancing. Some of his methods and systems were adopted as a standard on which others were to follow. Lowe's legal career deserves more than a paragraph here and it is hoped that someday a thorough article will be written about it.

115

Outside of his profession, Lowe loved studying languages and customs of other countries over the world and visiting the London Asylum in the Kent Road. Lowe's studies enabled him to become fluent in languages such as French (modern and Old Norman), Latin, Greek (ancient and modern), German, Italian, Spanish, Portuguese, Dutch and Danish. On top of that, Lowe obtained more than adequate knowledge of Swedish, Polish, Russian, Gaelic, Finnish, Hindustani and Sanskrit among others. Despite all that, Lowe's association with the Deaf had never been broken: he visited many gatherings of Deaf people and was at one time a member of the Edinburgh Congregational Deaf Church between 1836 and 1838 when he resided in Edinburgh.

Returning to London in 1839, Lowe married Frances Jellicoe on 13 June and went to live in North Brixton. This marriage lasted 20 years and produced two sons and two daughters. Lowe's wife Frances passed away on 29 October 1859 and this hit Lowe hard, but he devoted himself to both his legal work and social integration with his Deaf friends. He was seemingly forever obsessed with the raising of the standards of education in the London Asylum. It was well known that every time Lowe visited the Asylum, he always chatted to the pupils first, asking questions that would give him an idea of the standard of education they were receiving. Many pupils in later days would speak of Lowe frowning, shaking his head in despair and nodding with a mixture of sadness and frustration upon realising that the standard of education did not improve. He would continually take up this matter with the head and governors, but to very little avail.

Approaching his last years, Lowe developed various forms of pulmonary infections, which grew steadily worse, leading to his demise on 3 February 1876 at his home in 72 Hockforth Road, North Brixton. Lowe's lasting memorial, however, is his exercise book, which is in the archives of Royal School for the Deaf, Margate, which was formerly known as the London Asylum for the Deaf and Dumb. This exercise book dated 20 August 1813 is the oldest surviving exercise book in the world that belonged to a deaf pupil and yields a fascinating insight into the education he received as a private pupil of Joseph Watson.

Raymond Lee

**Samuel Bright Lucas
1840-1919**

Samuel Bright Lucas was born in London in 1840. Losing his hearing in infancy, he received his education partly under a private tutor and partly at Bristol, under Dr. Webster. He was a nephew of the John Bright who was a famous British politician.

In 1868 he married Miss Jessie Oliver, the daughter of Mr. Lewis Oliver, by whom he had two sons. A member of the National Liberal Club, he travelled widely in Norway, Sweden, Germany and Europe and was extremely well read. Also a keen billiards player and salmon fisherman, he achieved some distinction as a water-colour artist, exhibiting at the Royal Academy.

However, what distinguished Samuel Bright Lucas from others was his interest in the welfare of the deaf and dumb in London, and for many years, he was the Secretary of the Royal Association in Aid of the Deaf and Dumb (fore-runner of the present day Royal Association in Aid of Deaf People). He was forthright in expressing his opinions and in the defence of the RADD, believing passionately in the freedom of education by the most appropriate method, whether it is through the Oral Method or through Sign Language or Manualism. He once said in an interview:-

No matter by what method the deaf are taught, an Association such as ours will be absolutely necessary if they are to make any real spiritual progress. I believe in teaching the deaf to speak and lip-read wherever the probable results seem to justify the labour and expense involved, but to put them all through the same mill, regardless of their capacity or inclination, is utter foolishness.

He was also the secretary of the Charitable and Provident Society for granting pensions to the Aged and Infirm Deaf and Dumb, which was founded in 1836 by John William Lowe, the deaf solicitor. It had 300 pensioners and encouraged thrift among Deaf people.

More than any other person, it was Samuel Bright Lucas who was directly responsible for the collapse of the National Deaf and Dumb Society, seeing it as a rival to his beloved Royal Association, particularly the way the NDDS aimed to be setting up Missions throughout the country. He was less successful in confronting the newly formed British Deaf and Dumb Association a few years later.

After the death of his first wife in 1900, he met and married a Mrs. Parker, a native of Passage West near Cork in Ireland, and began to divide his time between Cork and London where he continued to be active in RADD business, especially with the Charitable Provident Society. In his sojourns in Cork, he would sometimes visit the Mission for the Deaf and Dumb, assisting in meetings. He died in Cork in 1919 after a short illness.

Peter W. Jackson

Francis Humberstone Mackenzie,
Lord Seaforth
1754-1815

Francis Mackenzie was born deaf, the second son of Major William Mackenzie, nephew of the 5th Earl of Seaforth. He was placed with Thomas Braidwood at his Academy in Edinburgh where he learnt to some extent to speak. However, for the major part of his life, Francis Mackenzie used sign language to communicate with his peers. He was a very fluent fingerspeller, and many of his associates such as Lord Melville and Lord Guildford acquired fluent fingerspelling skills. He was a highly intelligent and articulate man, given to writing numerous letters.

On 22 April 1782, he married Mary Proby, the daughter of the Dean of Lichfield, who bore him 4 sons and 6 daughters. In 1783, his elder brother Thomas, who had succeeded his second cousin Lord Seaforth in 1781 as Chief of the clan Mackenzie, died and Francis succeeded his brother as Chief of the clan and inherited the considerable Seaforth estates which were in a neglected state. Because of his interest in his Scottish estate, Mackenzie stood in 1784 against all expectation for Parliament against Lord Macleod, the sitting member for Ross-shire, and was elected, it is said, with a number of fictitious votes. He served as MP from 1784-1790 when he resigned because of his financial problems and gave his interest in the seat to a friend, William Adams.

On the outbreak of war with France, Mackenzie raised the 78th Regiment of Foot, Ross-shire Militia, with himself as Lieutenant-Colonel Commanding. In 1794, he added a second battalion. Although he rose to the rank of Lieutenant-General of the Army by 1808, he never joined his or any other regiment on active service. The impact of events in France on domestic politics drew him out of political retirement, and upon his friend Adams being offered a seat at Banbury, he stood again for Ross-shire and was handsomely re-elected. On his return to the House, he gave silent support to the government as a result of which the Seaforth peerage was revived and he was created 6th Lord Seaforth.

He was appointed Governor of Barbados in 1800 and during his governorship up to 1806, he strove to improve the conditions of slaves. He was reported to have been an able and vigorous governor.

On his return to Britain in 1806, Lord Seaforth played no further significant part in national politics, and his later years were blighted by misfortune. His financial embarrassments caused him to sell the 'gift land' of his house, as well as much of his estates. In addition, the only survivor of his four sons died unmarried in 1814 and Mackenzie himself died a few months later a physically and mentally broken man. These last tragic events fulfilled the words of a seer, Kenneth Mackenzie, prior to his execution by the 3rd Lady Seaforth in the 1660s: -

> *In the days of a deaf and dumb caberfeidh, the gift land would be sold and the male line of Seaforth will cease.*

Peter W. Jackson

118

George Annand Mackenzie
1868-1951

George Annand Mackenzie achieved the distinction of being the first born-deaf English graduate at a British University in 1910. One of three born-deaf brothers, the other two being James Wilson Mackenzie and Charles Douglas Mackenzie, he also had a hearing sister Annie and they were all born in Liverpool, George on 20 October 1868. Shy, awkward and moody as a young boy, he was sent away to Perthshire to stay with his uncle. On his return to Liverpool, he was found to be wild and unkempt. When he first met his eldest brother, James, he hid under the table! His father, R. B. Mackenzie, was the chief reporter for the *Liverpool Mercury* and was involved with the committee work of the Liverpool Deaf and Dumb Adult Society. On Sundays, George and his brothers would attend the nearest church where services for the deaf were conducted.

George received occasional lessons from Dr. Addison during the mornings at the Liverpool School for the Deaf. He also received lessons in grammatical English from Robert Armour, the Deaf missioner to the Deaf of Liverpool. George found the acquisition of English language very difficult in his teenage years, but his mother insisted on the use of complete sentences in conversation and would not allow broken English or bits of sentences. His mother encouraged him to attempt speech and at one time he received some instruction in articulation and lip-reading, but he found it impossible to improve beyond a certain point.

At the age of thirteen, after some irregular attendances at a junior school and partly taught at home by his mother who was fluent in fingerspelling and signing, George attended a large public hearing school in which he was the only deaf pupil. He found instruction difficult but during his two years there, he reached the top position of the school, excelling in athletics, rowing and swimming and he won several prizes. At first, his schoolmates made fun of him, waving their hands and fingers in mimicry of his only means of expression. His good-natured and responsive smiles soon turned them into understanding friends. As George's speech was not that good, he often resorted to pencil and paper for communication with hearing people. With deaf people, he used fingerspelling and signs. On leaving school, George wanted to go on to further education as he loved to read books, but he had to find ways to earn money. Therefore, he embarked on a practical career in art and took up the study of art at the Liverpool School of Art, where he did many paintings in oil and watercolour and drew portraits. His works were exhibited in the South Kensington national competitions and he won a number of prizes and medals. He exhibited his works at various art galleries between 1884 and 1898 and amongst his famous sitters were Lord Edward Russell, Dr. Robert Jones F.R.C.S. and other notable people of Liverpool. George's brothers, James and Charles, were also successful artists, notably James who had his works exhibited at the Royal Academy in London. Charles was a successful local portrait painter and a cartoonist for a Liverpool journal. For a short spell, Charles once designed pottery for the well-known Crown Derby Company but he disliked the monotonous factory life. In his leisure time, he learned poetry and studied French language.

The brothers regularly attended the Liverpool Deaf and Dumb Adult Society. George helped out with the work of the society, took classes and services, gave lectures and was the secretary of the Deaf and Dumb Young Men's Association for 9 years. In his spare time, he worked amongst the poorest in the slums of Liverpool for some years. He also organised some drama shows, including Shakespearean shows in which he trained the acting companies and painted scenarios. Such was his busy and varying early life in Liverpool before 1900.

Wishing to work with the adult deaf, George applied for, and obtained, the post of missioner with the Oxford Diocesan Mission to the Deaf. From his residence in Reading, he covered Berkshire, Oxfordshire and Buckinghamshire as part of his missionary work. He worked hard and he was keen to improve his academic qualifications. Whilst trying to obtain a place on a degree course at Oxford, he was snubbed with a curt and emphatic "Impossible". It was a harsh setback for him, but he did not allow this to deter him from achieving his goal. In 1905, he attended the World Congress of the Deaf and Dumb at Liege, Belgium, and found himself elected as the representative delegate for England at the inaugural meeting. He was able to converse with many Deaf foreigners. Young Mackenzie was by then an experienced missioner and he decided that it was time for him to transfer his professional activities and private hopes to Cambridge.

On his arrival at Cambridge in 1906, George continued his missionary work amongst the deaf but with a difference; he had to establish a new diocese within his catchment area. His house, St. Aubyn's in Hardwick Street in Cambridge, was often used as a meeting place for local Deaf people. In 1907, with the help of a local clergyman, Mackenzie successfully applied for a degree course in Classics at Fitzwilliam Hall, University of Cambridge. During the summer of the same year, he married a deaf lady artist, Miss Emily L. Kett, who came from a family of Cambridge builders and who received her education under the Sleight family at the Brighton Institution for the Deaf and Dumb. Whilst studying at Fitzwilliam Hall, George was practically self-taught and had no tutors to help him out with his academic work, and although encountering some innumerable and disheartening difficulties to overcome, George, with his characteristic determination, kept pressing on and never failed in any examination. Three years later, he achieved his objective and was duly awarded the coveted degree of Bachelor of Arts in the Theological Special on 18 June 1910. There was a blaze of publicity surrounding his wonderful achievement. The following year, he pocketed the Master of Arts degree. It was also the year that his son Alan F. Mackenzie was born.

In 1921, George moved to South Wales and continued his missionary work among the adult deaf in Glamorgan and Monmouthshire for ten more years before he retired. He died on 9 July 1951, leaving his son Alan to follow in his footsteps as a missioner to the Deaf with an M.A. degree.

Mackenzie's persistent and self-disciplined example and his unique achievement showed that deafness was not a handicap, or even a disqualification, for any Deaf person to attempt a University degree course. His example swept away the current belief in those days that oralism was the sole mode of communication possible for deaf children to progress in further and higher education. His life was always something of a continual struggle, always seeking a solution for the betterment of life for deaf people in all walks of life. For example, one of his many significant contributions that he made in 1911 was at the BDDA Aberdeen Congress, when he referred to the proposed universal sign language reform and suggested that reformers might eventually make sign language a World Language among the Deaf. This would eventually become today's *Gestuno*, a guidebook on the use of International Sign Language.

Anthony J. Boyce

120

Archibald MacLellan
1831-1902
Duncan MacLellan
1836-1920

The two Deaf brothers, Archibald and Duncan MacLellan were the sons of John MacLellan of Messrs. John MacLellan & Co., East India Merchants and Ship Owners, Greenock and Glasgow, a company which owned a large fleet of ships trading to the East and West Indies during the early part of the 19th century. Both boys were born deaf and were sent to the Glasgow Institution for the Deaf and Dumb, firstly as ordinary primary pupils but latterly as private pupils of one of the greatest teachers of the Deaf ever known, Duncan Anderson. Archibald started his education in September 1839 and Duncan in August 1844. The brothers became very well educated and were particularly proficient in written English.

Archibald MacLellan

Duncan MacLellan

Sometime after Duncan left the Glasgow Institution, the MacLellans emigrated to Canada where the brothers commenced studying law. The brothers studied by clerking in various solicitors' offices, gaining experience as they progressed, which ended in their acceptance onto the Roll as fully qualified lawyers. The brothers formed a partnership, specialising in equity and they were frequently employed by other lawyers to draft special bills of complaints and other papers peculiar to chancery practice.

The brothers' partnership moved to Madoc, north of Bellville, where they enjoyed a lucrative practice, often being relied on by other lawyers to draw up written titles with respect to disputes over lands and mines. This was at the time of the gold fever around 1880 but the mining industry did not last long and the brothers moved to Trenton where they enjoyed equally great income and constant amount of work.

Archibald died on 3 August 1902 and Duncan continued his practice independently until 1907 when he retired. Duncan died on 8 February 1920.

Raymond Lee

Murdoch Macleod
1872-1951

There can be few Deaf people who have lived a life of adventure that included taking part in two wars and trekking through hostile territory on their own. One such Deaf adventurer was Murdoch Macleod who was born in Edinburgh after his parents had moved there from Ullapool in Ross-shire. A direct descendant of the Clan Macleod of Harris and Dunvegan, Murdoch was educated at Donaldson's Hospital School, Edinburgh. On leaving school, Murdoch was apprenticed to a military tailor in Edinburgh, a job that offered little security and which was too mundane for his liking.

When his two elder hearing brothers, James and Angus, decided to emigrate to South Africa, Murdoch decided to join them and after scrapping together the fare of £13, he sailed with them on the "Lismore Castle" from Southampton, arriving in Cape Town in October 1892. His first job in Cape Town was again as a tailor, working in appalling conditions with Arabs, Greeks and Jews. Working hard and saving up to satisfy his wanderlust, Murdoch was soon able to purchase a four-wheeled ox wagon and eighteen oxen. Going first to Bloemfontein in the Orange Free State, he worked for a further year as a tailor to a German to acculumate more savings. With these savings, Murdoch was able to load his wagon with cheap merchandise, pots, pans, jewellery, tools, provisions, rifles and ammunition, which cost a total of £300.

Setting forth as a trader of merchandise in the native kraals, he passed through Basutoland, Bechuanaland and Matabeleland (now part of Zimbabwe). Trading was carried out through a system of barter; a blanket or two would exchange for a cow, some jewellery would produce a goat or some native handicrafts. Murdoch became well-known amongst the native Africans by the name of Seetu the Trader (Seetu means 'silent' in the native language), and after nearly three months wandering in the bush Murdoch arrived at his destination, Bulawayo.

With a partner, he purchased a farm near Bulawayo and set about stocking it. By chance, he was in Bulawayo getting provisions when the Matabele rebellion started. Around 450 white settlers were massacred as many farms and settlements were attacked and burnt to the ground, amongst these Murdoch's own farm. Murdoch saw six months hard service in the Matabele War as part of the group of white settlers fighting the Matabele before they were relieved by Government troops.

After this war, he resumed his trading activities around the kraals in Rhodesia. While staying in one kraal, smallpox broke out amongst the Africans. Murdoch rode to the nearest drug store 150 miles away to obtain vaccine and instructions in their use before returning with all speed to the kraal where he vaccinated all the natives, performing the operation by scratching the skin with a broken bottle. After doing this, the amateur surgeon was forced to flee for his life as the post-vaccination symptoms began to bite and the Africans were convinced he was trying to kill them all with his "magic". After their fears and pains had subsided, Murdoch was feasted and a special celebration put on in his honour.

122

Shortly after this, Murdoch himself became seriously ill with malaria and his life was in turn saved by the Africans who carried him on a litter to a hospital in Bulawayo where he took five weeks to recover from his illness at a cost of £45. After his recovery, Murdoch worked as a rigger in the Kimberley diamond mines and took on a brick-making contract, which earned him £1,600 in three months.

When the Zulu War broke out, Murdoch joined up again and was part of the famous Jamieson's Raid on Johannesburg which led to the outbreak of the Boer War. When these wars ended and Murdoch's mercenary duties were over, he returned to that part of Rhodesia where he had earlier saved the African tribe and set up a farm owned by a London syndicate. The farm was fenced by 25 miles of wiring and employed over 200 Africans producing crops of maize, tobacco and sweet potatoes. However, several years of bad drought in the 1930s ruined the farm and Murdoch decided it was time to retire back to his native Scotland. When he departed from Africa, his workers gathered to give him their own poignant farewell in the sign language they had learnt from him.

For about ten years after his return from Africa, Murdoch Macleod was a familiar figure in the Edinburgh Institute for the Deaf and Dumb where he gave several interesting lectures about his experiences in Africa. He died peacefully at his home in Kinghorn, Fife, on 16 February 1951.

Peter W. Jackson

Francis Maginn
1861-1917

Francis Maginn was born in Johnsgrove in Co. Cork, Ireland which was at that time still under the British control, on 21 April 1861 to the Rector and Rural Dean of Castletown, Roche, Cork, the Rev. C. A. Maginn. Francis' mother was a direct descendant of the poet Spenser. In 1866, Francis contracted scarlet fever and became deaf. He was sent to the Kent Road Asylum in London as a fee-paying pupil on 6 October 1870. After six years at the London Asylum, Francis was retained as a Pupil Teacher at twenty pounds per year at the Margate Institution on 6 August 1876. In 1878, he was promoted to a junior teachership. In 1883, three years after the infamous Milan Conference, there were only two deaf teachers on the staff at Margate Institution, Maginn and one Miss Reaby.

Maginn wrote a letter to Dr. Richard Elliott, the fourth headmaster of both London and Margate, that he wished to resign as a teacher. The reason for his resignation, on Saturday 17 March 1883, was noted by the headmaster Dr. Elliott, who wrote in his log book: -

> ... he was desirous of extending his education by matriculating at the London University and that he had not by the "stringent" rules of the place time to study – he therefore intended to endeavour to gain a place where he could have more opportunity.

Maginn spent a year studying at home before going to the National Deaf-Mute Institute in Washington, USA, in autumn 1884. During his time at home before leaving for the States, he helped to found the Southern branch of the Missions to the Adult Deaf and Dumb of Ireland in Cork.

In 1887, his father died and Maginn had to return to Ireland before he could complete his course at the National Deaf-Mute Institute. Instead of returning to the National Deaf-Mute Institute to complete his studies, he decided to become a missionary for the Belfast mission.

Francis Maginn was active in helping to set up the British Deaf and Dumb Association, becoming one of its first vice-presidents.

Maginn met his demise on 16 December 1917 under tragic circumstances. There was a gala evening attended by a large crowd of deaf people. At the end, when everyone left for home, a fight broke out between two deaf men. Maginn waded in to break up the fight. However, he received a heavy punch on his chest – and died a few days afterwards.

Peter R. Brown

Saul Magson
1813-1894

Saul Magson was born on 17 August 1813 at Horn Street, Manchester, one of five children of Joseph Magson, a journeyman spinner and became deaf at the age of two when he became severely ill with convulsions. In 1822, it was found that in the Manchester cotton mill where Saul's father worked, there were a total of 19 deaf children of various ages belonging to the employees of the mill. The number of deaf children discovered in this mill (plus six more in a nearby mill) led to the Manchester Institution for the Deaf and Dumb being founded in 1823 at Stanley Street, Salford.

Saul was one of the first batch of eight boys and six girls admitted to the Institution, and his pupil roll number was 10. The first headmaster of the new Institution was William Vaughan, who had been an assistant under Dr. Joseph Watson at the London Asylum for the Deaf and Dumb in Kent Road.

On leaving school, Magson found employment as an administration clerk in the Town Clerk's department in Manchester Town Hall, where he remained for the next forty years until his retirement. In his leisure time, Magson devoted himself to working with his fellow Deaf people. In one of the first reports of the Manchester Adult Deaf and Dumb Society, his is the very first name that is mentioned. The Society originated in 1850; and not only does his name appear in the first list of subscribers for 1854, but also it is stated that the operations of the Society up to 1893 had been *"performed by the voluntary services of Mr Magson and Mr Patterson and his assistants."*

Whilst working in his full time employment and living with his relations, Magson used Sundays to hold deaf church services at Ashton-under-Lyme, Oldham, Bury, Rochdale, and a few other places. He would leave home early in the morning and not return until the small hours. This was an additional voluntary task he undertook on top of his involvement with the Manchester Adult Deaf and Dumb Society, a work he enjoyed in company with other Deaf persons of renown, Hogg, Jones and Goodwin.

Magson, having retired from his employment in the Town Hall two years previously, decided to leave Manchester in 1880 and live in Southport. Magson, after a lifetime's work with the Deaf, sought peace and quiet in his retirement and he had hoped to fade into the background – into oblivion. However, this was not to be as the Deaf of Southport learnt of his arrival and persuaded him to renew his connections with the Deaf community. Magson relented and he occasionally conducted church services for the Deaf in the Congregational Church in Portland Street, Southport, up to 1890. Not only that, Magson participated in local gatherings and took keen interest in the welfare of the Deaf of Southport.

Magson died in April 1894 and was interred in the cemetery at Cheetham Hill, Manchester, on 16 April 1894.

Raymond Lee

The Crucifixion,
By Francis Ross Maguire

Francis Ross Maguire
1860-1932

Francis Ross Maguire was one of the best Irish/English professional religious painters although he was not as well known as other Deaf artists and there is no mention of his name in the numerous dictionaries of British Artists. Francis was born deaf in London in August 1860, the first son of the portrait painter Thomas H. Maguire (1821-1895) who lived at 6 Broomfield Crescent, Westbourne Terrace, London. Thomas excelled in portraits of historical characters and was a regular exhibitor to the Royal Academy of Arts from 1846 to 1887. He was also a good lithographer who did work for Queen Victoria. Thomas had seven children born in same place: Bertha, Edith, Helena, Theresa, Francis Ross, Sidney Calton and Adelaide Agnes. Teresa was born deaf. When they were small, their parents sent them to Dublin for their education as there was no Catholic school for deaf children in England at that time. Francis was admitted to St. Joseph's School for the Deaf boys at Cabra run by the Catholic Christian Brothers in August 1868 and Teresa to the St. Mary School for the Deaf girls, Cabra, in September 1869 run by the Dominican Nuns. Her number was no. 400 according to the Catholic Institution for the Deaf and Dumb Annual Report dated 31 May 1869.

Teresa stayed for only three years and was discharged in 1872 after she received her Holy Communion and she returned to London. For two years, teachers using the Irish Sign Language system educated Francis. He was discharged in 1870 after being admitted to the sacraments and returned home to London, where he worked with the religious firm Burns, Gills & Oates of London, for whom he painted many religious pictures, oil paintings and icons for Catholic Churches in the British Isles and abroad.

Francis Maguire attended old school reunions on a regular basis and for a period, he stayed in Cabra from 1912 to 1915 where he did several murals. In the school chapel, he painted the colour mural *"Antependium"* on the ceiling and *"Adoration of the Lamb of God"*, was painted on the altar. He also painted a 80" x 56" canvas of *"The Last Supper"*, signed and dated, Francis Maguire 16 January 1912 on the right bottom side, for the boy's refectory. A small beautiful watercolour, *"The Crucifixion"*, signed with his initials, F. R. Maguire 1915, still hangs in the school. Unfortunately, a billiards table-sized mural containing a chart of single and double-hands finger alphabet was destroyed after being thrown into a bonfire in 1914 by then Brother Superior who supported the oral system and banned the use of Irish Sign Language in the school. No photograph of this chart exists. Francis did not ask for payment for any of his work at St. Joseph's, Cabra, where he had as his good friend Thomas Mahon, the Deaf teacher and School Chart painter.

In 1932, St. Joseph's annual magazine reported his death. He never married and was buried in London.

David Breslin

Thomas Mahon
1864-1939

Thomas Mahon was born deaf in Baltinglass, Co. Wicklow, in 1864 and entered St. Joseph's School for Boys, Cabra, Dublin, in 1871 at the age of seven. According to the school records, Thomas was the 531st pupil admitted to the school. He was an unusually intelligent pupil and on completion of his education, his exceptional ability for sketching and painting was recognised and encouraged by the Christian Brothers teachers. From 1877 to 1882, he was a gardener and kitchen servant at the school. During this period (in 1880) Thomas attended an art school in Hawkins Street, Dublin, although no there is record of what he was learning. In 1884, he was selected to accompany the collector for the Catholic Institution for Deaf and Dumb (CIDD) committee, Mr John J. Roe, on a tour of the United States, to raise funds to continue the work in St. Joseph's. Thomas was a gifted artist and while Mr. Roe gave lectures, the young Deaf artist would astonish those around him with his quick sketches of great men, animals, scenery and other subjects drawn on a large blackboard. The tour was a great success and on his return to Ireland, Thomas was employed to assist in the educational activities of the school.

In 1888, Thomas became a full-time teacher of junior boys, a position which he was to hold for over 45 years. During his time as a teacher, he painted up to eighty beautiful charts under the instruction of Brother Matthew Reddington, who was compiling a comprehensive graded language course for the school at that time. The charts contained over six thousand illustrations. They were painted in brilliant colours on a batik black canvas background, which enabled every detail to be seen by a class group.

On 25 April 1922, three Christian Brothers from Cabra set sail for Australia to join the pioneer work of the newly-founded St. Gabriel's School for Deaf Boys in Castle Hill, New South Wales. Castle Hill, a former penal settlement for Irish political convicts, was the site selected for the future Cabra of Australia. The Brothers brought dozens of duplicated illustration charts by Thomas Mahon to St. Gabriel's.

Thomas Mahon died on 15 March 1939, at the age of 75 after a brief illness. He never married. On St. Patrick's Day, he was buried in the small community cemetery of St. Joseph's. There was no headstone placed on his grave until after World War Two when some former pupils decided to raise funds to cover the cost of a handsome headstone and the unveiling ceremony took place on Friday 6 August 1954. Thomas Mahon was a great Irish painter and teacher. Deaf and hearing people have been admiring his charts for over 90 years, and to commemorate his work, a new St. Joseph's Heritage Centre was set up and it opened in November 2000 with the Mahon Charts exhibited in the display cases.

David Breslin

Harriet Martineau
1802-1876

Harriet Martineau was born at home in Magdalen Street, Norwich, on Saturday, 12 June 1802, the third of eight known children of Thomas and Elizabeth Martineau. She was christened near her home at the Octagon Presbyterian Chapel in Colgate on 3 September 1802. She was nearly starved to death at the age of three months old when her mother discovered that the wet nurse did not feed her enough milk over a period of time. This caused her deafness and Harriet later became a sickly girl. She was afraid to drink milk for the rest of her life.

Harriet did not attend any of the Deaf and Dumb Institutions in England, but was taught at home by two of her brothers and a sister; Thomas in Latin, Henry in writing and arithmetic and Elizabeth in French, reading and exercises. She also had a private tuition with her two sisters, Rachel and Ellen, at Mr Drummond's house in Market Place, a walking distance from their home. They became acquainted with his two daughters. John Beckwith, an organist of Norwich Cathedral, also taught her music. In 1813, she was sent with her sister Rachel to a school kept in the town by the Rev. Isaac Perry at the Cherry Lane Chapel. When Perry left Norwich in 1815, Harriet left school, but continued her classical studies at home. While at Perry's, her deafness began to show itself and by the time she was sixteen, it had become very distressing. It was afterwards suddenly made worse *'by what might be called an accident'*. In her *Letter to the Deaf*, published in 1834, Harriet wrote:

> *I ought undoubtedly to have begun at that time to use a trumpet; but no one pressed it upon me; and I do not know that, if urged, I should have yielded; for I had an abundance of the false shame which hinders nine deaf people out of ten from doing their duty in that particular. The redeeming quality of personal infirmity is that it brings its special duty with it; but this privilege waits long to be recognised. The special duty of the deaf is, in the first place, to spare other people as much fatigue as possible; and, in the next, to preserve their own natural capacity for sound, and habit of receiving it, and true memory of it, as long as possible. It was long before I saw, or fully admitted this to myself; and it was ten years from this time before I began to use a trumpet.*

Devotional Exercises, with a *Guide to the Study of the Scriptures,* was her first work to be published, in 1823. During the next decade from 1830, she published at least eight known books between 1830 and 1834, mostly in religion and political matters. Her name was made with the publication of nine volumes of short stories under the title, *Illustrations of Political Economy,* which sold out quickly. Besides this, she wrote four 'poor-law tales' and five supplementary tales called *Illustrations of Taxation.*

Her health suffered from her labours, but the income she received from her successful tales enabled her to visit the United States of America with a female companion, sailing from Liverpool on 4 August 1834, and reaching New York after a voyage of forty-two days. She had already written against slavery whilst in England and she did not attempt to conceal her opinions in the States.

During that period, there was fierce opposition to the abolitionists of slavery who were constantly exposed to lynch-law. Harriet Martineau received threats of personal injury during her travels around the States, at one time being forced to abandon some journeys. She came home to England a determined abolitionist.

After she returned to Liverpool on the *Eurdrice* on 26 August 1836, she published two articles, *Society of America* in 1837 and *Retrospect of Western Travel* in 1838, an account of her trip to the States. She also wrote novels, two in 1838 and one called *Deerbrook* in 1839, which was extremely successful. During the next ten years, she published seven known articles and books, of which one of the articles was for the Anti-Corn-law League and the other for *Knight's Weekly Volumes*.

Harriet purchased two acres of decent land in 1846 and built her home, 'The Knoll', on Rothay Road, Ambleside, few miles north of Lake Windermere in the Lake District. During her time in the Lake District, she was a close friend of William Wordsworth, a native Lakelander, who was a poet and a writer and shared similar interests with her.

Harriet continued travelling, visiting France, Palestine, Lebabon and Egypt for eight months in 1847 and published an account of her travels in the Middle East in the following year.

Always a sickly woman, she was expected to die in 1855 after a doctor had pronounced a disease of the heart to be fatal and she quickly wrote her autobiography. However, she lingered until June 1876, preserving her mental powers to the last. Her *England and her Soldiers* in 1859 (written to help Miss Florence Nightingale) was followed by two other books in 1861 and 1869.

Harriet died at her home, The Knoll, on Tuesday, 27 June 1876 and was buried in a Martineau family plot in Old Cemetery in Smethwick, Birmingham. There is a commemorative plaque on the wall marking the house in Magadalen Street, Norwich, where Harriet was born.

Harriet Martineau's history and philosophical writings do not have the thoroughness of research or the originality of conception which could entitle her to greatness. However, as an interpreter of a rather rigid and prosaic school of thought, with an independence and solidarity of character that give a value to her more personal utterances, she certainly deserves a high place in English Literature.

Geoffrey J. Eagling & Peter W. Jackson

Claremont Institution for the Deaf and Dumb, Dublin

**Francis McDonnell
1822-c1885**

According to *A Dictionary of Irish Artists*, a deaf and dumb artist named Francis McDonnell studied at the Royal Academy School of Sculpture under Constantine Panorma (1805-1852), Sculptor, A.R.H.A., and he obtained a prize in 1843. Francis was born at 29 Francis Street, Dublin, in 1822, the son of a poor shoemaker. Little is known of his early years but the Claremont Institution for the Deaf and Dumb's admission book incorrectly records his name as McDonald. His pupil roll number was 280, and he was admitted aged 7½ years in 1829. Another famous Irish artist, Lawrence Fagan, was educated around the same time. Francis remained at Claremont until he was 16 in 1838.

As a young boy, Francis must have observed stonemasons carving many headstone sculptures in the monumental mason yards that operated on the busy Francis Street, and this may have led him to decide to apply to the Royal Dublin Society's School of Modelling to study sculpture and drawing studies. In 1839, he was accepted as a pupil of Panorma and studied under him for a number of years. After that, Francis McDonnell resided at 134 Francis Street, where there is now sited the Tivoli Theatre. From that address, he sent three marble sculptures to the Royal Hibernian Academy of Arts for exhibition.

In 1846, Francis left Dublin and settled at 5 Howland Street, off Fitzroy Square in London. He continued to send paintings and sculptures to the Royal Hibernan Academy for exhibition. One of his paintings, *The First Born*, was also exhibited at the Dublin Exhibition of 1853. He contributed another two sculptures to the Royal Academy of Arts in London in 1846 and 1852.

Most of his surviving works are believed to be in private collections as no trace of his work can be found in the National Gallery of Ireland or the National Museum of Ireland.

He is presumed to have died in London around 1885, but it is not known exactly where or when.

David Breslin

William McDougall
1865-1950

William McDougall was born in Tillicoultry in Clackmannanshire and became deaf through illness at the age of five. He was sent to Donaldson's Hospital School, Edinburgh, for his education. He proved such an excellent pupil that he was asked to stay on as a pupil-teacher and was at the time the only Deaf member of the teaching staff. Leaving temporarily, he went into partnership with his brother running a woollen mill in Alva, Clackmannanshire. Apparently, this was not very successful and he returned to Donaldson's after a few years to continue his teaching career.

William was by all accounts an excellent teacher, spoken of with affection and respect by his ex-pupils. His ideal was to give each of his pupils a workable command of language. He believed that language was the key that would open the doors of life to his pupils and he cared not what method was adopted in teaching so long as the acquisition of language, and the proficiency in its use, was attained. In pursuit of this ideal, William McDougall was a "bonnie fechter".

In 1904, he was offered, and accepted, the post of missioner at Carlisle which he was to hold until his retirement in 1935. Due largely to his good work, the activities of the Carlisle Diocesan Association assumed new proportions. Institutes were acquired in Carlisle and Barrow-in-Furness and a year before his retirement, William saw the fulfilment of one of his dearest ambitions - the dedication of a chapel for the Deaf in the Carlisle Institute.

Perhaps the height of William McDougall's prominence in the Deaf world was reached when he became Secretary-Treasurer of the British Deaf and Dumb Association in 1906. In that capacity, and also as representative of the National Institute for the Deaf (now the RNID), he crossed the Atlantic to address over 2000 delegates at a Congress for the Deaf in Buffalo, New York State. He was to retain the office of Secretary-Treasurer for a long period of 29 years. It was during his time at the helm that the BDDA experienced a tremendous growth in membership largely due to McDougall's unflagging efforts on its behalf.

But, for him, it was not all work and no play. He demonstrated on the rugby field a prowess that made him remembered well in Edinburgh. As a teacher, he played regularly for the old St. George's Club, taking with him onto the playing field the rugged, purposeful determination that was to characterise his every effort in life. When his playing days were over, he continued to interest himself in all forms of sport but was never happier than when parading the touchline as an super-enthusiastic and noisy spectator on the playing fields of Donaldson's Hospital. He was particularly keen on attending international rugby matches at Murrayfield and at Twickenham.

He died after a lingering illness in March 1950 and was buried in Carlisle Cemetery at a funeral attended by many friends in the Deaf world.

Peter W. Jackson

Dorothy Miles
1931-1993

Dorothy May Squire was born in Gwernaffield, near Mold in North Wales, on 19 August 1931. She attended a local school and revealed her talents both in drama and poetry. In 1939, she had an attack of cerebrospinal meningitis and after a long convalescence, she became totally deaf. She attended the Royal School for the Deaf, Manchester, in spring 1940 and developed her signing skills in story telling. After the World War II, she entered the Mary Hare Grammar School for the Deaf at Burgess Hill, Sussex. She passed her School Certificate examinations in 1949 and left in 1950 to become an assistant librarian for the Road Research Laboratory. A few years later, she was a welfare officer for a short spell at the Liverpool Benevolent Society for the Deaf and Dumb.

In 1957, Dorothy emigrated to the U.S.A. and went to Gallaudet College (now University) where she gained her B.A. degree in English. Whilst there, she won an award for the best actress of the year. At the same time, she started to write poetry with some encouragement from Rex Lowman. In 1960, she had her poem and prose published in "The Silent Muse". She went on to Howard University for her MA degree course in Sociology but did not complete it. Then she joined the newly established National Theatre of the Deaf as a professional actress at the O'Neill Theatre Centre in Waterford, Connecticut, and at the same time took an MA degree in Educational Theatre at Connecticut College with her thesis "A History of Theatre in the Deaf Community of the United States".

Dorothy married Mr. Miles, a Physical Education instructor but it was a short-lived marriage, which proved to be traumatic for her for a time. In January 1975, she went to California State University, Northridge, and concentrated on making use of her undoubted talents, which she inherited from her early childhood, but with a difference; she added a new dimensional perspective, the introduction of the sign language in poetry and putting it into practice. As a result, her book "Gestures" was published in 1976 and this was supplemented with videotapes in which her poems were read in terms of sign language. Performing her sign language poetry in public earned her wide acclaim throughout the United States.

Dorothy Miles returned to England in 1977 and very soon she undertook a research project on the teaching of sign language with the support from British Deaf Association and Department of Health and Social Security at Newcastle. At the completion of the project, she went to Durham University as a lecturer on sign language and worked on a new project on the training of sign language interpreters. She also took part in the drawing up of the constitution leading to the establishment of the Council of Advancement of Communication with Deaf People at Penrith in 1981. She then became a part time registered examiner with CACDP and travelled all over the United Kingdom examining candidates for the different stages of sign language qualifications. She was involved in the training and moderating of sign language Tutors with the University of Durham and also contributed towards the making of the BDA/University of Durham BSL dictionary.

Dorothy continued to experiment with her poetry and set up workshops on sign language poetry. From these workshops, involving Deaf participants of varying levels of age and intelligence, she could see that they could become stereotyped through her example of poetry in action and she felt the need to use a different approach. After a two-year course on improvisational drama in 1981, she went on to do many more workshops using improvisational methods with great success. In every case, she sought the best means of raising any performance to the highest theatrical level. During the BDA Centenary Congress at Brighton, she signed her specially written poem:

"The BDA is you and me,
Fighting for equality..."

She made many appearances giving sign language poetry for "See Hear" on BBC television and her performances on the theme of Christmas were memorable. She was a friend to all, giving a helping hand wherever she went and was involved in campaigning rights on behalf of the British Deaf community. Dorothy Miles died tragically in November 1993, leaving behind a saddened Deaf community to treasure her poems in writing and on video.

Don Read

One of the paintings by William Mitchell

**William Frederick Mitchell
1845-1914**

William Frederick Mitchell was born deaf and dumb at Calshot Castle, Hampshire, in 1845 and was educated at the Kent Road Institution in London. It was there that he acquired his talent for painting. He made his living as a lithographer but his first love was the sea and the ships that sailed on them. He started to paint pictures of ships for naval officers, who wanted to keep memoirs of the ships they served in. He also had an arrangement with Griffin's Bookshop in Portsmouth to take orders for his work, and the firm printed two volumes of *The Royal Navy in a Series of Illustrations*. The same firm framed and sold a lot of Mitchell's paintings. Fred Mitchell does not appear to have been paid very much for his naval paintings and he was never given the credit that was due to him.

Although Fred Mitchell led a fairly reclusive life on the Isle of Wight, he nonetheless took an active part in Deaf community life. He was one of the first Deaf people to join the British Deaf and Dumb Association in 1890 and was also active in the Hampshire Deaf community, helping to form the Mission at Portsmouth.

He died in Ryde, Isle of Wight, in 1914.

In 1987, Ashford Press printed a book by Conrad Dixon titled *Ships of the Victorian Navy*. There was hardly any text in the book and all 48-colour plates in the book were painted by Fred Mitchell, but the artist was barely mentioned in the acknowledgements.

Many of his paintings can be seen in the National Maritime Museum in Greenwich, London.

Peter W. Jackson

Reverend Benjamin Burton Morgan
1898-1984

Benjamin Morgan was born on 18 June 1898 in Aberystwyth, Wales. He was totally deaf from birth. He was educated at the Royal Schools for the Deaf, Old Trafford in Manchester, and stayed on until he was eighteen. During the First World War, he served his apprenticeship in mechanical dentistry in Manchester, and afterwards worked in different parts of North Wales as a dental mechanic, but he was never happy in his work.

In the summer of 1919, while celebrating his twenty-first birthday in London, he met a new friend, Mr Algernon J. M. Barnett, missioner at Northampton, with whom he formed a lifelong attachment. Later he began to make further friends with some of the leading men working for the Deaf, the Rev. Prebendary Albert Smith and Leslie Edwards, missioner at Leicester and Secretary of the British Deaf and Dumb Association. Through their encouragement, Benjamin became, at the early age of twenty-four, a missioner at Wolverhampton. In 1928, he was appointed missioner to the Deaf and Dumb of South Staffordshire and Shropshire, working from his Wolverhampton office and after a course of study, he was awarded the Diploma of the Joint Examination Board. There he found his work to be much congenial, for not only had he the satisfaction of helping his fellow Deaf in many ways, but also his work gave him regular opportunities for teaching. He had a real gift for teaching and explaining and the Deaf at Wolverhampton were fortunate to be able to watch his interesting sermons week by week. He served as superintendent for twenty-one years as successor to Agar Russell. During Benjamin's time, the office at Rupert Street was built and the Mission Centre opened at Shrewsbury.

Around 1938, Benjamin married Joan Seth-Smith, the second daughter of the very popular 'Zoo Man' Mr David Seth-Smith, a Fellow of Zoological Society, in St. Mary the Virgin Church, Primrose Hill. The marriage produced two children, John and Diana. Benjamin was the Honorary Treasurer of the St. Bedes Deaf Club's Tennis Section around 1937 or 1938.

In May 1950, the Royal Association in Aid of the Deaf and Dumb accepted Benjamin for the post of missioner to the Deaf and Dumb of the Guildford Diocese and the whole of Surrey. He was happy there as it brought him nearer to London. It also enabled him to take part in activities of the Deaf in that city, especially through membership of Spurs Club and National Deaf Club. His thirst for knowledge and the desire to equip himself more fully to serve Deaf people led him to seek ordination. During that time his family lived at 15 Ellis Avenue, Onslow Village, Guildford.

On 14 February 1954, Mr Morgan was admitted to the Diaconate in All Saint's, Norfolk Square, Paddington, by the Bishop of Kensington on Letter Dimissory from the Bishop of Guildford, in whose diocese Mr Morgan had the care of the Deaf. Later he was ordained priest by the Bishop of Guildford in Burgh Heath, Surrey. During that time he was ill with influenza and had to return to his bed after travelling through a blizzard of driving snow. He served the Deaf of Surrey as a Chaplain until his retirement in August 1963.

Benjamin founded Surbiton Deaf Club in February 1958 and remained its Chairman until 1962 when he became President of the Club for the next sixteen years.

In the wider field, Benjamin influenced Deaf people through the BDDA. He served on the Executive Council for many years, becoming a Grand Councillor and later Vice-President. He was also the Chairman of the BDDA Southern Region. His outstanding contribution was his advocating Further Education for adult Deaf people and pressing for the establishment of regular Summer Schools of one week's duration. He helped to bring these into being and he attended many of them. His special delight was to attend those held at Harlech in his beloved North Wales. He was the chairman of the Aldershot, Guildford and Woking Deaf Clubs from 1956 to 1957.

He was keen on hospital work, especially those who were psychiatric cases. Benjamin was also a champion of the Deaf-Blind. Even in retirement, his zest for promoting educational matters still continued, and through the BDDA, he organised visits to London museums, where interpreters were present to make lectures available to Deaf people.

Benjamin and his wife moved to their new home in Amersham, Buckinghamshire, in 1983 to be near their daughter. He died peacefully at home the following year on 3 March 1984, at the age of 85 years.

Geoffrey J. Eagling

Alexander Muirhead
1848-1920

The British Association for the Advancement of Science meeting held on 14 August 1894 at the Lecture Theatre of the University Museum of Natural History, Oxford, witnessed something both so innovative and revealing that no one present at that time had any inkling of the true potential of the demonstration. The exhibition presented at that meeting signalled the birth of broadcasting as everyone knows today in the 21st century. That day saw the world's first ever-public demonstration of wireless telegraphy by Sir Oliver Lodge, who had borrowed the apparatus from his deaf friend and telegraph equipment manufacturer, Alexander Muirhead.

Alexander was born in Saltoun in East Lothian, Scotland, in 1848. Due to an accidental fall at a very early age, which caused injury to his head, Alexander became profoundly deaf. His family moved to London when Alexander was very young. Alexander was educated privately until he was fifteen. According to *Chamber's Scottish Biographical Dictionary*, Alexander's speech, being of broad Scottish accent, was not easily understood, but obviously this was attributed to his deafness and inability to control his voice. Alexander entered University College, London, straight from school and graduated with honours. Afterwards, he joined his older brother, John, to work in their father's firm of telegraph engineers, Muirhead & Co., in Westminster.

In 1875, Alexander patented a method of duplexing – i.e. sending and receiving signals simultaneously in both directions – and he demonstrated a genius for accurate measurements, perfecting the standard of electrical capacity that was subsequently adopted by the National Physical Laboratory. Muirhead, as an electrical engineer, then established a partnership with the distinguished physician, Sir Oliver Lodge, in developing wireless telegraphy during the last two decades of the 19th century. In 1888, Muirhead manufactured Lodge's patent, the Lightning Guard, for telegraphic equipment. After a successful public demonstration in 1894, Lodge initially failed to notice the tremendous commercial potential of wireless telegraphy and Marconi seized on this opportunity, thus earning himself fame as the inventor of radio. However, after Marconi established himself, Alexander urged Lodge to mount a challenge and by the end of 1897, both Lodge and Muirhead submitted five patents for pieces of wireless telegraphy, compared with Marconi's two. In 1901, both Alexander and Lodge formally established the Lodge-Muirhead syndicate. However, by that time ship-to-ship and ship-to-shore communication was the main application and Marconi established a monopoly in that field. Nevertheless, Lodge and Muirhead did establish few installations, including those in Burma and the Andaman Islands.

Alexander Muirhead died in 1920. A permanent exhibition containing apparatus that Muirhead either patented or manufactured at the Oxford University Museum of Natural History commemorates the historic event of the 1894 meeting and ensures that his name is not forgotten.

John A. Hay

Samuel White North
1831-1892

Samuel White North was a distinguished Deaf wood-engraver and a well-known Deaf missioner of West London. He was born in 1831 at Coningsby, Lincolnshire, and was christened on 10 May in the same year. Samuel was the second son of Thomas and Mary North. His father was a hard-working farmer and an earnest Christian. When Samuel was six months old, his uncle visited him and carried him around the farm. Samuel's father had taken his gun with him, and "forgetting how tender an infant is," suddenly fired it at some bird or animal, the noise from the gun caused Samuel, who was close by, to start violently. He became stone-deaf as a result of that incident.

Samuel used to attend church regularly with his parents and on Sundays helped out placing chairs for the congregation, besides placing a soft pillow on a small table before putting a large Bible on it. He would then gesticulate, as he had seen the clergyman do at church, "holding out his little hands in an earnest manner to his *dumb* congregation." He seemed destined to become a preacher of the Gospel.

Samuel attended a local school and developed a love of reading, trying to understand as fast as he could read. At the age of nine, he was admitted to the Yorkshire Institution for the Deaf and Dumb in Doncaster. In this school, using signs and fingerspelling as the main means of communication, Samuel made rapid progress and showed exceptional talent for drawing. His drawings and engravings were exhibited in public examinations around Yorkshire. During his last year at school in 1847, he struck a great lifetime friendship with Samuel Smith, who was undergoing his five-year apprenticeship to become a teacher of the Deaf. Samuel's younger and hearing brother, John W. North, was a trainee teacher at the same school and later in 1883, he became a missioner at the Manchester Adult Deaf and Dumb Institute.

After leaving school and spending a few years at home, Samuel, at the age of twenty, went to London to train as a wood engraver, serving a number of years apprenticed to the well-known engraving firm, J. & G. Nicholls, in Paternoster Row. It was reported in 1869 that Samuel was doing very well in his engraving business for the prestigious *Art Journal*.

Samuel showed a taste for evangelism since early in his life, and he knew that Samuel Smith had arrived on the London scene in August 1855, to re-form an association in Aid of the Adult Deaf and Dumb. Smith found a lot of support from Samuel who joined and participated in the activities of the association during his spare hours away from engraving. Whilst Smith was taking his course for ordainship at King's College, London, for three years, Samuel helped by taking over Smith's Sunday services for the Deaf. By 1858, he was appointed Smith's assistant missioner for the Deaf and two years later, Smith was duly ordained.

On 1 July 1861, Samuel North married Ann Elizabeth Chappell, aged 39, a hearing governess at the Holy Trinity Church, Islington. Her deaf sister married Alexander Melville, who was one of Samuel's teachers at Doncaster. Samuel then concentrated on studying for the Church with a view to becoming ordained. He studied Latin, Greek and Hebrew, and took written examinations that he passed very satisfactorily and presented himself for ordination. The Bishop of London refused to ordain him because he was deaf and that it was not possible for him to enter the ministry. The Rev. Smith made an earnest plea on Samuel's behalf but to no avail. Samuel was deeply hurt and disappointed. This was followed by the death of his wife, Ann, in 1866.

However, Samuel continued to encourage the Deaf to take interest in Biblical studies. He visited Brussels twice, preaching to the Deaf Belgians who learned a lot from Samuel, whose knowledge of Greek and Hebrew helped to explain some difficult or interesting parts of scriptural statements. Samuel was responsible for missionary work for the Deaf in the district of West London from 1858 to 1892, holding regular church services for a small group of Deaf adults on Sunday mornings at St. John's schoolroom in Notting Hill and in the evenings at St. Jude's schoolroom in Chelsea. He often gave talks to members of the Deaf community on the curiosities of natural history at St. Saviour's Church in Oxford Street. Samuel did an engraving of the same church for the front cover of the *Deaf and Dumb Magazine*.

Samuel later met a lady who became deaf in early childhood and married her in 1872 at St. George's, Hanover Square, London. She was Jane Ann Hunt, who was a prolific artist and poetess. Over thirty of her oil paintings, mainly miniature portraits, under the name Jane A, North, were exhibited at the Royal Academy of Arts. Samuel engraved many of his wife Jane's sketches and drawings, as well as those of another renowned Deaf artist, Thomas Davidson, for various magazines.

In 1876, Samuel accompanied a group of Deaf Dutch and Belgians on their tour of the United Kingdom. They gave lectures in Deaf clubs and their sign language appeared to resemble that used by the British Deaf, who were able to catch the gist of their talks and appreciated Samuel's efforts to make them express themselves in international sign language. Samuel was one of the earliest members of the newly founded British Deaf and Dumb Association in 1890 and in one of his last articles in 1890, an extract on the subject of "Deaf and Dumb", he gave an insight into his clear and direct preference for sign language: -

> *Many who have learnt with painful difficulty at the oral schools prefer to drop the use of their speech and use finger and sign language on this account, and also because they have learnt so little variety of language, each word being so great a labour to articulate or read from the silent motion of the lips of other people, that they find it impossible to express all they think and feel that way, and have recourse to signs even more than those who have learnt altogether on the silent system. There are hearing people who prefer to be "deaf and dumb" spiritually.*

Samuel North became ill and died nine weeks later at his home in Kensington in the winter of 1892. Samuel's early pioneering efforts to pave the way for the Deaf to be ordained into the priesthood resulted in Edward Rowland and Richard Aslatt Pearce achieving the goal in 1882 and 1885 respectively.

Anthony J. Boyce

Robert Jones O'Keeffe
1811-1876

Robert Jones O'Keeffe was an extremely popular person with the members of the British Deaf community of his time. It was most likely that his humility and his simple wants of life endeared himself to everyone he met. However, behind him, his family had an illustrious history. His ancestor, Arthur O'Keeffe, was buried in Westminster Abbey, where a monumental tablet is placed, stating him to be the descendant of the Kings O'Keeffe of Ireland. O'Keeffe's father was an officer in the army (and then a clerk in the stamp office in Dublin) and his uncle was an officer in the British army who was killed in the Battle of Waterloo. O'Keeffe had an aunt who married one Farmer Wiseman and bore him a son, who grew up to become Cardinal Wiseman. O'Keeffe had two cousins. One was Lieutenant Robert O'Keeffe, who subsequently blew his brains out after shooting dead a creditor, to whom he owed a large debt. The other was Captain Charles O'Keeffe, who was accidentally shot by a soldier during a target practice!

Robert Jones O'Keeffe was born in Ireland on 29 October 1811. He became deaf at 2½ years old by falling into a lake. He was educated at Claremont, a Protestant school for the Deaf in Dublin under Joseph Humphreys. After leaving school, O'Keeffe found employment at a mail coach factory in Dublin and worked there for 15 years; but when railways were introduced to Ireland, he was made redundant. Desperate for work, he and his widowed mother left their native country and headed for London in 1843. O'Keeffe was fortunate to find employment with the builders, Cubitt's, in Grays Inn Road. The owner of the building firm, Cubitt, knew his father and uncle. Through Cubitt, O'Keeffe became a well-known personality among the wealthy classes of London, in particular the Lord Mayor, Sir W. Cubitt. O'Keeffe worked for the building company for 32 years until he was struck down with paralysis around 1875.

In 1855, some seven years after he arrived in England, O'Keeffe finally joined the Deaf community when he visited one church service organised by the Association in Aid of the Deaf and Dumb and became a frequent visitor at Saint Saviour's Church in Oxford Street, London. It was during that period that he met and married an English deaf widow (who died in 1870 and her name is yet unknown). O'Keeffe became an attendant at services and lecturers and it was in that role that he became very well-known and popular. He was respected by all who knew him until his death on 1 February 1876. He was buried in the Great Northern Cemetery, Colney Hatch, on Saturday 6 February.

Raymond Lee

140

Kate Oxley
1896-1978

There have been very few Deaf novelists who have published books for sale to the general public. One such person was Kate Oxley, who wrote five novels under the name of Kate Whitehead, her maiden name. Kate was born in Goole on 5 August 1896, the daughter of a dock labourer. She became totally deaf through scarlet fever at the age of eight. She was admitted to the Yorkshire Institution for the Deaf and Dumb in Doncaster in 1906 and left in 1912.

Although she never received training in writing in the accepted sense, she wrote a children's historical mystery novel *The King's Legacy,* a story about the French revolution and the Dauphin Louis XVII. The first book sold out and was favourably reviewed in *The Teacher's World* by Enid Blyton. In a short story competition in *The Bookman*, out of a thousand entries, Kate was placed 15th on the list to get an honourable mention, the judges not knowing that she was deaf. Her

Kate Oxley's first novel

next book, *For Prince Charlie,* depicted him as a soldier. One of the chief characters was Henry Baker, who was one of the earliest teachers of the deaf in England. The two books showed evidence of Kate's great interest and research into Deaf history.

While living in Hull in the early 1920s, Kate became great friends with William McCandlish, the Deaf missioner for the Hull and East Yorkshire Deaf and Dumb Institute, who introduced her to Selwyn Oxley. A man of private means, Oxley was an evangelist and a man with a mission to bring Christianity to deaf and hard-of-hearing people. His father founded the Guild of St. John of Beverley, and in time many missioners for Deaf people came to belong to this Guild. Selwyn Oxley also had another mission - to collect and build up a library of all literature relating to deafness, and Kate moved to London in 1924 to become his secretary. It was during her time with Oxley that Kate wrote and published her two historical mysteries. Selwyn and Kate were married quietly on 5 August 1929, and they set up home in Ephphatha House, Ealing. This building eventually became the home of the "Deaf Library" with a collection of over 5000 books, magazines and pamphlets. There were also over 4500 slides and photographs. It was the most comprehensive Deaf library in Britain at that time. Kate was so busy assisting her husband with this collection that she only wrote three more novels after her marriage, all about cats, and the last was published in 1933.

In 1940, Selwyn and Kate made a decision to relocate to Cheltenham in Gloucestershire in the interest of preserving the unique library from possible damage from wartime bombing. The relocation and the strain of packing all their valuable books took its toll on them both, and the library never functioned as such again. After the war, the library was systematically reduced with large batches of books going to deaf schools overseas, especially Australia, and to Selwyn's old college, Radley in Oxford. After Selwyn's death in 1951, what remained of the unique collection was bequeathed to the RNID Library. Kate wrote one further book after her husband's death – a biography of Selwyn, entitled *A Man with a Mission*, published in 1955. Kate passed away on 22 February 1978 at Northwood Pinner & District Hospital, London.

Anthony J. Boyce & Maureen A. Jackson

George Percy Patrick
Lord Carberry
1810-1890

One of the few aristocrats who felt the greatest affinity with his fellow Deaf was George Percy Patrick, later to become Lord Carberry of Laxton Hall, Northamptonshire. Born deaf in Co. Wexford, Ireland, Lord Carberry never spoke in his life. Educated privately at home in Northamptonshire in his early years, he was sent to France at the age of 10 to the "Institution Nationale des Sourds–Muets", Rue Saint-Jacques, Paris.

He married a Catherine Shuldham, the daughter of a general and had a daughter who later married the Earl of Brandon. Lord Carberry's estates in Northamptonshire and in Ireland made him a rich man. His shrewdness in improving and managing his properties increased their worth considerably.

His Irish birth and French education gave him a lifelong interest in the welfare of Deaf people in Ireland and in Europe, using his family wealth to support many schools for deaf children and organisations for deaf adults.

Lord Carberry became associated with St. Saviour's Church for the Deaf, contributing £110 to its building fund and a further £200 to enable the trustees to complete the chaplain's residence. He was present when the foundation stone of the church was laid in Oxford Street by the Prince of Wales.

When the National Deaf and Dumb Society, the forerunner to the British Deaf and Dumb Association, was formed in 1879, Lord Carberry gave financial support to the organisation, and was elected its first President.

Peter W. Jackson

Thomas Pattison
1805 -1898

DEAF and DUMB INSTITUTION,
152 Liverpool Street, near South Head Road.

This Institution is to be conducted by
Mr. THOMAS PATTISON,
late secretary and treasurer of the
Edinburgh
Deaf and Dumb Benevolent Society.

The School will open on Monday, the 22 October.

The Religious Meeting of the Mute Adults
commences on Sunday the 28 Instant.

Worship at 2 p.m. and 6 p m

This notice appeared in 1860 in the *Sydney Morning Herald* and announced the opening of the first school for deaf children in Australia, although Pattison had been teaching some children privately in his home. Pattison had been born in Edinburgh 54 years earlier on 5 January 1805 (and became deaf early in life) so that his life was divided almost into two halves, one half in Scotland and the second in Australia. Both halves were full of ups and downs!

He was one of the Macdonald Clan of Caledonians and was admitted as a pupil to the Edinburgh Institution for the Education of Deaf and Dumb Children in 1813 at the age of seven. His fees were paid by this school, which was itself very new, having been founded in 1810. He seems to have been a pupil for five years and then a "monitor" for two more years, leaving in 1820 when he was still only thirteen years old. On leaving school, he was apprenticed to a coach builder in Edinburgh and over the years he must have moved about in Scotland as he is known to have been identified with the missions in Dumfries and Dundee before becoming secretary and treasurer to the Edinburgh Deaf and Dumb Benevolent Society at a time for which there are no records.

Thomas' hearing brother Robert was a successful adventurer who visited Australia in 1837 and going again in 1858, became a prominent citizen of the colony. So it was not surprising that Thomas followed him. Whilst in Australia, Thomas decided to set up a school, possibly because he came into contact with the father of three deaf and dumb daughters who had no education and he realised there was no school at all in Australia for deaf children. He started with about eleven pupils, but the school grew slowly. George Lentz, the father of these three children, worked with him and they ran the school privately for a year. This proved very difficult and they were helped by the Rev. George King to set up a public institution for the Colony of New South Wales. One of the first pupils was Lentz's niece Anne. Lentz's hearing daughters taught in the school.

In 1861, Pattison started travelling to other parts of the country to find and bring in more pupils, and collect subscriptions, visiting his brother on the way. The school then moved to larger premises with the Governor of New South Wales as its Patron. Numbers still fluctuated and all the pupils came daily until 1868. The manual alphabet was used. There was a falling out between the Lentzes and Pattison. Then Thomas' marriage took place and after some problems, his wife was appointed Matron. As Miss Lentz had been dismissed, Thomas was the sole teacher, but his wife taught sewing. Too much money was being spent and after a year Mrs. Pattison's appointment was terminated. Pattison's hours were reduced and he was made a "daily teacher", until he left in 1866. He was then 60 years old.

Thomas went first to New Zealand and worked again as a coach painter and then to Victoria where he opened a shop, but soon became a coach-builder until the age of 80. He was a respected member of the Melbourne Adult Deaf and Dumb Mission. For four years he lived in a Benevolent Asylum, and then was supported by members of his family but looked after by deaf friends until his death in 1898 at the age of 92.

Thomas Pattison ranks with Braidwood, de l'Epee and other pioneers as a founder of a country's first school for deaf children. It was said that he had a desire *"to impart to others situated similarly to himself the benefits of that education which he had received in our fatherland."*

Doreen E. Woodford

James Paul
1848-1918

One of the giants of the Deaf Community in the late 19th Century was James Paul, who was born in Cardross, Dumbartonshire. He lost his hearing in infancy and was sent to the Glasgow Deaf and Dumb Institution when aged 8. At school, he proved to be a very able pupil, going on record as *"one of the brightest of a clever band of scholars"*.

On leaving school, Paul was apprenticed to the bookbinding trade, but as this did not altogether satisfy his youthful ambition, he wisely resolved to prepare himself for some higher career by devoting his leisure hours to study and self-culture. Consequently, he soon began to take a leading part in the affairs of the adult deaf and established a reputation as a leader and organizer. One of his greatest achievements in those early days was the formation of a National Deaf and Dumb Society, which he succeed in floating in 1879. This was the forerunner of the present-day British Deaf Association. For this reason, James Paul is regarded by many Deaf people as the true founder of the BDA. The Society did not hold together very long, having been torn asunder by internal dissensions, but before its collapse, it inaugurated two important undertakings, the Stockton-on-Tees Mission and the Ayrshire Mission to the Deaf and Dumb. James Paul himself became the missionary in the latter district, which was founded in 1881.

Despite the collapse of the National Deaf and Dumb Society in 1886, many Deaf people, including Francis Maginn, saw to the fallacy of the collapse which was caused by fierce resistance by Deaf supporters of the mainly London-based Association in Aid of the Deaf and Dumb and went about to restore it. James Paul was persuaded to step into the breach once again and became instrumental in the re-establishment of the organisation, under a different title of British Deaf and Dumb Association. James Paul's advice, expertise and inspiration had strong impact on Deaf people like Francis Maginn.

In 1894, mainly through his personal efforts, the mission acquired a fine property in Clark Terrace as its headquarters. The house was formerly the residence of the late Provost M'Lelland. In addition to a home for the missionary, the premises comprise various offices and a hall for meetings. A few months later a home for deaf girls was established in Ayr.

In these homes the work of sheltering and training the deaf was carried out with much efficiency; many girls, otherwise friendless, were sheltered and cared for while learning a trade, and also many deaf girls from all parts of the country had the opportunity of spending a cheap holiday by the seaside in congenial company.

James Paul died on 1 June 1918. He had been in failing health for about fifteen months, and in the previous October he underwent an operation, from which he never fully recovered and for the last six weeks he had been entirely confined to bed. He remained conscious to the very end and up till within ten minutes of his death signed fluently.

Peter W. Jackson

Benjamin H. Payne
1847-1926

Benjamin Payne was born on 23 January 1847 in Ireland. He received his early education in the Church of Ireland National School in Athlone, Ireland. He was a diligent pupil and at ten years of age, he won a scholarship for a place at the Raneleigh Institution, Athlone. The future seemed bright for him but a serious attack of scarlet fever completely destroyed his hearing. He was already familiar with the manual alphabet and this proved a great help to him. For a time he worked in the office of a local land agent and whilst there, he learned accountancy which proved a useful asset when he was destined to run a school for the deaf later on.

At the age of 13, Benjamin was admitted as a pupil at Claremont Institution for the Deaf and Dumb, Glasnevin, Dublin. After a few months, he became a pupil teacher and was later appointed an assistant teacher. He recalled his early days of hardship at Claremont when he received very low salary, plain food, and little time for leisure, and had to observe rigid economies in fuel and lighting.

At the age of 29, in an open competition with seven hearing candidates, Benjamin was chosen to become the head of the Cambrian Institution for the Deaf and Dumb Swansea. Following his appointment, he married Miss Florence Passant on 18 April 1876 at St. Mary's Church, Swansea. Florence was born in Slane, near Drogheda, Ireland, and had taught for three years at Claremont and then for another three years at Donaldson's Hospital, Edinburgh. Both Mr. and Mrs. Payne were at Swansea for nearly 40 years before they retired in July 1915. Benjamin ran his school well, giving his all to its success and taught deaf children using the combined method. He believed in adapting the method to the pupil rather than the pupil to the method. He was an eloquent signer, broad-minded and liberal, with an outlook that was always positive. Benjamin was a strong Churchman and undertook missionary work amongst the deaf in Swansea. He took service for them every Sunday at his school. He was a good friend and counsellor for the deaf. Mr. and Mrs. Payne had an only son, Arnold Hill Payne, who went to Oxford and gained his M.A degree in Divinity, and who later became a missionary worker amongst the deaf.

Benjamin was a ready advocate to champion the cause of the Deaf and Dumb, specially on religion and education. His chief interest was in the work of the BDDA and he was for many years a member of the BDDA Executive Committee and Vice-President for Wales. The British adult Deaf looked up to him as a leading defender of their freedom to converse by fingerspelling and signs.

During the First World War, Benjamin Payne worked for a time under the Royal Association in Aid of the Deaf and Dumb. In 1921, his wife died and was buried at Rede, Suffolk. Benjamin passed away on 20 August 1926 and was laid to rest in the same grave.

Anthony J. Boyce

146

The Reverend Richard Aslatt Pearce
1854-1928

Richard Aslatt Pearce, eldest child of Richard S. Pearce, a town clerk, and his wife Annie (née Patterson) was born deaf at the family home, 55 St. Mary, Northam, Southampton, on 9 January 1854. Richard was educated at the Brighton Institution for the Instruction of Deaf and Dumb as a private pupil. His father paid £50 a year for school fees. He was listed as admission no. 186 and was admitted on 16 August 1860. He spent twelve years under the personal care of Mr William Sleight, the headmaster. He obtained a high-class education and training, entirely on the manual system. His brother and sister, Walter Seaward and Pearce, were also born deaf and educated privately at the same Institution in 1869 and 1871. Mr Sleight reported that Richard spoke very well and possessed good speech.

In 1872, Richard left the Institution and entered his father's attorney office as his secretary. He soon began to employ his leisure hours in seeking out and instructing the deaf and dumb poor, especially in collecting adults together on Sunday afternoons for religious worship and services. His interest in religious work led to him being ordained by the Bishop of Winchester, with the approval of the Archbishop of Canterbury, on 21 May 1885. Richard was the first born-deaf person in Great Britain to be ordained by the Church of England.

Queen Victoria was always interested in the deaf and had heard much of the good work done by Rev. Pearce, who later had the honour of being presented to the Queen and Princess Beatrice at Osborne House in the Isle of Wight on 16 January 1886. The Queen spelled to him on her fingers and presented him her autographed portrait.

On 26 April 1888, Richard married Frances Mary Monck at St. Saviour's Church in London. She became deaf when she was two years old and was privately educated under the oral system. Her father, Viscount Monck, was Governor-General of Canada.

Richard Pearce conducted services in London and throughout Hampshire, Surrey and Sussex. He served the Winchester Diocesan Mission to the Deaf and Dumb for forty-three years. The Church (formerly mission hall) in Northam was converted in 1889 and funds were raised chiefly by Sir Arthur Henderson Fairbairn. The Rev. Pearce was one of the few who received a lifetime annuity for his mission work from his friend, Emma Constance Fairbairn, sister of Sir Arthur.

The Rev. Pearce retired from active service at the age of sixty-eight. At a farewell gathering held at the Fairbairn Centre in Southampton on 31 December 1921, Mr Arthur Sleight, son of William and second headmaster of Brighton Institution, thanked him for having sought out so many deaf children and sending them to the Institution. The Rev. Pearce died at the age of 75 on 20 July 1928 at his home, 'Homelands', The Heritage Street in Winchester, leaving a widow and three children.

Geoffrey J. Eagling

147

Bernard Lewis Pitcher
1909-2000

The only son of H. A. Pitcher, a civil servant, Bernard Pitcher was born deaf on 18 September 1909, in Worthing, West Sussex. At the age of four, Bernard received some private tuition at his home and two years later attended Miss Wehner's private school at Wallington. At the age of 9, he attended Dene Hollow School and was taught by Miss Mary Hare for seven years. He was grateful to her for enabling him to develop *a priceless possession of clear and unusually accurate, straightforward language*. He was then transferred to Spring Hill School, a private school for deaf boys in Northampton in 1925 and took an academic curriculum for seven years. He passed several School Certificate subjects with distinction, which led him to study scientific subjects at a higher level. He attended the Northampton Technical College for practical laboratory work and received specialised tutoring from Mr. Ince-Jones, the headmaster of Spring Hill School. By 1932, Bernard gained a number of credits sufficient for entry into a university. In all the years during which Bernard received his education, the oral method of was used. The *Sunday Times* dated 6 November 1932 reported that:

> *Bernard's examination successes would be an unusually good record for anyone possessed of all faculties but when it is remembered that he had to spend a large part of his time in the slow and tedious process of learning to speak, to read lips of others and to build up the elements of the English language, it is a remarkable achievement.*

In the autumn of 1932, Bernard entered the Royal College of Science, University of London, and embarked on a course for a degree in Science. In the 1933 issue *of Spring Hill* magazine, he explained how he overcame the problems of following lectures by getting *a student to write carbon copies of the lectures* for him. In the 1949 *Bluebird* magazine, he wrote that when he attended lectures where lantern slides were being shown in the dark, he resorted to *flashing torchlight on the notepaper of the student who was writing*. By his determination, persistence and courage, he sweated his way through and was duly awarded the B.Sc. degree in addition to the diploma of Associate of Royal College of Science in July 1936. Bernard continued his studies in geology at the Imperial College of Science and did his fieldwork in Shropshire where he collected and classified fossils, discovering a number of species of fossils, which had not been described before. His thesis on this work, titled *The Upper Valentian Gastropod Fauna of Shropshire,* earned him the Ph.D. degree in May 1939. He was the first born-deaf Briton to have achieved this distinction.

Bernard Pitcher was by nature quiet, unassuming and conscientious and he was a man of private means. Due to his delicate health, he never worked. During his early years, he was a regular at the Spurs Club for the Deaf in London. For the greater part of his life, he was the Secretary of his local Deaf Club in Worthing, where he died at the age of 90 on 17 April 2000 in a local nursing home.

Anthony J. Boyce and John A. Hay

148

Princess Katherine Plantagenet
1253-1257

It is not probably generally known that the daughter of one of the English Kings was deaf and dumb. Katherine Plantagenet, the youngest child of Henry III, was born on St. Katherine's Day, 25 November 1253. Her christening feast was celebrated with great pomp and rejoicing. Some items of the bill of fare consisted of 14 wild boars, 24 swans, 250 partridges, 1650 fowls, 61,000 eggs, etc. The little princess was styled as the Queen's beautiful daughter and was described as a remarkably lovely child. It was not till she was about 2 years old when her royal parents realised the sad fact that their daughter was deaf and dumb. The distressed King made large offerings to Westminster Abbey on numerous occasions on Katherine's behalf. The prayers of the sorrowing parents were surely answered, though not as they themselves hoped, for as the lovely little deaf mute was not to grow up in ignorance and helplessness which was the fate of all thus afflicted in those days. In 1257, the ears which had been deaf to all mortal sounds heard the voice of angels calling her to Paradise at the early age of three.

The tomb of Princess Katherine Plantagenet in Westminster Abbey

Katherine's health had always been delicate and the year before she died she had been sent for some time to the country to be under the charge of the widowed Lady Emma de St John, tenant of one of the Crown Manors in Berkshire known at the time as Swalefelle, later as the village of Swallowfield. The King sent, among other presents, a little kid from the Royal Forests to be her playfellow at Swallowfield. He continually despatched messengers to enquire about her health and once, when the report was better than usual, he bestowed in his delight a good robe to the messenger who brought the welcome tidings. But the child was fast fading away from the earth and she only returned to Windsor to die on 3 May 1257. The King and Queen were inconsolable in the loss of their daughter and Henry fretted himself into a low fever. Costly gifts were bestowed upon the nurses in remembrance of the sweet little maiden. A gorgeous funeral was held at Westminster Abbey and a silver statue as large as life was placed over her tomb as the last proof of love by her heartbroken parents. The statue was stolen during the dissolution and all that remains is the tomb devoid of any inscription of the deceased.

Who knows that she, being a Princess, might have had an instructor provided for her had she lived longer and might have supplied a chapter in history of the education of the deaf. Even in the rude era, England had its learned and compassionate priests such as St John of Beverley four centuries before Princess Katherine's time, and the opportunity would not have been lacking in the royal court or in the silence of Swallowfield for experiment in teaching the deaf and thus giving them a place of respect in society.

Arthur F. Dimmock

149

Jane Poole
1781-1860

This is the last Will of me Jane Poole Spinster of Ludlow in the County of Salop I give the several Legacies as following to Mrs. Dunne the wife of Thomas Dunne Esquire of Bitterley Hall the sum of One thousand pounds to Mr. Wilton the sum of One hundred pounds to the Reverend Charles Walcot the sum of One hundred pounds to my niece Isabella Fitzgerald the sum of One thousand pounds to my niece Caroline Hamilton the sum of One thousand pounds to my niece Constance Dunbar the sum of One thousand pounds to my Nephew Charles Benjamin Stevenson the sum of Seventeen hundred pounds to my maid Elizabeth Rufford the sum of Two hundred pounds and all my furniture and linen to my maid Ann Rufford the sum of Five hundred pounds and all my books I give unto my Executors the sum of One hundred pounds upon trust to pay the same out of my personal estate to the Treasurer of the School for the Deaf and Dumb Oxford Street East Liverpool which sum of One hundred pounds I desire may be applied for the Charity And I give and devise the rest of my personal estate and my real estate if any unto my said Nephews and Nieces to be divided equally between them I appoint the said Thomas Dunne and Mr. Wilton Executors of this my Will Signed by me this twentieth day of November one thousand eight hundred and fifty two — Jane Poole — The contents of this paper writing were communicated to the abovenamed Jane Poole by spelling the same word for word on her fingers and she repeated the same word for word on her fingers and being fully understood by her it was signed by her as her last Will and Testament in the presence of us present at the same time who at her request in her presence and in the presence of each other have hereunto subscribed our names as attesting witnesses — Sarah Rice of Bitterley Widow — David Buxton of Liverpool Principal of the Liverpool School for the Deaf & Dumb. —

Proved at London 31st May 1861 by the oath of George Mansell Wilton the surviving Executor to whom admon was granted. —

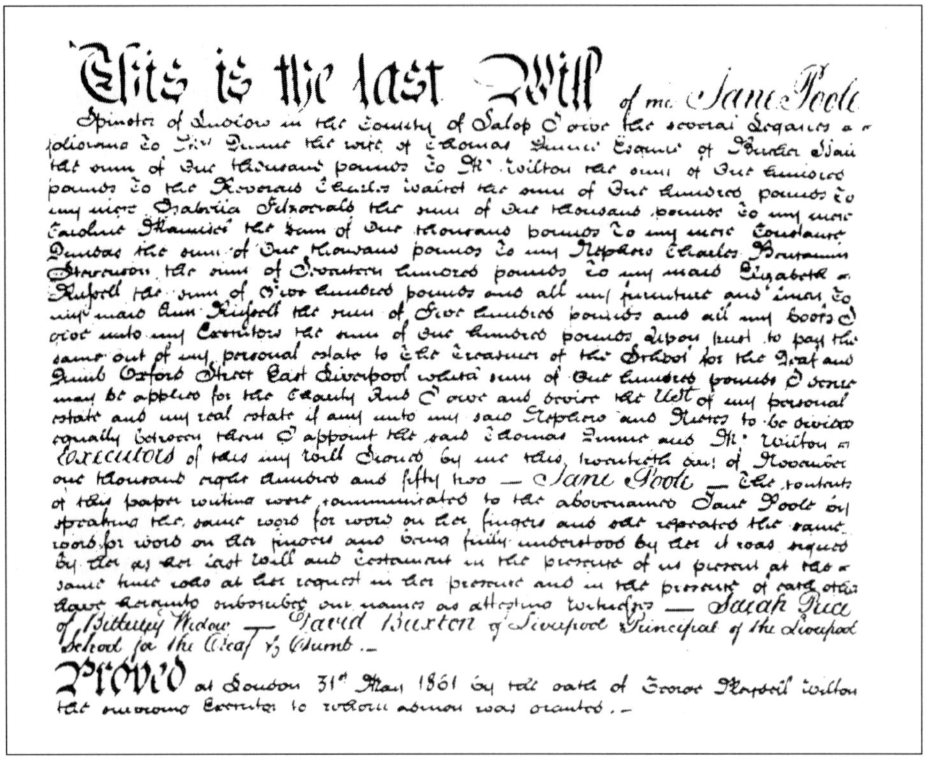

Jane Poole was born deaf in Ludlow in the county of Salop in July 1781. She was the youngest of six children of James Poole and Ann Cooper. Very little is known about the family and its members with the exception that the family was comfortably well off and also that the family's attitude to Jane's deafness was such that she was not as well treated as her hearing siblings. When Jane was barely six years old, her mother shunted her out of the family and she was taken into the care of her two maiden aunts, who loved her as if she was their own.

There came one day when a male member of the maiden aunt's side of the family passed away and he left a vast sum of money to Jane. The bequest enabled the two maiden aunts to set up a kind of trust fund on Jane's behalf to manage Jane's newly found wealth. The bequest was wisely used to send Jane to the fabulous Braidwood's Academy for the Deaf and Dumb based at Grove House, off Mare Street in Hackney in the county of Middlesex. The fee for her education was believed to have been initially £110 per annum when she commenced in 1787 and it rose to £150 per annum in 1791, remaining constant until her last year in 1795.

Jane was the only member of her own family to inherit from her uncle's will and this infuriated many members of her family, in particular her sister Caroline Stevenson, and this set the tone for Jane's future; her life was to be made as miserable and unbearable as could be by her spiteful sister.

Little is known of Jane's life except for that she acquainted herself with another Braidwoodian pupil, Ann Walcot. She was also deaf and hailed from Bitterley in the county of Salop. Jane never married, but Ann was married to her cousin, the Rev. Charles Walcot. During Jane's stay at the Braidwood Academy, one of her maiden aunts died. In 1826, Jane's surviving maiden aunt passed away and Jane took possession of her fortune from the trust.

With her money, Jane sought to rid of loneliness and engaged a former maid of her friend Ann Walcot as a servant. This maid, Elizabeth Russell, was fluent in the manual alphabet. They both went to live with Jane's mother and her spiteful sister, Caroline, at Henner and stayed with them for seven years until 1833 when her mother died. By that time, Caroline had married and returned to Ludlow. Jane returned to Ludlow with her servant and her daughter Ann Russell and rented a number of rooms in a house initially in 37 Broad Street. An elderly spinster, Miss Rogers, owned this house. The group later moved to 29 Broad Street.

Jane's life was marred by another misfortune when in 1841 she became blind. She was 60 years old and became increasingly dependent on her servants whom she trusted. Caroline, greedy and aware of Jane's wealth, tried without success to assume control of her financial affairs as Jane was able to prove that she could manage her affairs through the manual language with her servants and the assistance of her trusty cousin, Mr. Biddulph, who was connected to the firm of Cox and Biddulph. Eight years later in 1849, Mr. Biddulph died and left around £21,000 to be shared equally between the three sisters Jane, Mary Ann and Caroline. The sum was placed in the name of the Accountant-General of the Court of Chancery in London. A dispute arose caused by Caroline demanding a larger share and the dispute dragged on for two years. Caroline felt that Jane needed little of the share due to her condition as a Deafblind person and that she could manage her share, giving her money only for what she needed. However, Jane's friends mounted a challenge to Caroline and a court case to settle the dispute occurred on Wednesday 5 July 1851 in the Court of Chancery. The case took three days and the outcome was the three sisters ended up receiving equal shares, an amount of some £7,000 each.

A year after the case, Jane felt compelled to protect her wealth from Caroline and set about to write her own will. As she was Deafblind, she engaged the Rev. Charles Walcot, Sarah Price (the son and daughter of Ann Walcot) and Dr. David Buxton to assist her in compiling her will which was conducted via the manual language. The will was then formally written down, signed and sealed. Jane lived until 10 April 1860 when she died at her home in Broad Street.

On her death, her will was read and she left a total of £14,000 to various persons named, most of whom were the children of Caroline Stevenson, her sister! However, Caroline objected to the will and blocked probate on grounds that Jane, being a Deafblind person, could not possibly have written such a complicated legal statement. She further indicated that deaf people could not write wills. Jane's solicitor, George Pleydell Wilton, tried to reason with her. Failing this, he took the case to the Court of Probate in Westminster Hall. The case was heard on May 2 and 3 1861 under Sir Cresswell Cresswell and the outcome was a triumph for Jane and utter humiliation for Caroline Stevenson, in that a special jury ruled that the will by a Deafblind person was valid, provided that it was properly written, witnessed and sealed.

With this decision, a precedence was established unique in English jurisprudence. But the true victory was that it was a triumph over the attitude and blinkered concept of deafness harboured by members of the hearing society in general at that time. It was also a triumph in that the court recognised that the intellectual abilities of the deaf and Deafblind were not in any way inferior to that of hearing people because of the handicap.

Quiet and little known, and always facing misfortune in her life, Jane Poole had posthumously achieved on behalf of every deaf and Deafblind person in Britain recognition of their right to write their own wills, and destroyed the myth then circulating that such persons cannot, and were forbidden by law, to write their own wills.

Raymond Lee

Bourton House, Bourton-on-the-Hill, Gloucestershire.

Alexander Popham
1649-1708

Alexander Popham shares with Daniel Whalley the dubious distinction of being the first born-deaf person in Britain to have supposedly been taught to speak. Alexander was the second son of Colonel Edward Popham, a Member of Parliament for Minehead, Somerset, and Anne Wharton. Alexander's father died at sea of a fever in 1651, and his uncle, Colonel Alexander Popham, then brought up the boy.

At the age of 11 in 1659, Alexander was sent to Dr. William Holder, FRS (1616-1698) at Oxford after this eminent gentleman had undertaken to teach the boy how to speak.

However, his family was apparently not happy with the progress made by Dr. Holder, and in 1661, Alexander was sent to another Doctor of Divinity, Dr. John Wallis (1616-1703) who had already been teaching a young man named Daniel Whalley for about a year. Evidently, Alexander did not like Dr. Wallis very much and forgot much of what he had learnt through Dr. Holder's instruction.

Nonetheless, Dr. Wallis took the opportunity to present both Popham, then aged 14, and Whalley, then aged 25, before the Court of King Charles II in May 1662 where both young deaf men were said to have spoken before the King. However, Alexander apparently uttered only one or two words and was taciturn and ill disposed in front of the King. It may be that the young lad still had strong feelings towards Royalty given his family's strong Parliamentary links.

After this event, nothing more is heard of Alexander until 1679 when he married Brilliana Harley, the daughter of Sir Edward Harley of Hereford, and went to live with her at Bourton Manor, Bourton-on-the-Hill in Gloucestershire, which his family purchased for him.

He had three daughters and one son, Francis, by Brilliana. Family documents do not record whether Brilliana or any of the four children were deaf, only that one daughter died in infancy, the other two daughters remaining unmarried throughout their lives and Francis dying without any male issue.

Alexander Popham died in early 1708 and was buried on 9 February 1708, aged 59. He left little by way of family documents, apart from some land deeds and a Will, which is rather indecipherable. The latter gives some credence to the fact that Alexander was indeed taught to read and write and had an education of sorts, which enabled him to get married to a presumably hearing person and manage a Manor House.

Peter W. Jackson

152

Princess Joanna
c1428 -c1486

Within the ruins of the Collegiate Church Chancel attached to St Nicolas Buccleuch Parish Church in Dalkeith, near Edinburgh, stands the Morton Monument. This monument is in reality a tomb with two recumbent figures of the 1st Earl of Morton and his deaf and dumb wife, Princess Joanna of Scotland. Over five centuries, the features of the stone sculptured effigies are unfortunately almost obliterated, although the head shields representing their coats of arms are clearly identified.

Princess Joanna was a part of the Royal Stewart dynasty and was born deaf and dumb around 1428 to King James 1 of Scotland and his English wife, Joan Beaufort, the daughter of the Earl of Somerset. Joanna was one of eight Royal children. Princess Joanna was among the

The Morton Monument Effigies

chief characters in the Victorian historical novel entitled *Margery's Boy,* written by Emily Holt in 1879. The book gave an insight into the world of the 15th century Court of Scotland with Joanna leading a typical life as a lady of noble birth. Joanna enjoyed close companionship with her sister, Princess Eleanor, who acted as an interpreter in Holt's novel.

James II of Scotland succeeded his father who was assassinated in 1437. The new boy king had to face turbulent days as powerful nobles jostled for power and influence upon the king. He arranged political marriages for all his sisters to ward off these nobles. On 18 October 1440, Joanna, at the age of 13 years, was contracted with a tocher (dowry) of 3000 Scots merks, to marry James, the 3rd Earl of Angus, but he died before the intended wedding. Afterwards Joanna was sent to France in 1445 for her education. She spent some years at a nunnery at Aigueperse near Clermont-Ferrard.

In 1457, James II, anxious to secure support from the powerful Douglas Clan, arranged to have his deaf and dumb sister marry James Douglas, the 4th Lord Dalkeith. Lord James was a peace loving and pious person, very different from his warring brethren. This matrimonial alliance was to infuriate others who were avowed enemies of the Douglas family and paved the way for James to gain the upper hand. Nigel Tranter, the Scottish historical novelist, wrote episodes featuring Joanna and her fiancé in his *Black Douglas*, published in 1968.

Upon their wedding on 15 May 1459, James was created the Earl of Morton and his wife accorded the title of Countess. They bore four children. Little is known further about Joanna apart from a fact that she was so named as *Muta Domina de Dalkeith,* which simply translates as The Dumb Lady of Dalkeith. In various records she is always referred to with great esteem. The deaf and dumb Countess of Morton died sometime after 1486. Her effigy as a part of Morton Monument is probably the oldest known image of the named Deaf person in the world.

John A Hay

Cyril Reynolds
1904-1981

In the World Games for the Deaf (also known as 'Deaf Olympics') events, British Deaf athletes very often tended to struggle to stay on par with the great Deaf sportsmen of other countries. One Briton who managed to achieve respect and status as one of the great Deaf international athletes was Cyril Reynolds.

Cyril Reynolds was born in Grimsby, Humberside, in 1904. He became profoundly deaf at eighteen months after suffering from scarlet fever. When education beckoned, he attended the Royal School for the Deaf in Derby and went on to become its Head Boy in 1919.

When at school, Cyril showed great interest in athletics and maintained this eagerness after leaving school. He was eventually selected to represent Great Britain in the 1928 World Games for the Deaf at Amsterdam. He was the least fancied runner in the 200 metres, but ran a great race to win the gold medal. He showed blistering pace which surprised his opponents. In the next event, Cyril came second in the long jump, winning a silver medal. In the 4 x 100 metres relay, Cyril managed to come third, winning the bronze for Britain.

In 1930, at the European Games for the Deaf at Liege, Belgium, Cyril won a gold in the 400 metres and came second to claim his silver medal in the 100 metres. The following year saw the World Games for the Deaf held at Nuremberg in Germany. Cyril was obviously off-form, faring poorly in his events. However, he managed to come third in both the 100 metres and the 200 metres, bagging two bronze medals. In the 1935 World Games for the Deaf held at White City in London, Cyril won his final gold medal, captaining the winning team in the medley relay race. After that, he retired from international athletics.

Cyril was deeply involved with the British Deaf and Dumb Association (BDDA) as it was called then and he was one of the founder members of the Grimsby Branch in 1929. In the following year, he became the Honorary Secretary of the Grimsby Mission for the Deaf and held that position for 30 years. In recognition of his achievements to Deaf sport, the Grimsby Deaf Centre and the BDA, Cyril was awarded the BDA Medal of Honour in 1973.

Cyril was married with three children. His wife, Phyllis, died in 1981. Tragically in the same year, Cyril's condition deteriorated, complicated by kidney failure, thrombosis and Parkinson's disease. After being unconscious in a diabetic coma for 10 days, he passed away on Boxing Day – a complicated end to a man renowned for his speed and fitness.

Raymond Lee

Sir Joshua Reynolds
1723-1792

Joshua Reynolds was born in Plymouth, Devon, the son of the headmaster of the local grammar school where he was later to be educated. In 1740, he came to London to be apprenticed to the portraitist, Thomas Hudson, for four years before embarking on a two-year tour of Italy to study the Grand Masters. Most of the time was spent at Rome. Back in Devon, his early works were naval portraits, largely done at Plymouth. In 1749, Reynolds sailed with friends to Minorca, one of the Balearic islands off Spain. On the island a fall from a horse injured him and left him with a scarred lip. It was at the same time that his hearing problem started to manifest itself.

Reynolds attempted to lead the British painting away from the indigenous anecdotal pictures of the early 18th century towards the rhetoric of the continent *Grand Style*. His paintings were largely of fashionable women showing individual traits of character and personality. His style became increasingly classical from 1760 onwards and most famous pictures were of the Discourse series, Ugolino in 1773 and fine child portraits of noble families such as the Duke of Marlborough. The Prince of Wales patronised Reynolds extensively. It was a busy spell for Reynolds at his London studio so he used several assistant artists to help him.

In 1764, Reynolds founded the *Literary Club*, of which Dr. Johnson, Garrick, Burke, Goldsmith, Boswell and Sheridan were members. Reynolds was one of the earliest members of the Incorporated Society of Arts.

The Royal Academy of Arts was founded in 1768 and during the opening Reynolds delivered the *Discourses,* which contained his artistic theories and he spoke of connecting the academy with a scheme, which he promoted to help young artists. The eloquent speeches revealed him as a fine scholar as well as a talented artist. Despite strong competition from Thomas Gainsborough (1727-1788) and the handicap of deafness, which had become worse, Reynolds was elected the academy's first president. King George III knighted him in 1769. In 1784, Reynolds became painter to the King.

Sir Joshua Reynolds, when asked about his deafness, replied that it sharpened his vision and enabled him to have clearer insight into the characters of his sitters. Reynolds never married but his sister, Frances, kept his house. It was believed that she acted as his interpreter using gestures and mouthing words. Furthermore he befriended David Garrick (1717-1779) who was a great actor and it is believed that Garrick's mime talents were used to convey meaning to Reynolds. Garrick's portrait along with that of his friend, Dr. Samuel Johnson (1709-1784), were Reynold's masterpieces. In 1782, he suffered a stroke and his eyesight declined from 1789 and he ceased to paint. Reynolds died in 1792 and was buried in St. Paul's Cathedral, London.

Arthur F. Dimmock.

Sampson Towgood Roch
1759-1847

One of the most interesting miniature painters of the 18th century was Sampson Towgood Roch, who was born deaf in his family's home at Woodbine, near Youghal in County Waterford in 1759. He was the eldest son of William and Mary Roch,, a grandson of James Roch of Glyn Castle, near Carrick-on-Suir, Co. Tipperary, and a great-grandson of James Roch, a High Sheriff of County Waterford. While on a visit to some relations in Cashel, Tipperary, in 1773, Sampson first showed indications of a talent for drawing, making some sketches of scenery and drawing some small portraits of his friends.

Roch's father sent Sampson to Dublin to study but he showed no interest for study and began to paint miniatures. An advertisement in the *Dublin Evening Post* of 18 December 1781 announced that Roch, miniature painter, had *removed from Exchange Street to Mr Rice's, 13 Capel Street, where he continues to draw like-nesses for bracelets and rings at his usual price of two guineas each.* It is believed that he knew two other Deaf engravers who worked in same street and visited each other for conversation in those years. Roch's name as an artist first gained renown in 1784 when he was practising as a miniature painter when resident at 152 Capel Street. However, Roch left two years later for Cork. His family soon arranged his marriage to his first cousin, Melian Roch, the only daughter of his uncle, James Roch. They were married on Tuesday 29 May 1787 in St. Mary's Collegiate Church, Youghal.

Roch had a miniaturist friend Charles Byrne (1757-1810) who acted as his interpreter for many years. From around 1789-1792, Roch was in Grafton Street and seems to have been well patronised, but he left in 1792 and took up residence in Bath, England, where he remained until 1822, working successfully as a miniaturist. In 1817, he was living at 11 Pierpoint Street, Bath. Roch sent two miniatures (his only contribution) to the Royal Academy of Arts. Around 1819-1822, his address is recorded as 12 Pierpoint Street. He painted several members of the Royal Family, naval officers, aristocrats and numerous wealthy actresses who patronised Bath in those days. In 1822, Roch eventually returned to Ireland

Roch's wife, Melian, died on 21 September 1837. Sampson Roch lived for another ten years before he met his demise at his home on 18 February 1847. He was buried in the family plot at Ardmore, Co. Waterford. There is no headstone on his grave and they did not have any children.

The National Gallery of Ireland has numerous miniatures by Sampson Roch and they are among the best produced by Irish artists. In England, the Holbourne Museum in Bath has several miniatures painted by Roch during his time there.

David Breslin

156

Frederick John Rose
1831-1920

Frederick John Rose was born hearing to an organ maker on 21 September 1831 in Oxford. In about 1835, he contracted scarlatina (scarlet fever) and became totally deaf. He was admitted to the London Asylum for the Deaf and Dumb on 30 September 1840 as a charity pupil. He left the Asylum on 24 December 1845. In 1852, he and his younger brother, Francis, emigrated to Australia, departing on the ship *Gloriana*.

Frederick worked as a cabinetmaker in Emerald Hill (now Melbourne) and four years later in 1856, he drifted to the gold digging region at Mount Alexander and Forest River (near Bendigo) but met with no success. He settled down at Sandhurst (now Bendigo) and worked as a carpenter. In 1859, while in Sandhurst, he saw letters in the newspaper *Argus* (14 and 16 February) written by a widow called Mrs Sarah Lewis, who appealed to the public for a school for the deaf in the colony. Mrs Lewis had a deaf daughter called Lucy Ann. Sarah concluded the letter *"... if nothing can be done speedily in the colony I shall be put to the peril and danger of the sea to get her educated in Old England."* (J. H. Burchett in his book *Utmost for the Highest* claimed that Frederick was the only person in the colony qualified to give the necessary aid. It was not true as some deaf people were already in the colony, like Thomas Pattison who came to Australia in 1858 and later opened a deaf school in Sydney in 1860).

Frederick replied to the *Argus* on 24 February 1859, offering to establish a school for the deaf in the colony. Two months later Frederick and Sarah Lewis met for the first time and they formed a long standing partnership which led to the establishment of deaf education in Victoria.

In 1860, Frederick returned to England to marry Elizabeth Manning Telfer in Oxford on 27 June. In the same year, he brought his wife back to Australia and on 12 November 1860, he opened the first school for deaf children in Victoria at his rented home with one pupil, Lucy Ann Lewis. Within a year after opening the school, the number of children had increased to eight. In 1866, after the fourth move, they settled down at a purpose built school for the deaf known as *The Victoria Deaf and Dumb Institution*. Frederick became its first superintendent and headmaster.

Frederick retired as headmaster in 1882 due to ill-health. In 1920, a film was made of Frederick, conversing with Mr. Ernest Abraham, through fingerspelling and signs. Some months later in the same year, he died at the age of 89 at his home in Malvern, Australia.

Peter R. Brown

The Reverend Edward Rowland
1846-1904

The Glamorgan Mission to the Deaf and Dumb owe their origin to the energetic and enterprising efforts of one Deaf man, Edward Rowland. Rowland was born in Pontnewydd, Wales, in January 1846. He was the youngest of nine children. At the age of four and a half years, he was stricken with scarlet fever from which he became deaf upon recovery. In 1855, he was sent to the Cambrian Institution for the Deaf and Dumb in Swansea. On leaving school, he was apprenticed to a tailor; a work that he disliked and took on only to please his mother. At the same time, his master sometimes forced Rowland to work as much as sixteen hours a day. During his apprenticeship, Rowland developed a desire to acquire knowledge and indulged himself in books. So great was his desire that it was no unusual thing for Rowland to stay up studying after having worked sixteen hours at his trade. When Rowland's apprenticeship ended, he stayed with his employer only for a few months before he sought and obtained employment in London. His parents were taken aback by the news that their son would be with them no more, but they reluctantly had to let him go as Rowland was now his own man.

Whilst in London, Rowland regularly attended church services conducted for the Deaf by Matthew Robert Burns and the Rev. Samuel Smith and he haunted old bookstalls, ever on the watch for religious literature. It was said that when Rowland came across a book that appeared to be interesting, he would hurry home rejoicing, spending many hours pouring over the difficult language with the aid of a dictionary; explaining it to himself word by word. Matthew Robert Burns invited him to address the Deaf congregation at one service. Rowland took up the invitation and from that day he made up his mind to become a missioner with the Deaf.

In 1865, Rowland left London and opened a non-church related business in Abertillery, which he carried on for three years. However, his desire to become a priest was strong and in the spring of 1869, he closed his business and set out to become a man of the cloth. Equipped with a few pounds and two brass-framed pocket slates, Rowland set out for Cardiff where he collected a few Deaf people together. Having secured a room for Sunday meetings, a committee was formed and the Mission was an accomplished fact, although on a very small scale, but when it became gradually known that the mission was doing a good work amongst the neglected adult Deaf, it obtained the support of a number of religious and benevolent organisations.

Rowland was not content with his accomplishment at Cardiff. He proceeded to do the same task at Merthyr and a branch of the Mission was founded in 1872. Aberdare in 1874 and then Bristol in 1876 followed Merthyr. Rowland did not stop there. He knew that there were many Deaf people in Pontypridd and the Rhondda Valley and he proceeded to open a branch at Pontypridd in September 1881. On 26 June 1882, Rowland was ordained at Cardiff and he became the first British Deaf person to be ordained to the priesthood.

Early in 1883, Rowland saw an empty house for sale in the centre of Cardiff for £700. He set his heart on purchasing that house and embarked on a fundraising venture that was to last three years. In early1885, he achieved his aim of raising the amount and duly purchased the house, which became a meeting-house for the Deaf as well as a residence for the missioner, R. Bird. This house, known as Mission House, was situated at 25 Windsor Place, Cardiff. It was officially opened in March 1885. The fundraising venture ended in early 1886 and the Mission funds rose to just over £254. By 1888, the Glamorgan Mission had grown to such a size that the Mission had to divide the work into two districts. As a result of this, Rowland left Cardiff for Pontypridd, which was the other district and he worked from that base.

Rowland was a well known preacher in Deaf church services all over Britain, having preached in large towns such as London, Manchester, Liverpool, Dublin and Glasgow. He was described as an energetic, vigorous and sympathetic man. His enterprise and devotion won him a place in the hearts of all Welsh Deaf and he was also greatly respected by many hearing people who were aware of his relentless work. Rowland died at his home in Hill Villa, Pontypridd, on 23 September 1904 after a brief illness.

Raymond Lee

Philip Sambell
1798-1874

Philip Sambell, named after his father, was born deaf in Devonport in 1798, and was to spend the rest of his life in the West Country devoted to architecture. His early life is obscure, but his family were probably Baptists, since most of the churches he built were Baptist chapels and he contributed to the *Baptist Magazine*.

In 1835, he stood, unsuccessfully, for a local seat in the House of Commons, but his main interest was in architecture – both the creation of new buildings and research into the history of architecture. These factors suggest that his family had some means, since it would otherwise have been impossible to try and raise the money to try and enter Parliament and he could afford leisure time to undertake research. He had relatively few commissions for buildings, indicating perhaps that he did not need to earn money.

Baptist Chapel, River Street, Truro
Last known building designed by Philip
Sambell 1849-50

In the 17th and 18th centuries most 'good' architecture had been expected to take the Classical examples of Greece and Rome as their model, other styles being condemned as 'barbarian'. Just before Queen Victoria came to the throne, when Sambell was starting out on his architectural career, there was a revival of interest in other historical styles. Sambell was one of many young architects who researched buildings from other periods and countries, e.g. those of mediaeval Europe. This was to have a strong influence on his own work. The Classical influence is still evident in his early work in Truro; St. John's Church (his only Church of England building) with its Grecian domed cupola, for example, reflecting contemporary fashions in architecture.

In the 1830s, Sambell began to use a variety of different styles, based on his architectural researches. In his Baptist chapels of the mid-1830s in Penzance and Helston, he translated the heavy stone carving of the Norman style into the wood, plaster and brick of a Victorian church, as in the characteristic Norman zigzag or 'chevron' arch over the door of Clarence Street Baptist Chapel, Penzance. As part of the Victorian religious revival, more churches were needed, and many architects looked to medieval styles for inspiration, feeling that the great piety of the Middle Ages would be revived by providing a similar environment for Victorian worshippers. All denominations, Anglican, Catholic and Nonconformist, participated in this revival, known in architectural terms as the 'Gothic Revival'. Sambell's work was an early example of this trend, before the works of the famous Pugin and Sir George Gilbert Scott, who were both a dozen years younger than Sambell.

In 1839, Sambell explained his views on architecture at the Royal Institution of Cornwall, of which he was not only a member but a proprietor, with a financial interest in its management and whose meetings he attended regularly. A report of this lecture is interesting in showing that his work was read out on his behalf:

160

"An essay on architecture by Mr. Philip Sambell Jr. was read to the meeting by the Secretary, in consequence of the physical defects under which Mr. Sambell labours, precluding him from reading it himself."

In this essay, Sambell explored the geometric quality of Egyptian architecture, praising its simplicity and lack of excessive decoration. The report on the lecture states:

The essay was illustrated by a large series of beautiful drawings of the principal buildings and structures referred to, which excited the admiration of the meeting.

This was to be the first of several lectures on the subject of architecture; Caroline Fox, the diarist, who was acquainted with many men of science and letters, attended another lecture in her home town of Falmouth in 1840, *"written by Sambell, the deaf and dumb architect and read by young Ellis."* She, too, mentions his beautiful illustrations to accompany the lecture.

This emphasis on geometrical simplicity in his lectures influenced Sambell's own buildings, as in the symmetrical south front of River Street Baptist Chapel, Truro. The centre rounded-headed window is given extra height to break into the triangular pediment, whose outline is emphasised by projecting stones; providing an interesting contrast of shapes in an otherwise severe and regular frontage.

In a letter to the *Baptist Magazine* in 1841, Sambell discussed the unusual topic of *"acoustics and the philosophy of sound"* approaching the practical problem of the positioning of pulpits so that the congregation could best hear the minister. He went on to suggest that the minister should be visible and audible to all: *"... the dispenser of the word of life embracing all at a glance, and when he speaks the sound radiates clear and distinct ..."* Whether or not Sambell had other deaf people specifically in mind when he wrote this letter, in the days before loops and hearing aids, it is certain he was eager to improve communication between the minister and the worshippers.

In this respect, Sambell was very much an architect of the Victorian age, interested in experimenting with different styles and problems, and bringing older styles to a new audience.

In view of his connections with the Royal Institution of Cornwall, it is appropriate that his Savings Bank in Truro, of 1845-7, now houses the Royal Institution. His last known building was the Baptist Chapel in Truro, 1849-50, although he was listed in the *Architects, Engineers, and Building Trades' Directory, 1868*, six years before his death at Stonehouse in Devon in 1874.

Serena Cant

Charlotte Angas Scott
1858-1931

Charlotte Angas Scott was born in Lincoln on 8 June 1858, the second of seven children of a Congregational minister, Walter Scott. She received private home tutoring during her childhood and this enabled her to attend the first college for women in England, Girton College. Scott, like all women at Girton, could only attend lectures if chaperoned. She excelled in mathematics and in 1880 took the mathematics Tripos examinations, which ran for a total of fifty hours over a period of nine days. Her result equalled that of the eighth man in Cambridge and it caused a sensation at that time. The fact that a woman had mastered a "man's" subject belittled the then traditional policy that a woman cannot be granted a degree. Charlotte Scott's achievement sparked public pressure on Cambridge University to administer all university examinations to female students as a matter of policy, not just special privilege. This notable impact is also referred to as a turning point in British history when feminism began to yield educational and political power. There was a petition advocating the admission of women to Cambridge examinations and it carried over eight thousand signatures. The following year on 24 February 1881, a vote on revision of the policy was taken and passed by 398 votes to 32. However, it was not to be until 1948 that Cambridge would grant a degree to a woman.

Scott's hearing had never been good since she was very young; she was most likely to have been very hard of hearing and people noted that her deafness increased during her college years. However, this did not put her off from her graduate studies and she had a good mentor in Arthur Cayley and she achieved an "external" bachelor's degree in 1882 and worked her way to her doctoral degree in 1885, both with a "First class" from the University of London.

On the recommendation of Cayley, in 1885 Scott applied for a position as Associate Professor at Bryn Mawr College in Pennsylvania, USA. At this college, not only did Scott become the first mathematics department head, she was the only woman with a Ph.D. in mathematics whose native language was English. Despite her gradually worsening hearing, Scott's classes grew in size and she became a popular and respected teacher. Scott was a progressive teacher and very much ahead of her time. Students under her gained achievements – three of her students gained doctorates in mathematics before 1900. Not only that, Scott fought against dismissals of students who were unable to stay on part of their courses due to illnesses, saying that their work was more important than the illnesses themselves which would deprive the students' right to resume their courses once they were well again. Scott was particularly caring and considerate to students and their needs; students found her accessibility as a teacher and willingness to counsel inspirationally. In fact, Scott's female students received three times the percentage of American Ph.D.'s in mathematics before 1940 (in her immediate footsteps) than they did in the 1950s.

In 1891, Scott helped to organise the American Mathematical Society (AMS), serving on its council for seven years, and for two years as its vice-president. When the AMS celebrated its 50th anniversary, thirty people were honoured and of these, only one was a woman – Scott.

162

In 1899, Scott became the co-editor of *American Journal of Mathematics* and she held that position for twenty-seven years. On top of that, Scott had numerous papers published. Her book, *An Introductory Account of Certain Modern Ideas and Methods in Plane Analytical Geometry* (1894) was reprinted thirty years later and acclaimed especially for its distinction between a general proof and a particular example.

Scott became completely deaf by the turn of the 20th century, but she continued to lecture perfectly well. She would train graduate student protégés to answer questions from undergraduates. In case of any difficulty, the protégé would be practised in communicating with Scott, who would answer the question orally. The Bryn Mawr faculty even approved payment of $600 for a "lipreader" who helped her to communicate in class and to correct papers as her eyesight worsened.

In 1901, Scott's efforts contributed to the establishment of the College Entrance Examination Board and she served as the Chief Examiner in Mathematics in 1902 and 1903.

Scott retired in 1925 and returned to Cambridge in England, where she spent her remaining years. She had maintained ties with her friends and contacts in Cambridge whilst she was working in the USA. It is known that while Scott enjoyed working in the United States, she had grown increasingly lonely and homesick. Spending her final years gardening and betting on the Turf, Scott even found an area for further mathematical research – on the statistics of previous race winners and the mathematics of horse-breeding.

Scott died on 10 November 1931 and was interred in St. Giles churchyard in Cambridge. A fine woman, she was called by Rebiére (Paris, 1894) "one of the best living mathematicians" and Marguerite Lehr, Scott's last doctoral student, remarked that ... *few people ... have contributed significantly to research mathematics, making it especially remarkable that one was a deaf woman.*

Peter W. Jackson and Raymond Lee

Robert Menzies Scott
at work as a young man

Robert Menzies Scott
1891-1977
&
George Scott
1904-1998

The Scott family in Glasgow was a large one. Both Robert Menzies and George were born to Deaf parents and there were two other brothers and a sister who were also Deaf. The intelligence and fluent language of the children gave them an enormous advantage and ensured them an excellent education at a time before the unfortunate banning of sign language in schools made this impossible. Their use of elegantly written, grammatical English would be unusual in schoolchildren, Deaf or hearing, today.

All the Deaf siblings were educated at Donaldson's Hospital School, Edinburgh (as Donaldson's College was then called). Already outstanding communicators in sign language through use at home, they soon excelled in the rapid fingerspelling of the English language that was then used in the education of deaf children at Donaldson's. George was still at Donaldson's in April 1916 when the school was attacked by a German Zeppelin that flew over Edinburgh. It received a near miss that rocked the school and shattered many windows and wrecked furniture inside the building. It could have been worse as many deaf children were fast asleep during the attack. George wrote home and said:

> ... A German Zeppelin flew over but I felt nothing. I was fast asleep. Next morning I awoke to chaos – everything overturned, furniture all over, beds moved, tables tipped over...

Much later in life, George became the first President of the Donaldsonian Former Pupils Association.

After they had left school, Robert and George developed separate interests and pursuits. Robert began work as a litho artist in Glasgow, but in his spare time, he also developed a reputation as a fine painter. Painting both in oils and in water colours, many of his pictures reflected Glasgow's Clydeside industrial scene. He married his wife, Mary, the same year that he started his job: she had been his childhood sweetheart at the same school in Donaldson's and they were to remain together all their lives, later moving to live in the Scottish town of Hamilton. After his death in 1977, Hamilton District Museum held a special exhibition of over 200 of his oil and water colour paintings, and charcoal, pencil, pen and wash drawings.

George took a different route. At the time that he left school, it was assumed wrongly that Deaf young men could hope, at best, for a trade apprenticeship. He became a carpenter whereas today he would have been a strong candidate for a place in a university. Like many Deaf people of his day, he compensated for lack of opportunity in the world of work by an active social and sporting life. He became a prominent member of Maryhill Harriers, an athletic club in Glasgow, and

164

developed further the footballing skills in which he had excelled at school, going on to captain the Great Britain football team that thrashed Belgium 12-0 in the final of the 1928 World Games for the Deaf.

George was also a keen scout with the 154th (Glasgow) Rover Scouts and had the honour of being among the group of scouts presented before HRH the Prince of Wales at a parade at Ibrox Park in 1931.

George Scott was not just a heartless, mindless gladiator living only for sport and social activities. At the peak of his physical fitness, he found time to notice the haphazard, or non-existent, care arrangements for elderly Deaf people in Glasgow and together with a missioner, the Reverend W. Grieg, he founded the Craigholme Residential Home for the Elderly, which still stands today.

When research into the linguistic structure of sign language started up at Moray House, Edinburgh, in the late 1970s, George was a key contributor to their studies because of his excellent narration of sign language, which was described as comparable to the artistic talent of a Raeburn or a Geikie.

George Scott, as captain of the British football team in the 1928 World Games

Unlike his brother Robert, George married late in life at the age of 55 to Cissie Borland, who survived him.

Peter W. Jackson

Kathleen Trousdell Shaw
1865-1958

Kathleen Shaw was born in 1865, the youngest of two daughters of Alfred Shaw, an Irish doctor working in London. Her father returned to Dublin in 1870, and it was in the same year that it was noticed Kathleen had trouble hearing after a childhood illness. This grew progressively worse until she was completely deaf in her mid-teens.

When she was aged 9, she spent a lot of her time in the local churchyard watching stonemasons at work on tombstones. One day, one of the stonemasons gave her two chisels and a piece of stone to keep her occupied, and she scuplted a remarkable copy of an engraving of Michaelangelo. To encourage her newly-found talent in sculpture, she was sent to the Dublin School of Art at the age of ten where she learnt to draw and to sculpt. She was so good that she won a number of medals and prizes in exhibitions and was sent to Paris where she lived in the Latin quarter with her elder sister. To her great joy, she was accepted as a student in the Ecole des Beaux Arts where she could study under the most eminent French artists and sculptors. After a brief spell in Rome where she studied under the scupltor Charles Desvergne, she worked for a time in the British Museum.

Setting up a studio in Knutsford, Cheshire, she frequently travelled back to Ireland where she scuplted many works in marble and stone, including the bust of Archbishop Alexander, Primate of All-Ireland, for Armagh Cathedral. She also did a War Memorial to the officers and men of the Royal Irish Fusiliers who fell in the Boer War in South Africa.

Her work was recognised and honoured when she was made a member of the Royal Hibernian Academy in 1907. She was the first woman scupltor to be made a member of any Royal Academy in the British Isles.

After the 1914-18 war, she retired to the little village of Cadmore End, near High Wycombe. By then, her eyesight was failing and her last work was to design and scuplt a memorial font in marble, silver and bronze to the nine men of the village who had been killed in the war. This can still be seen in the pretty parish church.

For the remaining thirty-odd years of her life, she was completely deaf and blind and relied on the deafblind method of communication. She died in 1958 in her cottage in Cadmore End.

Peter W. Jackson

Memorial Font in marble, silver and bronze of Mother and Baby in Cadmore End Parish Church.

Charles Shirreff
1750-1831

The name Charles Shirreff (at times spelt variously as Sherrif, Sherriff and Shirref) has a special niche in British Deaf history. He was the first deaf pupil of Thomas Braidwood, and his progress was such that Braidwood forsook his previous calling as a mathematical teacher, and devoted the rest of his life to the education of deaf children, founding a school in Edinburgh in the first quarter of 1760, which came to be known as Braidwood's Academy.

Craigside House, better known as Dumbie House, where Thomas Braidwood's Academy, the first deaf school in the world was sited.

The son of Alexander Shirreff, a wealthy merchant of South Leith, Edinburgh, Charles left Braidwood's Academy at the age of 18 to go to the Royal Academy Schools in August 1769 from which he graduated with a silver medal in 1772 to make a career as a miniature painter. He successfully exhibited at the Free Society of Artists and at the Royal Academy, as well as others, and built up a clientele that was mainly theatrical, forming a strong friendship with Caleb Whitefoord and David Garrick. Shirreff, however, had a charm that many ladies found attractive and this caused a scent of jealousy among the men. Whitefoord later turned against Shirreff, bitterly regretting his acquaintance, as he was no competition to Shirreff when it came to women!

Shirreff worked from London after graduating from the Royal Academy, and applied to go to India in 1778. In his application to the East India Company, he stated that he had no speech but was able to make himself understood by signs and requested that he be accompanied by his father and his sister Mary to act as interpreters. However, the failure of the Fordyce's Bank ruined his father; and his plan to visit India was abandoned as Charles had to stay to support his family.

He lived and worked in Bath from 1791-1795 where he was no doubt acquainted with two other deaf miniaturists, Sampson Towgood Roch and Richard Crosse. Certainly, all three shared at various times the same people whom they painted.

In 1795, he renewed his application to go to India, and left England in the *Lord Hawkesbury* which reached Madras in January 1797. He painted in Madras for some years before moving to Calcutta, where he worked on his *Illustrations of Signs*. In 1807, he announced it was nearly completed and would be available to subscribers as soon as possible. This work has never been traced and is presumed lost *en passage* from India, a great pity as it might well have been the first sign dictionary.

Shirreff returned from India in 1809, and painted in London for a number of years before retiring to Bath where he died unmarried in 1831.

Peter W. Jackson

The "Bohemian"

John Smith
1849-1880

On Sunday night 6 February 1880, a cargo steamer the *"Bohemian"* went down in a fierce gale in Dunlough Bay, Crookhaven, Ireland, when en route from Boston, USA, to Liverpool with the loss of 35 lives. Another 18 men were saved by the efforts of people on the shore. When the news reached Liverpool, numerous newspaper readers could be seen everywhere, anxiously scanning the lists of "saved" and "lost". This included Deaf people who knew that a Deaf man, John Smith, was one of the crew of the ill-fated steamship. In the first edition of one of the evening papers that came out, his name indeed, appeared in the list of "saved", while the others ignored it altogether hence arousing in a weeping wife and sorrowing friends a most agonising conflict between hope and fear regarding his fate. Relying on the proverbial accuracy of the *Evening Express,* the first paper mentioned, however, the preacher George Healey sped to Mrs. Smith's home to offer her his congratulations on what he reasonably enough deemed her husband's hair-breadth escape from a watery grave. Hope flickered on until the following morning, when a different tale was told it left considerable room for a feeling of fear. After one anxious week had gone by, it was accepted that John Smith was lost at sea.

John Smith, a son of a fisherman, was born in Kirkwall in the Orkney Isles, on 9 July 1849. Brought up for about 10 years in Orkney, and close to the Arctic Ocean which washes its shores, he early displayed that taste for sea-faring pursuits which neither the lapse of time nor any subsequent change of circumstances and scenes could ever remove. When a boy, he had the good fortune to be sent to Donaldson's Hospital School in Edinburgh. And two years later, his younger brother James, also deaf, was, for reasons unknown, shunted into the dingy, but historic institution in Henderson Row, over which the fame of Braidwood and Kinniburgh still lived. Under conditions so different, the two brothers contrasted in their development.

John profited from the great facilities available at Donaldson, developing into a young man of splendid physique. However, his brother James, long accustomed to the cramped proportions of the old Institution in Henderson Row, became stunted in his physical growth, whilst at the same time assuming unconsciously the aspect of a regular bookworm, immersed in a book or newspaper. After completing his education, John was apprenticed as a printer but disliked it so much he quit and after a spell in a Glasgow iron foundry, he went to sea as a coal-trimmer in September 1871. Later he was promoted to the position of fireman which he held for 8 years until his death. In his travels around the world, John Smith gathered a wealth of information about the various countries and on his return to Liverpool, he would give lectures in the Deaf Institute about the places he had visited. He was also shipwrecked twice and this life of hard seafaring adventure made him an interesting speaker to watch.

John Smith was a staunch teetotaller, a rarity among seamen, and was also an avid Bible reader, attending George Healey's Bible classes whenever he was in Liverpool. Through these Bible classes, he met his wife, Hannah Webster, and they were married in August 1879 but only to be wed for seven months before he was lost at sea. Healey conducted John Smith's memorial service at the Liverpool Deaf & Dumb Institute, which was well attended by many friends.

Maureen A. Jackson

168

John Guthrie Spence Smith
1880-1951

John Guthrie Spence Smith was born at Rose Terrace in Perth on St. Valentine's Day 1880. He was the fourth and youngest of the family of Joseph Smith and Grace Farquharson. Spence Smith's father was prone to heavy drinking and this took a toll on him, causing him to die a few weeks before Spence Smith's first birthday. When Spence Smith was 2½ years old, he had a severe attack of scarlet fever and this caused him to become deaf.

Spence Smith's education was unclear; there are accounts that from around 1887 he was probably educated at Donaldson's Hospital School in Edinburgh. After leaving school, he took an interest in art and attended the Edinburgh College of Art in 1904. During that year, some of his paintings were exhibited at the Perth Arts and Crafts Exhibition and he won a bronze medal for one of his four exhibits, a series of watercolour postcards depicting a gardener, along with a prize for one guinea for syllabus cover design.

In the following year, Spence Smith attended the Royal Scottish Academy (RSA) Life Class, where he studied under Robert Burns RSA and Charles Mackie RSA. In 1909, Spence Smith exhibited for the first time at the RSA. At that time he was living with his mother at 6 St. Vincent Street, Edinburgh. Spence Smith obtained an unkind nickname from his fellow artist pupils, "Dummy Smith". In 1912, Spence Smith co-founded The Edinburgh Group with fellow artists at the RSA; David Alison, Eric Robertson, Alick Sturrock, William Mervyn Glass and David Sutherland. This group had its first exhibition in 1912 and again in 1913. The war ended the exhibitions until 1919 and after that the group exhibited annually until 1921, when the group appeared to fade away. Spence Smith took to watercolour painting and concentrated mainly on landscape themes. His work was much admired and in 1930 he was made an Associate of the RSA. Nine years later, he became a full Academician of the RSA, the second Deaf person to have achieved such prestige since Walter Geikie. Spence Smith had a unique distinction in that his works were exhibited practically annually at the RSA until 1949, two years before his death. The exhibition of his works were not only confined to the RSA, but were staged in Edinburgh, Glasgow, Perth, Liverpool, Bradford, Birmingham and Stirling amongst others. In his lifetime, Spence Smith contributed over 130 paintings.

Spence Smith's mother died in 1933 at the age of 87 and consequently he moved to live with the artist William Mervyn Glass ARSA at 38 Drummond Street, Edinburgh, where he lived until his death on 22 October 1951.

Raymond Lee

John Thomas Alysius Spearing
c1927-1994

John Spearing was born to a London docker who had seven children. The father had a great love for beer and he frequented the taverns in the docklands. This indulgence precipitated a huge stuggle in the family that meant scarcity in food and clothing. During childhood John was found to have a slight hearing defect so much to the pleasure of his father. It meant he qualified for admission to the St. John's Institution for the Deaf and Dumb, Boston Spa, Yorkshire, where board was free and attire provided. John did not distinguish himself as a scholar; in fact all the knowledge he gleaned came through hearing. While there, he learned bootmaking and on leaving he worked as a cobbler in East London. He frequented a variety of Deaf clubs in the north and east of the city. Cobbling did not appeal to him and he taught himself accountancy and managed to find work as a bookkeeper in the City.

While working in a firm, he encountered Maud Randle, a product of the old Fitzroy Square oralist school, who supervised the typist's pool. She once worked as a stenographer and sometime writer for the defunct *Globe*. At that time she was the secretary of the Society for the Higher Education of the Deaf (SHED) and entered Spearing in the committee who were impressed with his potential. In 1947 a huge conflict ensued between Spearing and Randle over the latter's stand for an oralist system in education. Most of the committee sided with Spearing, and Maud Randle walked out and was never seen again. Spearing took over as the secretary and a year later he organised an excellent banquet at the Society of Vincent de Paul in Holland Park. Among the participants were A. R. Thomson, the Royal Academician and Edward Evans, MP, a former headmaster of the East Anglian School for Blind and Deaf Children, Gorleston, near Great Yarmouth. Substantial funds were raised.

Around 1950, Spearing became the secretary of the Independent London Deaf Club. In 1953, he launched the *Independent Courier*, which he jointly edited with A. F. Dimmock. The paper was alas short-lived, going out of existence at the end of 1954, through being too costly for the club to run.

The Society for Higher Education of the Deaf was officially disbanded in April 1959 when the committee recognised that SHED's aims had been achieved.

In 1955, Spearing organised the Grand Celebrity Ball in London. Several society and entertainment celebrities came and the ball was a huge success. Spearing was dressed in a red tunic with epaulettes and blue ribbon across his chest. This exposed his eccentricity that was his hallmark for some time. He organised a tourist venture for a hundred or so to the International Games for the Deaf at Brussels in 1953 and a year later, Lucerne in Switzerland was the venue, but the latter resulted in police intervention over unpaid hotel charges. It was his last tourist venture. However, in 1965, Spearing went to the Washington Games under British Deaf Tourists Movement (BDTM). He hired a car that enabled him and his companion, Nora Uwins, to go to places instead of joining the coach parties. In 1973, the BDTM hired him as one of the interpreters for the Island of Paradise cruise that had 203 participants, all deaf. He was a success, not only as an interpreter but an entertainer, which enhanced his popularity.

Spearing inherited the estates of three elderly ladies, one of whom was Maud Randle, but all the money went on fast cars and failed enterprises, one of which was a large frozen food company in Norfolk. Back in London, Spearing joined a jewellery firm ran by his brother. He supervised the jobbing jewellers and did accounts but he did not last long in this position, due to disputes. He did jobbing accounts for various firms and this line of inconsistent work heralded the end of his labours. With his knowledge of finance he could have made life comfortable and prosperous for himself, but instead he died in poverty, in mysterious circumstances, believed to be from cirrhosis in 1994. He left a pile of writings meant for publication which could have been quite interesting, but his few effects and the papers were left to one of his sisters and she had the papers destroyed, thus much insight into his life and perceptions was lost for ever.

John Spearing was actually more hearing than deaf, but he associated with Deaf people most of his life so he was made to feel that he belonged to Deaf society. He was one of the instigators of the Brothers and Sisters Club that has grown to be the largest gay and lesbian club in Britain, but little or nothing has been done to honour him for his involvement.

Arthur F. Dimmock

*The ruins of the house built by Betty Steel
on Norfolk Island*

**Elizabeth Steel
1764-1795**

Betty Steel, as she was known, was born deaf in Holborn in London, the eldest child of John and Sarah Steel. Her mother died when she was nine years old and her father was a frequent inmate of the local workhouse, where he died in 1786. Betty Steel therefore had a hard childhood, living often in poverty and this no doubt shaped her life as a young deaf woman growing up in London.

The London where she lived was poor, unhealthy and smelly, especially in the district of Shoe Lane where she grew up as a young girl. It was full of alleyways and courtyards, drinking dens and places where vagrants slept. For centuries, these alleys had been home to the poor, thieves on the run, street sellers and prostitutes.

For Betty Steel, perhaps there was no choice but to go the same way. Perhaps being deaf did not help either. For her, without a mother and a father who was in the workhouse, it was a desperate struggle to survive. She became a thief and a prostitute. Sometimes she would rob her punters of jewellery and money and get away before the sex act even took place. It would only be a matter of time before she made a mistake and got caught.

She made her mistake one winter's night in January 1787 when, with another prostitute, she met two men named John Mills and George Childs (who was himself deaf) in a public house near Holborn and arranged separately to go upstairs to rooms to have sex. Shortly afterwards, Childs was seen staggering down the stairs, bleeding from his mouth. He alleged he had been assaulted and his expensive watch stolen. Of Betty Steel, there was no sign. However, it had been a mistake to rob another deaf person as they would have known of each other, and Betty Steel was found an hour later. The watch was not with her, and she would not say where it was but she had money with her she did not have before and obviously it had already been sold.

Betty was arrested, and in court in October 1787, she was found guilty and sentenced to be transported to the British Penal colony in Australia for seven years. After 18 months, she was taken to a ship, *Lady Juliana,* and began her one-way journey to Australia. The *Lady Juliana* set sail from the Thames in June 1789, and after collecting prisoners from other ports on the South Coast, left Plymouth on 29 July 1789. The journey to Australia involved three stops for supplies, at Tenerife, Rio de Janiero and Table Bay on the southern tip of Africa. The ship arrived in Sydney Cove on 6 June 1790 after an 11 - month voyage.

Less than two months later, Betty Steel was in another ship, the *Surprize*, being transported again, this time to Norfolk Island about 1000 miles out in the Pacific. With her went 156 other female convicts and 37 male convicts.

Betty was to spend the remainder of her sentence on the Norfolk Island penal colony. This was a much better place than the penal settlement at Sydney Cove, but the first part of her stay there was blighted by the cruelty of the commandant, Major Ross, who delighted in flogging any convict he judged to have slighted him. One day, Betty Steel misunderstood something that Major Ross said to her and in his anger the Major accused Betty of telling him a lie and ordered her to receive fifty lashes. Tied to a triangle with her back exposed to receive the whip, Betty passed out before the full fifty lashes were delivered. Her back, and her health, never recovered from the flogging and although she formed a relationship with another convict, James Mackey, she spent the last part of her sentence an ill woman.

With James Mackey (who had also been sentenced to 7 years transportation), Betty was allocated a piece of land upon which they built a cottage and grew crops such as maize and vegetables.

When the end of his sentence was up, James Mackey applied to join the army and was sent to Australia. Betty's sentence ended more or less at the same time and as the "wife" of a soldier, she was entitled to a passage to Australia to join her "husband" and left Norfolk Island on 22 July 1794 for Sydney Cove.

Once in Australia, Betty joined up again with James and they were given a plot of land on which they erected a wooden hut. However, Betty's health was failing and she died on 7 June 1795, and aged 30.

Betty Steel's tombstone was found underneath the floor of Sydney Town Hall during renovations in 1991 and its removal was filmed by Australia TV.

She is the first known deaf person (apart from the indigenous Aborigines) to settle in Australia.

Peter W. Jackson

**Alexander Fairley Strathern
1844-1890**

Alexander Fairley Strathern was a literary giant in the Deaf world in the late 19th century. Born in West George Street, Glasgow, in 1844, he was the son of the Sheriff of Glasgow. He lost his hearing at an early age, and was for some time a day scholar at the Glasgow Institution, under Duncan Anderson. Prior to that, he had been at an ordinary day school.

After leaving school, he was apprenticed to the wood engraving trade to which, however, he never took kindly. After serving his time, he went to London seeking to further improve himself in the art. However, on the death of his father, being pretty much thrown on his resources, he threw up wood engraving and placed himself under the care of Messrs Dalziel Brothers, London, where he was taught the details of a painter's business.

While in London he interested himself in all matters connected with the Deaf, was a prominent member of the debating class connected with the Royal Association, gave many a lecture and thoroughly identified himself with the Deaf community there. However, it is perhaps in his native city, Glasgow, to which he returned in 1872, that Alexander worked most for Deaf people.

He was one of the originators of the Glasgow Mission for the Deaf and Dumb which was the result of amalgamation of the two rival societies then existent in the city in 1872. Alexander Strathern acted as the secretary, but on the appointment of Mr. James Howard (later to be Headmaster of the Yorkshire Institution for the Deaf and Dumb at Doncaster) as missionary, a post which also included that of secretary, he took the responsible duties of treasurer.

For three years, besides performing the duties of secretary to the Mission, he conducted the Sabbath services, and in general looked after the welfare of local Deaf people. Previous to the appointment of a regular missionary, Mr. Strathern was practically "guide, philosopher, and friend" to the Deaf of Glasgow, and the value of his labours were gratefully recognised by the presentation of a testimonial by them.

Owing to differences with the then committee, Alexander withdrew from all active participation in the work of the Mission in the mid-1880s, but still took a great interest in all matters pertaining to Deaf people. Probably he was best known throughout the kingdom by his connection with the *Deaf and Dumb Magazine*, which he edited and published for some time after the Rev. Samuel Smith gave it up. A great politician, a sound Tory and high churchman, his debates in the *Magazine* and *Deaf and Dumb Herald* with "Robertus" (Robert Armour) and "Nil Desperandum" (Alex McGregor) were particularly looked forward to. With an inexhaustible fund of humour and repartee, and a great command of the "Queen's English", he had *nearly*, if not quite, always the better of his opponents. The pages of the magazine were also occasionally enlivened with entertaining articles from his facile pen on local, public, or personal matters relating to Deaf people.

With James Paul, of Kilmarnock, he was instrumental in forming the National Deaf and Dumb Society (NDDS), which although having a short life-span, did some good work in its day, founding the Durham, Winchester, and Kilmarnock missions. The NDDS was also indirectly the means of promoting others, and to a great extent, through its operations, familiarising the public with Deaf people.

Alexander was married on 16 July 1873, in London, to a Miss Mary Bellars, daughter of William Bellars, Esq., of Canonbury, London, by whom he had two sons and two daughters, another son having died in infancy.

Alexander Strathern died on the evening of 16 December 1890 after a lingering illness. For more than a year prior to his death, he had been in indifferent health, and in August 1890, he and his wife spent a short period in Peebles Hydropathic, hoping that the rest from business cares and worries, and the change of scene and air, would do much towards improving his health. He had only, however, been there a few days when he became quite ill and found it necessary to come home, not wishing to be laid up in a strange place. This was but the beginning of the end for upon getting home he took to bed from which he never rose again.

Peter W. Jackson

Emil Stryker
1917-1990

Emil Stryker was born the youngest of four children, three hearing sisters and one deaf brother, at Wurzburg in southern Germany on 23 December 1917. He was totally deaf in his left ear and had extremely limited hearing in his right ear. Not realising that Emil was deaf, his parents initially sent him to a Jewish school for normal hearing children. Whilst there, Emil was considered educationally backward and his school reports were dismal. His parents were advised to have him transferred to a school for the Deaf. This was done, and Emil progressed, but did not fare well with his speech, even though he used hearing aids and was put in a class with the hard of hearing.

When Emil left school, he became apprentice bookkeeper in his father's business as a wine merchant. Emil's mother died in 1935. His two sisters married before the death of their mother and followed their husbands to Paris. The rise of the Nazis in Germany at that time was bringing fear, terror and hardship to the Jews. The situation became so bad and unbearable that every person who was a Jew was persecuted and in danger of losing their lives. Mass exodus from Nazi Germany took place, but many were captured. Emil's father escaped to Paris but was later arrested and taken to the Teresienstadt concentration camp when the Nazis later occupied France; he died there shortly afterwards. Emil's father's business was closed down by the Nazi police and handed over to non-Jews.

In November 1938, Emil went into hiding. Early in 1939, came the *Polenabschielbung*, the expulsion of all Polish Jews to Poland from Germany. As Emil held a Polish as well as a German passport, Emil was expelled and imprisoned in harrowing conditions. The German and Polish governments, however, later came to an agreement, which resulted in Emil being sent back to Germany. Starved and exhausted, Emil was put into a hospital where he met his older brother Sam again. His youngest sister, Molly, made arrangements for both of them to escape from hospital. With the assistance of a refugee committee working under the auspices of the Chief Rabbi of Great Britain, Emil and his brother were taken to England. Emil found England a very friendly and tolerant place and settled in east London. Shortly afterwards, he fell in love with the English language and studied it with great enthusiasm.

Whilst trying to settle in east London, Emil chanced to meet two Deaf men, a father and son, walking in the street and communicating with each other in sign language. Referring to his German-English dictionary, Emil informed them that he wanted to go to a club for the Deaf and to meet Deaf people. He met them again the next day and they all went to a reading room in Adler Street, where a group of Jewish Deaf people were congregating. He was made very welcome and one person in particular, Jane Gedlovitch, took a shine upon him. They both married in 1941.

However, the trials and ordeals of Emil's experience caused him distress and, in spite of living in happy and secure circumstances in England, Emil suffered a breakdown and had to be admitted to a sanatorium in Surrey for several months until he recovered sufficiently to be discharged. From thence, he became a strong and independent person, joining Green Star Deaf Club, becoming a member of its tennis team. He continued to study English vigorously and was consequently able to

176

achieve an above-standard command of English. Emil was elected as honorary secretary of Green Star Club, a post which he held for nine years.

In 1951, the Festival of Britain was celebrated all over the country. Emil organised the first-ever Deaf Tennis tournament. It attracted many players from Europe as well as Britain and the tournament turned out to be a hugely successful event. Emil's wife, Jane, played tennis for the British team in the 1953 World Deaf Games in Brussels. With her partner Miss Berman, she won a Gold Medal in Ladies' Doubles.

Emil became closely associated with the Jewish Deaf Association (JDA) when its new premises at Cazenove Road, Stoke Newington, London, opened. He held various official positions within the JDA for many years, establishing links and friendships with other Jewish organisations and individuals all over the world. This worldwide contact culminated in an historical moment in 1977 when Emil founded the World Organisation of Jewish Deaf (WOJD) and established its head office in Israel.

In 1977, Emil joined the National Union of the Deaf (NUD) and became a long time member of its committee, representing the views of the Deafblind and Deaf ethnic/religious minorities. His contribution within the NUD was immense, bringing awareness of the need to establish a charter of rights of the Deaf.

In 1984, Emil was the vice-Chair of the 3rd WOJD Conference held in London between 2 – 6 September. His endeavours and dedication in his work with that conference paid off when the participants voted the event a rousing success. Such was the popularity and respect for Emil that he was awarded life membership of the Jewish Deaf Club in Paris and vice-Presidency of the Jewish Deaf Association.

On 28 April 1988, Emil was awarded Certificate of High Merit and recognition as founder of the WOJD by the Board and Bureau of WOJD in Israel.

Emil's interests went a bit further in sports. He loved football and introduced the inter-country football matches between teams from London and Germany. The clubs involved were St. Vincents Deaf Club, Lewisham, Cologne and Wuppertal.

Emil passed away peacefully in his sleep on 31 January 1990 and he was buried in the Jewish Cemetery at Enfield.

Emil Stryker was robbed of his home and nationality by the Nazis and adopted England as his home. England, nay Britain, is indeed proud to have accepted this amiable and charismatic person as one of its adopted sons.

Jack Hart
(Nephew of Emil Stryker)

Revd. Canon Thomas Henry Sutcliffe
1907-1996

For anyone who lost hearing and faced the world of silence as an adult must have been a traumatic experience as was in Tom Sutcliffe's case, yet he would not let his deafness deter him. He devoted much of his long life to helping other people and he opened the world wide and educated both Deaf and hearing people in all aspects of deafness. Born in Blackburn in 1907, Tom was a graduate of Cambridge University. He chose to enter the ministry and was ordained at Blackburn Cathedral in 1932. While serving as a curate in his second year, he began to lose his hearing and became totally deaf at the age of 28.

He then received a 'calling' to work as a Chaplain for the then Royal Association in Aid of the Deaf and Dumb in 1935 at St. Saviour's Church, Acton. This was a big change in his vocation, switching his ministry from hearing people to profoundly Deaf people. One could imagine Tom who had no connection with Deaf people prior to his deafness, facing a crowd of Deaf people and to watch them signing could be a frightening experience. Yet Tom was determined to get through to them and from that day forward he ably ministered to Deaf people spiritually. In 1937, he was transferred to St. Barnabas Church in Deptford, South London, for the same organisation, RADD, where he held his office until 1942.

Tom was introduced to his future wife, Brenda Sainsbury of Brighton, by correspondence through the Revd Canon and Mrs Alan Mackenzie. Tom and Brenda liked to tell friends about their first romantic date under the Charing Cross Station clock. They were married four months later in 1950 at Rottingdean, Brighton, and they bore three children, David, Roger and Ruth.

Tom was persuaded later by the Bishop of Blackburn to return to his birthplace to serve as a chaplain among Deaf people in the Blackburn area. He continued to broaden his horizons and in 1952, he was offered a position as the Secretary for the Church of England General Synod Council for the Deaf, which he faithfully served for 23 years until his retirement in 1974. His wife, Brenda, became his official interpreter and secretary. With the aid of Brenda, he set up a numerous courses and became an inspiration to younger chaplains. He was responsible for setting up the Chaplains to the Deaf Examination Board, an ecumenical body which awarded a diploma to successful candidates. He also played a big part in the training of lay helpers and lay readers for Deaf people to enable them to be better qualified to assist their Deaf churches. It was through Tom that the National Deaf Church Conference for Deaf people was formed in 1967 and it still exists today.

In 1966, Tom was appointed an Honorary Canon of Canterbury Cathedral by Archbishop Ramsey in recognition of his work for Deaf people. Throughout all the centuries that Canterbury Cathedral stood, this was the first time that a totally Deaf man had been installed as a Canon and possibly the first in the world.

For many years Tom was actively involved with most of the national and international organisations for the Deaf, and was awarded honours by the British Deaf Association, the Royal National Institute for the Deaf, Gallaudet University and the World Federation of the Deaf. He was a gifted speaker at many functions and for some years a visiting lecturer to the course for Social

178

Workers with the Deaf at the North London Polytechnic, Highbury. He was also a member of the Standing Conference of Interpreting Trainers which was part of the British Deaf Association and Department of Health and Social Security Communication Skills project and which led to the formation of the Council for the Advancement of Communication with Deaf People (CACDP). It was Tom who proposed at a meeting of the Standing Conference that *CACDP be formed here and now*.

Over the years Tom wrote numerous articles for journals and conferences and he was author of several books both on the issues of deafness and religious teachings. His last book published in 1990 was *The Challenge of Deafness* and it was *dedicated to the memory of my late wife, Brenda and to my family, who for many years, have patiently shared deafness with me*.

Tom's great joy was fellwalking and rockclimbing and he was a member of the Deaf Mountaineering Club for over 35 years. When he retired, he and Brenda went to live at Reigate. Tom actually never retired from his life long involvement with Deaf people. He was in a great demand preaching Harvest and Thanksgiving Services far and wide and was a regular visiting preacher at a Reigate church for Deaf people, near his home. He was a born traveller and enjoyed travelling around the world meeting friends in his retirement.

Tom and Brenda then moved to Taunton in 1987 to be near their elder son David and their two grandchildren. Sadly, Brenda died very soon after. Apart from David and his family, Tom did not know anyone in his new surroundings. In time, Tom made friends and found peace and comfort by attending the Religious Society of Friends (Quakers). Tom was grateful to have the help from the worshippers by writing notes on what was said.

Lewisham Deaf Football Club organised their reunion and Exhibition in 1994 and the footballers so wanted Tom to attend as a guest of honour. To their delight he was able to make the long journey from Taunton to attend and he was overwhelmed by the warm welcome received from many people present from his Deptford days.

For all Tom's 89 years, he was YOUNG. His fresh mind was kept alert by reading and the open air. Tom Sutcliffe lived life to the full and certainly a much loved man of God and a founding father of many other achievements for Deaf people.

Elaine Lavery

George Tait
1828-1904

George Tait was born at Watten in Caithness, Scotland, in 1828. Deafened at an early age, he was educated at Edinburgh Deaf and Dumb Institution from 1842 to 1849 with financial support given by the school's Ladies Auxiliary Committee.

For reasons as yet unknown to us, Tait had always yearned to live in the United States of America. In 1851, Tait obtained a job as assistant carpenter on an American ship docked at Liverpool. Since he was not allowed to set foot upon ship, the ship's captain disguised Tait so that he would pass as an American seaman and get past unsuspecting customs officers. The voyage brought Tait to the West Indies and Boston before disembarking at Maine, where he spent two or three years working in the shipyards.

In 1856, Tait moved on to Nova Scotia to work alongside his uncle, who was also a carpenter in Halifax. While staying at lodgings, the landlord asked Tait to teach his deaf and dumb daughter, Mary Ann Fletcher, in his spare time, thus making him as the first teacher of the deaf in the province. The girl therefore became the first deaf person in Nova Scotia to be educated. Fletcher urged Tait to seek out other deaf children in Halifax with an idea of setting up a school for the deaf, but Tait, not wishing to give up his carpentry trade, decided against the idea unless he found someone else to teach full time before establishing the school.

By a strange quirk of fate, Tait, while walking along the street, encountered a trio of people *talking with their fingers* in the manner of the British two-handed manual system. They turned out to be William Gray, his deaf wife and their hearing daughter, all being *friendless and penniless*. Gray attended the same school as Tait in Edinburgh, but a considerable number of years before with both having Robert Kinniburgh as their headmaster. The Gray family was so pleased to meet someone who could communicate fluently with them. Tait invited them to his lodgings and both Deaf men discussed the possibility of setting up a school for deaf children. Gray would take responsibility for teaching while Tait would be responsible for fundraising.

After raising £40 in ten days, George Tait subsequently secured further sufficient funding to achieve the wishes of his deaf pupil. On 4 August 1856, the new school for the deaf in Argyle Street in Halifax opened with William Gray as its first teacher, along with two deaf children in attendance, one of them Mary Ann Fletcher.

Tait married a hearing woman named Cynthia Tupper in 1859 and they had 9 children over the next thirteen years. In 1873, the Tait family moved to Dartmouth, Nova Scotia, where George, relying on his carpentry skills, built his own home. The house in Mackay Street still stands today.

When the 1877 Annual Report of the Halifax Deaf and Dumb Institution came out, Tait became upset when he read that his efforts which contributed to the founding of the school were not mentioned and that the honour as founder was credited to William Gray. This drove Tait to write and privately publish a booklet entitled *Autobiography of George Tait, A Deaf Mute who gave Instruction to the Deaf and Dumb in the City of Halifax* and he promoted himself as the true founder of the school for the Deaf. This booklet underwent 14 editions between 1877 and 1896 and outlined Tait's life and contributions towards the establishment of the school for the Deaf. During the depression of the 1880s, Tait earned few pennies by peddling his booklet throughout three provinces of Nova Scotia, Quebec and New Brunswick. Tait used his editions to convince *"some who doubt the validity of my statement concerning my first starting the Deaf and Dumb School in Halifax"*.

George Tait died on 25 July 1904 at Dartmouth, leaving a legacy for the Nova Scotia Deaf community to argue over who was actually the founder of the school – either George Tait or William Gray.

The controversy was "resolved" when a committee was specially convened to decide on the question of which man should be named the school's founder at the 3rd Annual Convention of the Maritime Deaf Mute Association in 1907. After listening to supporters of both Tait and Gray, the committee cast their ballots, resulting in 6 votes for Gray and two for Tait.

In 1976, the Canadian Cultural Society of the Deaf honoured the initial efforts made by George Tait towards the establishment of the deaf school in Halifax by adding his name to its Deaf Hall of Fame, along with his co-founder, William Gray

Clifton Carbin in his *Deaf Heritage in Canada,* (published in 1996), stated that *despite this decision, however, historians still argue over which of the two is the actual founder, or whether Tait and Gray should be considered co-founders of the institution.*

John A Hay

Frederick Lawrence Tavaré
1846-1930

Frederick Lawrence Tavaré was born in Cheetham in Manchester on 13 December 1846. His family had an illustrious history, boasting descent from a Spanish Cardinal, John (Pardo) de Tavera who died in 1545. Frederick's great grandfather was Dr. Daniel Nines de Tavarez, M.D., LL.D., a French physician and citizen of Zwolle, Overysell; a complimentary letter to him from Benjamin Franklin existed among the family treasures. Frederick's grandfather, M. Charles de Tavaré, came to England from his native Amsterdam as a refugee during the rebellion of 1789, together with his favourite sister, Mlle. Caroline Tavaré, who was later to become Mrs. Swain, the mother of Charles Swain, a notable Manchester poet. Charles Tavaré, who dropped the "de" on coming to England, knew twelve languages and was proficient in nine. Frederick's father was a landscape artist and a teacher of drawing.

When Frederick was eighteen months old, an artist friend of his father noted that he was not responding to sounds and alerted his parents. Such a lack of reaction to sound and noise indicated, as always, the presence of deafness and this came as a great shock and grief to Frederick's parents. In desperation for a remedy for deafness, they took their son to some of the most noted London aurists in 1849. Disappointment came upon the parents when every aurist could do nothing to cure Frederick's deafness: in fact, every one of them could see nothing organically wrong with his hearing, but came to a decision that the cause of deafness was apparently due to a difficult dentition and inflammation of the brain.

In October 1854, Frederick was sent as a pupil and boarder to the Manchester Institution for the Deaf and Dumb, where he remained until December 1861. At school, Frederick studied drawing under Mr. G. F. C. Goodwin. On leaving school, he pursued his studies alone and in 1863 and 1865 won certificates in freehand and modern drawing from the Science and Art department of the Committee of Council on Education examination. When his father died on 17 June 1868, Frederick and his younger brother, Charles, succeeded to his connection as teacher of drawing and maintained it until 13 December 1872.

It is known that Frederick was employed in connection with the Post Office from 11 September 1899 when he was 53 years old. A brief article in the February 1900 issue of *British Deaf Monthly* reported:

> *Intelligence, honesty, the ability to read and good walking powers are the chief requirements of a letter-carrier, which is thus evidently an employment for which the deaf are well-suited. This is practically recognised at the Post Office of Mere, near Knutsford, Cheshire, where the well-known Manchester deaf artist and antiquary, Frederick L. Tavaré, has been employed since September 11 last as letter-carrier and messenger.*

Every morning Mr Tavaré takes round the letters – a task that occupies an hour or so; the rest of his working day is given up to carrying telegrams and other occasional Post Office duties. In his leisure time he still works with brush and pencil and has made many watercolour sketches of houses, farms, lodges, etc. for Mere residents. The Mere artist-postman-antiquary is quite a man of renown.

Frederick L. Tavaré, however, was best known for his pictures and sketches taken from quaint, tumbledown, timber-fronted relics of Old Manchester that were doomed to destruction. The artistic merit and antiquarian interest of his works created praise and favourable comments in the local press. Frederick also excelled in still life. Between 1867 and 1880, Frederick exhibited fourteen works in oil and watercolour at the Royal Manchester Institution, and another in 1885. From 1873 to 1884, he exhibited 39 works at Whaite's Art Gallery in Bridge Street: in the latter year the annual exhibitions ceased. Frederick's other exhibited works were displayed at the following venues - Darwen Art Treasures Exhibition (1868); Cardiff Fine Art and Industrial Exhibition (1870); "Old Manchester" Department of the Royal Jubilee Exhibition (1887); London International Health Exhibition (1884).

Frederick was quite an authority on the antiquities and annals of his native city and county. To the "Notes and Queries" department of *The Manchester Weekly Times*, he contributed about 180 replies and notes, illustrated by nine woodcuts from his own sketches. Frederick also contributed in the same way to *The Manchester City News*, *Notes and Queries* (London) and to *Cheshire Notes and Queries*. The editor of *The Dictionary of National Biography* applied to Mr. Tavaré for assistance in the compilation on the brief of Charles Swain, and duly acknowledged the source of his information.

Frederick L. Tavaré lived to a long age, moving to Salford where he passed away sometime during the first quarter of 1930, according to the Family Records Centre.

Raymond Lee

Alfred Reginald Thomson
1894-1979

Alfred Reginald Thomson was born at Bangalore, Mysore in India to George Thomson, a major in the army pay corps. His deafness was discovered during infancy and this caused the father to be thunderstruck. Later after queries, he was told about a school for the deaf in England. When the boy was seven, he was admitted to the Royal Asylum for the Deaf and Dumb Poor at Margate, Kent, as a paying pupil. As a scholar he made no significant progress but he was found to be able to sketch well. A teacher asked the class what they wanted to be when leaving school. *"Cobbler, very good, carpenter, very good."* Thomson wanted to be an artist. *"How foolish"* retorted the teacher, *"who wants pictures?"*. Thomson's father came to the school and found his son unable to speak so he had him transferred to Mr Barber's oral school at Brondesbury, North London. Thomson, then 14 years old, did not progress well, but one lady teacher noticed his talent in art and he was sent to Kilburn Polytechnic to learn, and later a place was found for him at London New Art School in Kensington, where he had Orchardson as his teacher whose father was a famous artist. When his father heard of the move, he went into a blind rage and had his son sent to a farmer, Mr Kitchen, at Lenham in Kent, to learn farming.

Thomson's father paid for the instruction and Thomson got nothing but food, board and clothes. He was banned from using pencil and paper and worked more as a slave than as learner for two years before fleeing to Radcliffe Road, known as the "Road of the Hopefuls", in Chelsea. He managed to find work as a commercial artist in Long Acre and re-enlisted in the London New Art School. This time he had John Hassall as his tutor. When George Thomson heard about it, he disowned his son and never wanted to see him again. This outburst upset his mother who died apparently from a broken heart.

Sometimes there was no work and no money and when this happened, Thomson used the St. Martin-in-the-Field crypts near Trafalgar Square where board and food was given freely, mostly to tramps. One night while at the Ham Bone in Denham Street, off Shaftesbury Avenue, he encountered a lady who took pity on him and invited him to her house. Thomson called her "The Rich Harlot" but she rescued him from poverty. His breakthrough came when he was commissioned to do murals in the Duncannon public house opposite St. Martin's crypts. The paintings depicted Dickensian characters and became famous. Later they were bought by a wealthy art enthusiast and transported to America. The work came to the recognition of Augustus John, William Orpen and Alfred Munnings who got together and enabled Thomson to be accepted as a member of the exclusive Chelsea Art Club.

Around 1936, the Essex County Council sent out invitations for a painting reflecting on the Pilgrim Fathers who were mostly Essex men. Several artists entered and the final number was downgraded to four among which two were famous and Thomson was the last on the list. After stringent judging he was eventually declared the winner and his painting of the *Pilgrim Fathers Embarking at Plymouth* was exhibited on the Royal Wall in the central hall of the Royal Academy

184

Summer Exhibition in 1937. Soon afterwards Thomson was elected a Royal Academician (RA). He wanted to confront the teacher who said, "Who wants pictures?" but he was by then dead and unaware of the rising fame of his former pupil. Work became plentiful and he became the official RAF artist during the war, but an accidental shooting wounded him.

During the Olympic Games held at London in 1948, Thomson won the gold medal for his painting of a seated boxer. Many of his paintings appeared on the front of the weekly magazine, *John Bull*. He became a close friend of Augustus John and sometimes stayed at his house in South France.

In 1958, H.M. the Queen and Duke of Edinburgh came to his studio for the Commemoration Dinner of the RAF picture and later he did the interiors of the House of Commons and the House of Lords for Harold Macmillan, then Prime Minister.

Thomson married twice but his first marriage failed. His second to a German-born woman was very happy. They had two children. She was an excellent interpreter and manager who served her husband well. Thomson's death was recorded on 26 October 1979.

Arthur F. Dimmock

Raymond Banks Thorpe
1910-1997

Ray Thorpe, as he was known, was born in 1910 at Market Deeping, near Peterborough. His parents were shopkeepers, firstly in the town of Ray's birth and later at Sandy in Bedfordshire. An attack of whooping cough at the age of two and half resulted in his deafness. They contacted the Leicester School for the Deaf for advice on the boy's education and chose having a governess, a Welsh lady, to educate him by oral means. She stayed until he was eleven before he entered Spring Hill School, at Northampton. There were 26 pupils, all boys, and they were taught some academic subjects, including French. During holidays, Ray's father sometimes induced him to do some work which was delivering goods for shopkeepers and farm work.

In 1927, Ray Thorpe managed to get accepted at the Derby Technical College and had four tutors with whom he communicated fairly well and two years later he became an articled pupil to a firm of architects at Reading. While there, he attended Reading University on part time basis and later the Royal Institute of British Architects in London. His first job was as an architectural assistant at Simmond's Brewery at two pounds and ten shillings a week. He moved to Leicester and served in William Keay's firm of architects and civil engineers, which had a staff of 45 and a year later, he took part in the RIBA studies and examinations. He won a first prize of £175 in a competition under the Architect's Journal and finally became an ARIBA in 1940. His salary increased which enabled him to enjoy his passion for vintage motor cars and get married to May Worsell, an oralist hard of hearing lady who was educated at the Derby School for the Deaf. They had one daughter, Carolyn, who later helped them as an interpreter.

After the war, Ray worked on the survey and reconstruction of bombed sites, particularly Coventry. About 1950, he accepted a post as an architect and surveyor in the Leicester department of the footwear specialists, Freeman, Hardy and Willis. Later, Ray joined the Warwickshire County Council and worked extensively on the Shire Hall in Warwick. He also did the restoration of the nearby Chesterton Windmill, a creation of Inigo Jones.

When Ray Thorpe retired in 1975, he and his wife May moved back to Leicester but May's time there was short-lived and she died in 1976. A few years later, Ray met up again with Doreen Auger, a widow who had been one of his wife's friends. Together these two friends toured the globe and finally settled in the pleasant village of Catisfield, near Fareham, Hampshire. Ray and Doreen died within days of each other in 1997, he from prostrate cancer on 21 January, aged 87 years and Doreen from leukaemia on 30 January, aged 81 years.

Leicester Deaf Centre is one of the architectural legacies that still stand as a significant testimonial to a totally deaf architect.

Arthur F. Dimmock

Charlotte Elizabeth Tonna
1790-1846

Charlotte Elizabeth Tonna was born in Norwich on 1 October 1790 and died in Ramsgate on 12 July 1846. In those 56 years, she made her mark on her generation in a variety of ways, but mainly by her pen, with about 100 works to her credit. During her time, she was also writing as Charlotte Elizabeth Phelan and Charlotte Elizabeth.

Her father, the Reverend Michael Browne, was a Canon of Norwich Cathedral and she had one much loved brother. Charlotte's childhood was very happy and unusually free for that time. Many distinguished visitors came to the house and the young, clever girl listened closely to conversations. She read beyond her years newspapers and books, and shared her father's love of music.

At the age of eight, Charlotte became seriously ill, being blind for a short while. The physicians used a popular drug of the day, mercury, for her. It appears that they over-dosed her and this led to total deafness at the age of ten. From then on, Charlotte withdrew into her books and her imagination, which was very strong. She was a person very reluctant to reveal her feelings, she saying only little about her deafness and nothing about her communication, though she later mentioned being cut off from music and conversation. Her father would no longer listen to music because she could no longer listen with him.

It is, however, clear that Charlotte continued to talk and learned fingerspelling to receive what others said. From this time, it seems there was always someone with her who could act as an interpreter for her. After her death, her widower wrote: -

> The reader is doubtless aware that all communication was made to her by means of the finger alphabet, but so quick was her apprehension of what was said, and so easy was it for those about her to acquire great rapidity in this art, that her total deafness was hardly felt to be ever an inconvenience.

When Charlotte was still ill in her teens, her father died. A little later, she married a soldier, Captain Phelan, travelling with him first to Nova Scotia and then to Kilkenny in Ireland. The marriage was unhappy and she left her husband in 1824. She developed a very strong Evangelical Protestant point of view, accompanied by deep hatred of Catholic beliefs and practices. She never let these beliefs affect her thoughtful, kind approach to all people, whatever their denomination. This extended to Jewish people and a great interest in Zionism.

However, her beliefs influenced her writing. Protestant hymns, tracts, articles and poems came from her ready pen. She edited and contributed to two Protestant magazines for many years, often using the pseudonym "The Watchman". She took an interest in deaf children, running a small school for deaf boys in her Kilkenny home, besides supporting the Claremont Institution in Ireland.

Charlotte moved to England to live with her much-loved brother, taking one of the Irish deaf boys with her. In England, she took an interest in the living conditions of Irish immigrants. Her brother died in a drowning accident. After Captain Phelan's death in 1837, Charlotte married another soldier, much younger than herself. She never had children.

Among her influential writings were those that drew attention to the effects of the Industrial Revolution on the lives of poor workers and on children. She also wrote about the rights of women. Much of her influence, ranked with other writers such as Mrs. Gaskill, Charles Kingsley and Disraeli, lay in her ability to read and understand the many dry statistical reports and other documents, and use them in novels that were readable. As Charlotte said, women could not vote, but they could interest the men in the family. Women would not read any dry reports, but they would read fiction that was about ordinary human beings and their lives.

A writer of her memoir, after her death, said: -

> ... for no inconsiderable period the subject of our sketch, by the influence of her writings, filled a most important position in society – a position she had fairly won by her undoubted talents, and maintained by the strength of her religious principle.

Charlotte had many friends and admirers, including Hannah Moore and Harriet Beecher Stowe. In 1864, the latter published, in America, the only collected works of Charlotte Tonna, saying in the preface ... *the authoress is a woman of strong mind, powerful feeling and of no inconsiderable share of tact in influencing the popular mind.*

Charlotte's second marriage, though short, was very happy; her husband sharing her Protestant fervour and himself being a writer. She continued to write, surrounded by her pets and tending her much-loved garden. Her time was divided between their two residences, Sandhurst and Whitehall, until she developed cancer.

The writings of Charlotte Elizabeth Tonna had an influence in both religious and social fields. She did not live to see the Factory Act passed in 1850, bringing about some of the reforms for which she hoped. But such was the respect in which she was held, a meeting in her honour in Ramsgate Town Hall was called a few days after her death.

Doreen E. Woodford

William Henry Hamilton Trood
1859-1899

William H. H. Trood was born in Taunton, Somerset, the son of a wealthy coal merchant. He became totally deaf at the age of five following a severe childhood illness.

Of his education, very little is known except that for a period he went to a college in Taunton. He may also have been a private fee-paying pupil at the Royal West of England School for the Deaf in Exeter. His wealthy father also provided a private tutor for him. As a young boy Trood loved to draw animals and developed such remarkable talent that he was sent to study art in South Kensington, London.

He started painting professionally from an early age and was soon contributing regularly to publications such as *Punch, Illustrated London News* and *Graphic Magazine*. Many of his paintings were of dogs, generally in humorous and sentimental situations. One of his special gifts was to draw pictures of political satire, where politician's faces were imposed on dogs' or other animals' bodies. These were much sought-after and earned Trood a good living.

The income from his paintings and satirical drawings enabled Trood to travel widely. On his travels, he would continue to paint and present his work to local dignitaries. On one visit to Morocco, the Sultan of Morocco was so impressed with one of Trood's paintings that he presented Trood a silver Damascus sword in-laid with jewels.

Some of Trood's paintings occasionally surface, especially in the West Country. One painting was sold in 1987 for £7,500.

William H. H. Trood died unexpectedly in the Phoenix Hotel, Taunton, after a very short illness, aged 39.

Peter W. Jackson

The Edinburgh Institution for the Deaf and Dumb,
from a school magazine engraving.

Joseph Turner
c.1799- ?

Joseph Turner was born in Woodside, Dumfrieshire, around 1799. His father was a farmer of humble means and had a large family. Joseph was admitted to the Edinburgh Institution for the Deaf and Dumb on 5 June 1811 under the headship of John Braidwood, the grandson of Thomas Braidwood. The fee for Joseph's education was partly met by the school to the cost of £5 with the rest met by his brother. When John Braidwood departed for America later in the year, he was succeeded by his assistant, Robert Kinniburgh who found Joseph to be a quick learner, always diligent and persevering in all his school exercises. In 1815, Joseph wrote three letters, which were published in the annual report as a demonstration of language attainments far developed from the state of ignorance when he first joined the Institution. During the school holidays, Joseph would work with bee-hives on his large home farm.

Alexander Atkinson, who was educated at the same Institution from 1815 to 1820, had the privilege of knowing Joseph Turner and profiting from his skilful teaching. He wrote: -

> *Turner was during the rest of the day employed in accelerating the snail-like progress of many scholars, as well as advancing his own; simplifying, and varying his explanations, with a pantomimic tact which none but himself could possess according to their different capacities. Indeed they needed not tell their little difficulties. He at once saw them, or to use a common saying "he hit the right nail on their perplexed heads."*

Kinniburgh found Joseph, who had been a general monitor on his behalf in his last year, a valuable asset in the instruction of his deaf pupils. In 1817, Kinniburgh offered Joseph the post of a permanent assistant teacher. Joseph had, however, expressed a wish to become a baker in the hope that the trade would bring him more money and domestic comfort with a lovely girl of his own heart. Kinniburgh offered him a regular salary from the funds of the Institution and a certain share of his private pupils' fees. After some consideration, Joseph wrote a letter of acceptance to the Institution Committee. He was the first Deaf teacher to work in Scotland.

In 1819, Joseph Humphreys, the headmaster of the Claremont Institution for the Deaf and Dumb in Dublin, visited Edinburgh and spent at least a month learning teaching skills from Mr. Kinniburgh and found himself admiring Turner's work. Evidence shows that in 1823-1824 Joseph was given an allowance of £30 for his duties carried out as assistant teacher, presumably his salary for a year's work. In 1826-1827, in view of the increasing number of deaf pupils, he worked with two more assistants. Thereafter no more was heard of him. Joseph Turner was indeed a Deaf teacher par excellence.

Anthony J. Boyce & John A. Hay

Daniel Whalley
1636-1695

Daniel Whalley has a special place in British Deaf History as one of the first two *named* prelingually deaf persons taught to speak. Dr. John Wallis, who subsequently wrote about these experiences, taught Daniel Whalley. Dr. Wallis took the opportunity to present Daniel, together with another youth he was teaching, Alexander Popham, to a special gathering in Whitehall in May 1662 of the court of King Charles II. Daniel Whalley was then 25 years old. The King was reported to have asked both young men their names, which were mouthed by Dr. Wallis, and the two youths told their names and where they lived.

John Wallis

Daniel Whalley was the sixth child of Peter and Hannah Whaley* of Northampton who had a total of 13 children, four of whom died in infancy. His father was a wealthy stationer and bookbinder who was a freeman of the town of Northampton and served as Mayor in 1646-7 and again in 1655-6, during which term he died in office. At the time of his death, Peter Whaley was also member of Parliament for Northampton. Peter Whaley's wealth is evident by the bequests in his Will. Apart from the third-born son, also named Peter who evidently fell out with his father and only received £20, all the other surviving children with the exception of Daniel himself received handsome legacies, including land and sums of money not less than £200. In contrast, Daniel was left an annuity of £15 per annum out of the rents of Tower House.

In the Will of Hannah Whaley, his mother, who died in 1671, all children also received handsome bequests and legacies except Daniel, who only received a silver spoon and one of his mother's little silver cups, plus a burial plot.

Hannah's Will concludes with this injunction:-

> … *And I charge you all my children with whom I have travailed in birth that you take especial care of your poor brother Daniel, and if any affliction befall him, that you succour and comforte him all the dayes of his life* …

For all that Dr. Wallis is supposed to have taught Daniel Whalley to read, write and to speak, it is evident that this education was insufficient to enable Daniel to support and look after himself (unlike Alexander Popham).

Daniel Whalley never married, and died at Cogenhoe, Northampton, in March 1695 and was buried in his brother, the Rev. Peter Whaley's, church.

*The family name was spelt Whaley with 1 up to the deaths of Peter and Hannah Whaley. Some of their children spelt the family name Whalley, including Daniel – others retained the original spelling.

Peter W. Jackson

191

Thomas Widd
1839 - 1906

Thomas Widd was a teacher, author and missionary and well-known for his public campaigning efforts and for his founding of the Sheffield Association for the Deaf and Dumb, the Montreal Protestant Institution for Deaf Mutes in Canada and the Los Angeles Association of the Deaf of Southern California.

Thomas was baptised on 4 August 1839 at Great Driffield in East Riding of Yorkshire, the son of John Hall Widd, a local saddler, and Elizabeth Widd. He had normal hearing and received a year's early education until at the age of five, when he became totally deaf after an illness resulting from an accidental fall off a horse into the river. Although efforts were made to educate him in a local hearing school, Thomas' speech gradually deteriorated. In 1852, he went to the Yorkshire Institution for the Deaf and Dumb (YIDD) at Doncaster where the celebrated Charles Baker was the headmaster. He progressed quickly under two well-known teachers, Alexander Melville and Samuel Smith, who used both sign language and fingerspelling. After two years' stay, Thomas's father thought his education was just enough to procure him a job and Thomas returned to Driffield.

In Driffield, whilst searching for a suitable job in his first six months with the help of his father, Thomas spent his time reading, developing a love of reading and improved his writing skills. He then found work in a sawmill not far from his family home and progressed to the responsible position of engine-driver. During that time, his employer encouraged Thomas to use his library during lunch break in order to study further. Later Thomas bought some books and local papers out of his earnings and set up his own small library in the engine room. The mill employees often visited to take advantage of reading his papers and to discuss the latest news of the Crimean War. The engine room was a very popular meeting place for lunch but one day someone labelled it "Dummy's Library". Thomas was shocked and did not like it, but he never found the person responsible.

In 1859, Thomas took up the position of a gardener's assistant at his old school in Doncaster. He eventually became interested in the printing trade and Charles Baker allowed him to take up this vocation. Thomas progressed so rapidly that he was asked to become an instructor in printing. For three years he was able to profit much from Charles Baker's literary works and thereby improved his reading and writing skills to an advanced stage.

In 1862, Thomas left the YIDD and met James Foulston, the secretary of the Leeds Society for the Adult Deaf and Dumb, and they discussed the possibility of setting up one in Sheffield for deaf adults. Thomas was interested but was not given any financial support at first. Undaunted, Thomas went to Sheffield and drew up a long list of deaf Sheffielders. Meanwhile, he noticed that many Deaf frequented a certain public house from which its landlord made huge profits from them. The ruse of the landlord was soon exposed by Thomas who gathered a group of Deaf frequenters outside the inn. Soon the police made orders for the Deaf group to move on. It was a difficult time for Thomas because he did not have the financial support from Leeds and he badly wanted to have a meeting-house for the Deaf. Thomas wrote an a letter of appeal to the local paper for help and went around to see some wealthy philanthropists but failed. In the meantime, he became friends with Joseph Askew who was also educated at the Doncaster school and they eventually rented between themselves a small house in a seedy area in Sheffield, thus starting regular Sunday meetings for the Deaf, which grew and became very popular. This attracted attention from the Mayor of Sheffield, Mr. John Brown, and the idea of the founding of the Sheffield Association for the Deaf and Dumb began to take shape. Thomas had achieved his objective and it was time for him to move on. In March 1863, the grateful group of Sheffield Deaf people presented Thomas a writing desk with a plaque to commemorate the founding of the association.

On 1 January 1864 at the Sheffield Union Workhouse, Thomas married Margaret Fitzakerly who was educated at the same Doncaster school and after a very trying time as a journeyman printer, they travelled to Driffield, Grantham and London over the next three years. Whilst in London, his wife, having lost her first son at Whitehaven, had a second son. Thomas had been working on one of Charles Dickens' books in a printing firm and met the celebrated author who agreed to be the godfather of his son, christened Arthur Charles.

After the newspaper strikes during the early months of 1867 and unable to obtain any employment in London, Thomas and his family, with financial support from Charles Dickens and his old teacher the Rev. Samuel Smith, emigrated to Canada on 19 September 1867. Thomas visited Montreal, which was a French-speaking and Catholic town and saw some deaf children wandering in the streets and found that their parents were Protestants. He decided to found a school for them. Working as an assistant editor on the Montreal local paper *The Daily Witness* for a year, Thomas seized the chance to write articles and letters appealing for funds and had them published in the newspapers. His successful public campaign led to the founding of the school for the Protestant Deaf Mutes in Montreal. He was its first principal and ran the school capably for twelve years. His school eventually became the Mackay Centre for Deaf Children. In 1882, Thomas became ill and after a year resigned his post. He and his family then moved away to Los Angeles for sun and health.

Whilst in Los Angeles, Thomas bought a ten-acre plot and had a house built and his family settled down. In 1886, the Rev. Thomas Gallaudet visited Thomas Widd and asked him to set up a new Association of the Deaf of South California. He did so with much success in spite of objections from rival local Deaf religious groups. Thomas issued an occasional publication, *Philocophus,* and he was made a licensed church lay-reader in May 1896. He died on 5 December 1906.

Thomas was quiet and studious and lived through his life, struggling from the lowest depth at the saw mill in Driffield to the great heights as a founder and principal of a school for the Deaf. He did it through sheer hard work, going about it with hardly any financial support in the first place. He was probably the first Deaf person to make use of the newspapers to carry out his campaign in public on behalf of his Deaf groups. For example, he wrote a newspaper article appealing for financial support for the establishment of a new church for the Deaf in London on behalf of his old teacher, the Rev. Samuel Smith. Finally, he is remembered today with great respect by the Deaf of Canada.

Mary Hayes (nee Widd)

Richard Rowland Williams
1825-1879

Richard Williams was born hearing of Welsh parents in Liverpool in 1825, and did not become deaf until he was aged 8. The incident which caused his deafness was unusual. It happened in the playground of his local school where another boy got hold of a bottle of chemical vitriol during a squabble and threw it at Richard, hitting him in the face. As a result, the young boy lost his hearing completely, as well as the sight of his right eye and carried a disfigurement, which was to remain with him for the rest of his life. His vocal cords were also damaged, causing him difficulty in speaking.

There is nothing remarkable or spectacular about Richard Williams's life. He was born in, grew up in and died in the same area of Liverpool all his life. What is exceptional about him is what he made of his life after that terrible childhood tragedy. He was enrolled as a day scholar in the Liverpool Institution for the Deaf and Dumb where he proved to be an exceptional student. He was the first pupil of that institution to become a pupil teacher and then assistant teacher. However, in 1844, Richard sought better employment as the pay at the Liverpool Institution was very low and he obtained a position as wages clerk with the Mersey Docks and Harbour Board. He was to remain in their employment for the rest of his working life.

He proved to be such a hard-working and exceptional wages clerk that by the time he was aged 30, he was the Chief Clerk of the Mersey Docks and Harbour Board, with responsibility for over 500 men. Exceptionally, he communicated with them by speech after training his damaged vocal cords to produce some resemblance of sound that could be understood. He was regular, prompt and extremely quick at calculation and was said to be able to remember every one of the 500-plus employees by face, and to be able to tell off the working time and wages due to each man from memory.

Richard did not mingle much with other Deaf people in the years after he left the Liverpool Institution. However, he got to know and remained on good terms with George Healey who founded the Adult Deaf and Dumb Society in Liverpool. His was the first name on the list of people who attended the first gathering in 1864. He served as a committee member and then as chairman from 1870 onwards until his death.

Richard met his wife, a hearing person, whilst both were working as clerks in the Docks and Harbour Board offices, and they had three sons that survived infancy. Although his position with his employer entitled him to a comfortable pension, he preferred to carry on working - often until late at night. He died in his sleep on 3 July 1879 after a lingering illness caused by overwork.

At his funeral, hundreds of his colleagues in the Docks and Harbour Board joined the family and Deaf friends. The funeral cortege stretched over a hundred yards behind the coffin as it moved the two and half miles from his home to the Toxteth Park Cemetery. Few deaf people can have had such a funeral procession.

Peter W. Jackson

194

Arthur James Wilson
1858-1945

Arthur James Wilson was born in Camden Town, London, the son of a schoolmaster. At the age of twelve, he contracted scarlet fever, which rendered him profoundly deaf. It became impossible for him to continue his attendance at school, and he was confined to his home where book reading became his main occupation. The question of sending Wilson to a special school for the Deaf was not raised as he already had gained literary competence and by the age of fourteen he wrote an excellent article that appeared in *A Magazine Intended Chiefly for the Deaf and Dumb,* which was edited by the Rev. Samuel Smith. Wilson's learning from reading books became an issue of controversy since literacy among deaf children declined through oral enforcement and it was suggested that they would benefit more from books than from classroom instructions.

At fifteen Wilson was apprenticed to a wood engraver but had to relinquish the post owing to eye strain. Having to begin the world anew, he took up journalism and a number of his writings were found in several Deaf magazines. His main hobby at the time was cycling and he used a wooden structure known as the "boneshakers" and associated himself with Dan Albone, a bicycle maker, which afforded him practical experience in the cycle trade. He organised cycle races, which included tough hill climbs. Wilson met J. R. Mecredy, the Irish champion, and beat him in a race and soon afterwards they became the best of friends. At the time Mecredy and his brother were running the *Irish Cycle.* However, a newspaper controversy written by Wilson interested Mecredy who recognised Wilson's talent as a writer and he offered Wilson partnership after the brothers split up.

Wilson's early breakthrough to prominence was as a cycling journalist. He used the pen-name of "Faed" which is "deaf" spelt backwards. In 1889, the pneumatic tyre was invented by the Pneumatic Tyre Company in Dublin and Wilson became the general manager despite what Mecredy called a terrible handicap. While working in Dublin, he married a hearing lady but she did not like living in the Irish city so they moved to London. Wilson opened a workshop with thirty hands in Farringdon Street and later used larger premises in the area. In 1899, he took up 168 Clerkenwell Road and the company was known as the Dunlop Pneumatic Tyre Campany. About 200 people were employed and all had to master the manual alphabet, which Wilson relied upon, as he was a very poor lipreader. All were sworn to secrecy in the making of the world's renowned air-blown tyres. Several years were to pass before the company became known as A. J. Wilson & Co Ltd. Further premises in the same road were taken over. In 1896, Wilson purchased a motor car and became the world's first Deaf motorist and later he acquired a motor boat and engaged in boat races. He lost the boat to the Royal Navy during the first World War. The business made him a wealthy man, but money was no good to him. He became a philanthropist and about 1905, he founded the Cycle and Motor Trades Benevolent Fund which was for rendering assistance to workers of the cycle and motor trade who, through illness or other causes, had fallen on bad times. The fund was also instrumental in the founding of the Home for Orphaned Children of Workers of the Allied Trades. The place situated at Sydenham, South London, cared and educated 50 children.

The safety bicycle appeared around the turn of the century and Wilson managed to get the Prince of Wales, later Edward V11, interested in cycling as an exercise. He and the prince became good friends and later he taught King George V and Queen Mary to ride bicycles and got the couple to become the patrons of the Cyclists Touring Club. He became the president of Great North Road Cycling Club and restored the old Paddington race track for cyclists to train as tracksmen.

During the war years the demand for tyres of army vehicles increased and this kept Wilson and his workers busy. The casualties of the war were traumatic which touched Wilson's philanthropic passion, causing him to launch the Hospital Motor Squadron and he became its Commandant, a position he held for 5 years. He organised half-a-million war-wounded patients from London hospitals for health drives and taking them to various entertainments. Wilson once hired the Albert Hall and filled them with eight thousand wounded men for an afternoon concert. Getting them back to their respective hospitals took hours and much sweat, but Wilson did not flinch. For his good deeds, the City of London made him a Freeman. After the war he established the Frederick Milner Hostel for deafened soldiers and became its chairman.

In 1918, Wilson founded the Federation of London Deaf Clubs (FLDC), an organisation which enabled sporting events between the eight major clubs in the London area to take place. The Wilson trophy for Billiards was keenly fought for and the contest resulted in some players becoming outstanding and century breaks were not uncommon. He also donated trophies for tennis, golf and football. In 1924, together with the Rev. Vernon Jones, he took the FLDC to the first Deaf International Games held in Paris. It is interesting to record that the FLDC was the first major sports organisation and at the time it was founded there were nearly 9,000 Deaf people living within the area. By 1930, Wilson's contributions, as founder and organiser, were curtailed and almost forgotten.

At the end of the second decade of the century, Wilson found himself widowed. He hired a Miss Sayer, who was the stenographer to the American Ambassador in London. She became Wilson's greatest employment asset and interpreter, using the manual alphabet proficiently. Eventually he married her. In 1926, the Cycle and Motor Trades Benevolent Fund had became large and influential. During the year Wilson invited Edward, Prince of Wales, to the annual banquet and his long speech was delivered by his wife. Also invited was a Mr Morris, a motor manufacturer who later became Lord Nuffield, and at the time Wilson was offered the OBE which he declined. Others who had done much less than what he had done were made lords and knights. Naturally Wilson felt insulted, but at the time offering a peerage to an individual handicapped by deafness was highly controversial. His business declined in 1928 and two years later the firm of A.J. Wilson & Co Ltd ceased to exist. Wilson and his family moved to Leamington Spa where he founded the Coventry Institute for the Deaf and from there he promoted sport and social gatherings in the Midlands. He died at his home in 1945, aged 87.

Mecredy, Wilson's close associate, best summed up the character of this unique man - *"Versatility is one of his characteristics. He appears to turn his hand to anything and do it well. His quickness of perception and grasp of a subject are most remarkable"*.

Arthur F. Dimmock

Dorothy Mary Stanton Wise
c1880-1918

Dorothy Stanton Wise was born deaf at Dover where she was educated at home by her mother who had taken her to see the Rev. Thomas Arnold at Northampton for advice on her education. She also attended a kindergarten school where she first demonstrated her talent for modelling with clay. When her kindergarten time was up, her parents engaged a modelling tutor to come in twice a week and she was so good that at the age of 7 she was admitted to the Dover School of Art where she stayed until she was eighteen. Her parents then moved to London and admitted her as a free scholar to the sculpture studio in the Royal College of Art, where she stayed for four years and graduated an A.R.C.A.

Then she started to earn her living by designing and sculpting many items of distinction and merit, earning gold medals at exhibitions at the Royal Academy, Manchester Art Gallery and Liverpool's Walker Art Gallery. A number of her sculptures were also sold to Queen Alexandra.

One of her best-known works is a marble memorial to Bishop John Prideaux who had led the impeachment and imprisonment of Charles I. Wise had done considerable research, copying the portrait of Prideaux from a miniature plaster medallion completed in 1638 by Claude Warin. The white marble medallion eighteen inches long was embedded in a plain slab of beautiful gray Pentelican marble with a long inscription incised below it.

Dorothy Stanton Wise discovered the Deaf community in her late teens and was a strong supporter of the BDDA. She contributed regularly to the *British Deaf Times*, mostly about travel in France.

Dorothy Stanton Wise stopped producing whilst in her prime in 1918. It is believed that she may have died a victim of the influenza epidemic. In her Will, probated on 16 April 1919 in London, her death date is given as 25 December 1918 and she lived at 46 Temple Fortune-Hill, Hendon, Middlesex.

Peter W. Jackson

John Philp Wood
1762-1838

Sir Walter Scott wrote in his *Journal* dated 27 June 1830: *Honest John, my old friend, dined with us. I only regret I cannot understand him, as he has a very powerful and much more curious information.* Scott was referring to John Philp Wood, a deaf and dumb editor of *Douglas' Peerage of Scotland.*

John Philp Wood was born in March 1762 in the parish of Cramond, a small township some 7 kilometres northwest of Edinburgh. He became deaf at very early age through scarlet fever, an infectious disease prevalent in his days. His parents then sent Wood to the celebrated Thomas Braidwood's Academy for the Deaf and Dumb situated near St. Leonard's Hill in the southeast part of Edinburgh. Along with some of his illustrious Braidwoodian pupils such as Charles Sheriff, John Goodricke, Francis Humberstone McKenzie and Sarah Dashwood among many others, Wood was taught under the combined system with a strong emphasis on reading, writing and manualism. Wood was proficient in fingerspelling like many Deaf people of his time, but was to excel in reading and writing.

In 1778, Wood was sufficiently educated to be able to obtain a post of clerk to the Accountant at the Scottish Excise Office in Chessels Court, Edinburgh, and he showed good aptitude for figures. Within a year, Wood was transferred to another department, that of the Solicitor of Excise, where he remained as a clerk for six years, after which he was given responsibility to maintain and distribute auctioneers' bonds and also to register lawyers' opinions. In 1797, he returned to his first department where he became an assistant Accountant for the next three years. After that period he became a fully-fledged accountant and in 1802 was promoted to the post of Over Deputy for signing licences.

Away from the steady climb in his career in the Excise Office, Wood began his literary work with a 1791 publication of his biography on John Law entitled *A Sketch of the Life of John Law of Lauriston, Comptroller General of the Finances of France.* This was followed by another publication in 1794, *The Ancient and Modern State of the Parish of Cramond.* This work, which spanned from 1790 to mid-1793, was highly acclaimed and credited Wood as Scotland's first ever person to write a parochial history. This book was a precursor of the technique employed by Sir John Sinclair for his monumental *The Statistical Account of Scotland*, published in volumes over the years between 1791 and 1799. Sinclair's work is recognised as the first statistical survey of any nation in history.

In 1794, the Excise Officer moved to Dundas House in St. Andrew's Square. Through the influence of one eminent judge of the Court of Session, Charles Hay (later Lord Newton), Wood became Auditor of Excise in 1809 when the Prime Minister, Spencer Percival, appointed Wood to the post. In the same year, a meeting was gathered in Fortune's, a pub in Edinburgh, to discuss the formation of a national school for Scottish Deaf children. At that time, there were no schools for the Deaf and the famous Braidwood's Academy had moved to Hackney on the outskirts of London in 1783. The outcome of the meeting was that Wood and James Farquhar Gordon, a writer of *The Signet*, appointed joint secretaries of the newly formed Edinburgh Institution for the Education of

198

the Deaf and Dumb and it was formally established on 25 June 1810 with John Braidwood as its headmaster.

Wood took to genealogy in his spare time and he later found it an asset when he was persuaded in 1813 to prepare the second edition of *The Peerage of Scotland*. Wood's work on that book gained him recognition as Scotland's leading genealogist of his time, having attended to several amendments and modifications to the original 1764 edition by Sir Robert Douglas. However, Wood's responsibilities as Auditor of Excise increased and in 1817, he resigned his post as joint secretary of the Edinburgh Institution. Wood, however, made legal history when Robert Kinniburgh, the headmaster of the Edinburgh Institution, engaged him as a relay interpreter in the famous Jean Campbell case in Glasgow.

In 1824, the Excise Office moved again to Bellevue House in Drummond Street and in the same year there was renewed interest in John Law and Wood brought out his fourth and final book, *Memoirs of John Law of Lauriston*. It was a much more detailed biography than the 1791 original and it covered the 'Mississippi Bubble' burst which saw Law slipping into oblivion and his subsequent death as an exiled penniless vagrant in Vienna.

Wood's career and work at the Excise Office was much respected and gained approval from the government of the day. Wood earned the tag of being "Honest", as regarded by Scott, for his sincere and diligent auditioning. From the time of his appointment in 1809 to his retirement in 1832, Wood put in an equivalent of 30 years work into 22 years, catching up with neglected and overlooked audits done eight years previously. On one occasion, he discovered that some £36,000 was incorrectly attributed as £12,000. On numerous times, he chased people into paying up their taxes and duties to balance the books and along the way he exposed corruption, both within and outside of the Civil Service. There was an occasion when Wood opposed a grant to the Commissioners of the Excise Office towards the payment of their private expenses made out of the public purse and he succeeded. Wood's action and conduct in this incident won praise and admiration from the Barons of the Court of the Exchequer.

Wood displayed his writing talents further by contributing to several learned magazines of his day, *The Analytical Review, The Critical Review, The Annual Register* and *The Gentlemen's Magazine*. In June 1830, Matthew Robert Burns conducted the world's first Deaf-led church services in a small room lit only by a small window in Lady Stairs Close. On that memorable day, John Philp Wood was one of the Deaf worshippers along with other prominent figures such as Walter Geikie and Alexander Blackwood. Wood's connection with the Deaf had always been strong in spite of his marriage to a hearing woman. His marriage yielded seven children and the eldest of his three sons, John George Wood, turned out to be one of the leading lights in the Disruption of the Church of Scotland in 1843.

Wood died on 25 October 1838 at 8 South Charlotte Street, which was his home for the last 28 years of his life. By a strange quirk of fate, in 1847 in a house, a few doors up the street, a baby born to an elocutionist and his partially deaf wife was destined to revolutionise the world of communication – Alexander Graham Bell.

John Philp Wood, truly one of the illustrious Braidwoodian pupils in British Deaf History, deserves better recognition from both Deaf and hearing communities for his remarkable achievements and outstanding contributions to both groups in society in spite of his deafness and total inability to speak. He was truly a man of many parts.

Raymond Lee

Peter George Spencer Woodcock
1929-1986

Peter Woodcock was born in the Hornsey area in North London on 12 January 1929 and he went to school there. During the war he became an evacuee at Hatfield, Hertfordshire, where he proved to be an excellent scholar. It was felt that he was predestined for higher learning and the Dartmouth Naval College was considered for him. But at the age of 15, a blow to the head resulted in total loss of hearing and the prospect of becoming an admiral receded into oblivion. Instead he was sent to Talbot House in Manchester to be taught tailoring. While there, he frequented the Deaf Club in Grosvenor Street and took up snooker, which enabled him to become a potential player among the north-west Deaf cuemen, who were at the time the best of the Deaf players in Britain.

Returning to London, Peter worked as a tailor and was lodged at the old RNID lodgings for Deaf working men at Highbury Quadrant. Soon, however, he quit the tailoring trade and became some sort of teaboy, running errands about the streets of London for the firm of Jonathan Fallowfield, a photographic supplier. He was sometimes allowed to serve customers at the counter but had to rely upon written orders, as he was no great lipreader, just like A. J. Wilson, the businessman, before him. It was discovered that when ordering stock, Peter proved to be proficient and sales increased significantly and eventually he was given the post of stock buyer. Some years were to elapse before he was made a company director.

Peter Woodcock married Naomi Harrison, the Deaf daughter of Sir Archibald and Lady Harrison, on 23 March 1957. Her father was knighted for his involvement in the Munich War Crime Trails. The Woodcock family settled in the Anerley area and Peter made friends with Doctors Pickvance and Turner who ran a surgery near their home. He taught Dr. Pickvance sign language and took both of them frequently to the Redhill Deaf Club to play snooker. In 1950 on Whit Monday at Salisbury, he won a shot put event in a regional match between the Deaf of the south and London. In 1970 at Lewisham, he was selected to play snooker against the World Professional Champion, John Spencer. He did not win but his name status as a player was enhanced. He helped the Redhill snooker team to win a national event.

Peter, his wife and four daughters, all hearing, took over Sir Arthur's old home in Rickmansworth on the latter's death. The owners of the firm he worked for decided to retire and it was taken over by a large concern. Woodcock was considered an expensive employee because he needed an interpreter able to do fast fingerspelling at meetings and conferences; therefore he was severed at the age of 53. However, he was able to live fairly comfortably on the severance payment. He frequented the local Conservative Club and taught some members sign language. He died on 28 September 1986 through cancer. Peter Woodcock had a remarkable brain and it was most unfortunate that he failed to reach a high position in society through being deaf.

Arthur F. Dimmock

200

Stan Woodhouse
1920-1983

Stan Woodhouse was born in South Shields, County Durham, on 20 October 1920. He did not become deaf until he was six years old after an attack of measles. Stan was later sent to the Northern Counties School for the Deaf in Newcastle-upon-Tyne. He was 9½ years old when he started school and had to begin in the lowest class with the five and six year olds!

After leaving school, Stan became an apprentice welder with the giant shipbuilder, Swans, in early 1937. However, during his time with Swans, Stan started to complain of chest pains caused by fumes when undertaking welding tasks. His chest was so bad that Stan had to quit his apprenticeship and he decided to train as a draughtsman. For his training, the then Ministry of Labour sent Stan to a training centre in Slough, Berkshire. After successfully completing his course in 1943, Stan could not find employment in his native North East, but one company, Scatchwell, in Slough offered him employment as a draughtsman and Stan took up the offer and stayed with the same company for 37 years until his voluntary early retirement in December 1980.

Before Stan went to Slough, he married Vera Hunter in South Shields. After settling down in Slough, Stan met members of the local Deaf community and was amazed to see that the local Deaf club was nothing but a small twelve-feet square room above a shoe shop in the High Street. This club opened only once a month on Saturday evenings for the Deaf and the room belonged to a charitable organisation. It was at one of the monthly meetings when Stan met Cyril Robbins, a Deaf architect employed by the local authority. The Deaf people had to move out of the room as it was claimed that the floor could not hold the weight of 20-30 people at any one time! Stan and Cyril Robbins decided that the local Deaf community needed a new Deaf centre of its own and set about achieving that aim. They applied to the local authorities for land and permission to build a centre, which Cyril Robbins had designed. There was indifference and poor response from the authorities and Stan took to arguing and demanding that the Deaf be given a place of their own, and at the same time he started a campaign appealing to local companies and influential individuals for funds. Surprisingly, funds poured in and that gave Stan and Cyril hope. Eventually, Slough City Council agreed to lease land for the purpose of building a Deaf centre and a £250 mortgage was taken out by a group of local Deaf people to purchase the land in 1967. With Stan as the foreman and Cyril as the architect, Deaf people were recruited on voluntary basis to build the new Deaf centre and it saw completion in 1968. For this work, Cyril Robbins was awarded the MBE in 1968 and there were protests that Stan should have received the same. Arthur F. Dimmock took up the battle and four years later Stan was deservedly awarded his MBE in the Queen's Birthday Honours in 1972. This award was a fitting tribute to a humble man who worked hard to give the Deaf a club of their own.

In 1976, the National Union of the Deaf (NUD) was formed and invited Stan to become its President. Stan was elated and accepted quickly. In the early years of the NUD, Stan's advice, experience and guidance, along with that of the NUD's Chair, Arthur F. Dimmock, proved great

201

help and influence to the organisation. However, Stan became increasingly ill with bronchitis and various forms of lung diseases that were not helped by his heavy smoking. Consequently, his role with the NUD gradually diminished, with the exception that he wanted to see a charter of rights for all Deaf people published. This triggered work on that subject – and the first publication, *Charter of Rights of the Deaf: Part One -The Rights of the Deaf Child*, got to him in good time in August 1982. However, Stan was never able to participate in the second part as his health deteriorated alarmingly, the man fast becoming a pale shadow of his former self. On 27 December, he was rushed to hospital with serious breathing problems and was pronounced dead on 1 January 1983.

Stan Woodhouse's strength was in his humility and generosity. He saw humility as a powerful weapon; he always called the Deaf people "the little people" and the hearing "the big people". Stan Woodhouse was indeed a little man, small in stature and very humble. Yet, this was the very man who was the inspiration, fighter and builder of Slough Deaf Centre and also he was the same man who took up the Presidency of a radical Deaf pressure group, National Union of the Deaf, and inspired changes he never lived to see.

Raymond Lee

David John Murray Wright
1920-1994

David Wright was born on 23 February 1920 in Orange Grove, Johannesburg, South Africa, the son of Gordon Alfred Wright, an Insurance Executive. His parents were married in London in 1919 and shortly afterwards emigrated to Johannesburg. David became totally deaf at the age of 7 years old through scarlet fever and started his education at St. John's Preparatory School in Johannesburg in 1927, before being sent to Miss Blanche Nevile's Private Deaf School in Regent's Park Crescent, London. He returned to South Africa briefly where he received private tuition under a Miss Holland who had been a Teacher of the Deaf under Miss Nevile. He also went to Park Town School in Johannesburg before he returned to England to attend the Spring Hill School for Deaf Boys in Northampton on his fourteenth birthday.

David became one of the editors of the Spring Hill School Magazine, which had been in existence for some fours years. This was the first time that David published his poems and he continued to contribute poems for the school magazine until he left school in 1939. He played first team football and cricket for the school from 1937 to 1939, and one of his team mates was David Hyslop, later to become one of the founders of Breakthrough Trust Deaf-Hearing Integration

David matriculated the Oxford Junior Local Examination with four distinctions, with a first place in English and a second and a third in two others in 1935. This enabled him to attend Oriel College, Oxford University, from which he graduated in 1942 with a Bachelor of Arts honours degree in English Language and Literature. Whilst a student at Oxford, he joined the Boat Club and rowed for the 1st Oriel team.

After leaving Oxford, David decided to move to London to seek employment. He joined the staff of *The Sunday Times* from 1942 to 1947. His first collection, *Poems*, was published in 1949 and led to him being awarded the Atlantic Award in 1950. He was also to win the Guinness Poetry Prize in 1958 and 1960 for his work in Literature. His second collection, *Moral Stories*, appeared in 1954 and David was to have a long career in literature, mainly as a poet and an editor. He was co-author on three books about Portugal, and as an anthologist, he edited a number of excellent volumes of poetry, among them *Longer Contemporary Poems*, the *Penguin Book of English Romantic Verse* and the *Penguin Book of Everyday Verse*.

David Wright's poetry was remarkable for its quiet intelligence and humour, and the integrity of its style, creating a lively curve of an eminently humane mind's thinking and speaking. The perceptions were romantic, elegiac and exact, the subjects various and diverse. He also wrote two autobiographies, *Monologue of a Deaf Man*, and *Deafness*.

David married Phillipa Reid, a divorced actress of St. Pancras, London, at Holborn Registry Office on 6 October 1951 and they went to live in Keswick in 1965, the same year that he became Gregory Fellow in Poetry at the University of Leeds, a position which he held until 1967. He was elected a member of the Royal Society of Literature in 1967 and gained a Master of Arts degree at Oriel University in Oxford in 1985. He was elected an Honorary Fellow of Oriel College in 1991 and Honorary Doctor of Literature at Leicester University in 1993.

Following the death of his first wife Phillipa, in 1985, David married Agnes Mary Swift, a widow and a director of a pottery company, in Penrith Registry Office, Cumbria, on 13 March 1987 and they went to reside at Bongate Mill Farmhouse, Appleby-in-Westmoreland. Sometime in the early 1990s, they also lived in Alfanzina, Portugal, but returned to England in 1993.

David died on 28 August 1994 in his home at Appleby at the age of 74 years. His ashes were interred beside his first wife's in her grave at St. Bega's Church, Bassenthwaite Lake in Cumbria.

Geoffrey J. Eagling

Editors' Note:

It was clear in the early stages of the *Deaf Lives* project that there might be some difficulty in compiling a bibliography because of the nature of the work. There were several reasons for this. A number of articles were written by contributors with personal knowledge of the subject concerned; others were written by people who had never before contributed anything in print and their contributions had to be re-written and properly structured by the editors. Such articles were usually submitted without sources or references. However, in keeping with the spirit of the project as required by the Lottery grant, these articles were still attributed to the contributors even if the details were sometimes corrected and changed using the editors' own personal knowledge and sources.

Another difficulty was that for a large number of contributed articles, particularly of Deaf people who had been very prominent in Deaf community matters, there was a wide variety of sources from which the information could have been obtained. Listing all these sources and references would have been very repetitive. Therefore in order to assist readers to trace sources and references, the editors have decided on a bibliographical format which they feel will give the best possible assistance in looking for these sources.

Primary Sources: *Journals, Periodicals and Newspapers*

There are numerous references to deaf people in a wide range of journals and magazines published for deaf people. Although much of the information is sometimes limited and repetitive, any source specific enough to be linked with articles in this book are given in the Specific Sources sub-section below. These mostly take the form of biographies or obituaries in the deaf magazines mentioned and also refer to sources such as publications outside the Deaf community.

The Deaf community sources where there are numerous references are as stated below:

American Annals for the Deaf
British Deaf & Dumb Times 1889-1908
British Deaf Monthly 1896-1903
British Deaf Mute & Deaf Chronicle 1891-1895
British Deaf News 1955-2000
British Deaf Times 1903-1954
Deaf & Dumb Magazine 1879-1885
Deaf & Dumb Times 1889-1891
Deaf News 1950-54
Deaf Quarterly News 1905-1950
Deaf History Journal 1997-2001
Deaf History Journal Supplements 1997-2001
Ephphatha 1896-1959
Glasgow Evening News 1891-1907 (containing 'Deaf Notes')
Glasgow Evening Times 1871-1893 (containing regular a deaf column)
Glasgow Herald 1871-1895 (containing a regular deaf column)
Magazine for the Scottish Deaf 1929-1931
One-in-Seven Magazine 1997-2000
See Hear! Magazine 1992-1997
Soundbarrier 1987-1992
The Teacher of the Deaf 1906-1956

Dictionaries and Reference Books

Readers will find a considerable wealth of information in a number of dictionaries and reference books, mostly of people linked with art or those who have aristocratic connections or those who have made significant scientific discoveries. These books are:

Burke's Extinct & Dormant Baronetcies, Burke's Peerage (Genealogical Books) Ltd, 1841.
Dictionary of British 18th Century Painters, Antique Club, 1981.
Dictionary of British Animal Painters, F. Lewis, Publishers, Leigh-on-Sea, 1973.
Dictionary of British Artists 1880-1940, Antique Collectors Club, 1952.
Dictionary of British Artists Working 1900-1950, Eastbourne Fine Art, Eastbourne, 1975.
Dictionary of British Historical Painters, F. Lewis, Publishers, Leigh-on-Sea, 1979.
Dictionary of British Landscape Painters, F. Lewis, Publishers, Leigh-on-Sea, 1952.
Dictionary of British Marine Painters, F. Lewis, Publishers, Leigh-on-Sea, 1967.
Dictionary of British Miniature Painters, Faber & Faber, London, 1972.
Dictionary of Irish Artists, Walter Strickland (1913)
Dictionary of National Biography
Dictionary of Painters of Miniatures, Philip Allan Co, London, 1926.
Dictionary of Victorian Painters, Antique Collectors Club, 1971.

People who are in *Deaf Lives* that are in these books include:

Alexandra, Queen	Arrowsmith, Thomas	Cavendish, William S.
Clemo, Jack	Close, Samuel	Cooley, Thomas
Crosse, Richard	Davidson, Thomas	Dent, Rupert
Docharty, James	Fagan, Lawrence	Fagan, Robert
Fleming, Sir John A.	Gaudy, Sir John	Geikie, Walter
Goodricke, John	Gostwicke, Sir Edward	Graham, Sir James
Gubbins, Beatrice	Heaviside, Oliver	Howe, James
Kitto, John	Mackenzie, Francis H.	Martineau, Harriet
Mitchell, William	Reynolds, Sir Joshua	Roch, Sampson T.
Scott, Charlotte A.	Shaw, Kathleen T.	Shirreff, Charles
Smith, John G. Spence	Thomson, Alfred R.	Tonna, Charlotte E.
Trood, William H. H.	Wood, John P.	Wright, David J. M.

Official Sources: Family Records Centre, 1 Myddelton Street, Islington, London & Probate Search Room, First Avenue House, 42-49 High Holborn, London.

For a number of contributions to *Deaf Lives*, it has been necessary to obtain birth, marriage or death certificates from the Family Records Centre and copies of Wills and/or probate from the Probate Search Room, in order to complete information on the subjects concerned. These include:

Bloomfield, Frederick A.	Blount, Hiram	Carr, Cyril
Fenning, Oliver	Mackenzie, George A.	Martineau, Harriet
Oxley, Kate	Pearce, Richard Aslatt	Popham, Alexander
Tavaré, Frederick L.	Wise, Dorothy M. S.	Wright, David J. M.

Books containing information about deaf people

There are five books that recur throughout the references that appear to have been consulted by contributors. To save repeating the full details throughout the Specific Sources sub-section, we are printing the full bibliographical details here. Subsequently, these books will only be referred to by their title. These books are:

Braddock, Gilbert C.: *Notable Deaf Persons,* Gallaudet College Alumni Association, Washington DC, USA (1975)
Carbin, Clifton: *Deaf Heritage in Canada*, Toronto Engraving Company (1996)
Firth, George C.: *Chosen Vessels*, Papyrus Printers, Exeter (1988)
Jackson, Peter W.: *Britain's Deaf Heritage,* Pentland Press, Edinburgh (1990)
Roe, W.: *Peeps into the Deaf World,* Bemrose, Derby (1916)

Specific Sources & References

Agnew, William	Glasgow & West of Scotland Royal Visit 1935 brochure
Alexandra, Queen	*The Deaf American*, April 1970 *Scottish Magazine for the Deaf,* Dec/Jan 1930 *British Deaf Times*, 1914 *Queen Alexandra*, Georgina Battiscombe (1984), Constable, London
Armour, Robert	*British Deaf Times* 1914
Arrowsmith, Thomas	*The Art of Instructing the Deaf & Dumb*, John Paunceforth Arrowsmith (1819), The British Library Collection
Ash, Harry	*The British Deaf-Mute*, June 1895
Atkinson, Alexander	*Memoirs of My Youth* (1865) J. W. Swanson, Newcastle-on-Tyne
Bain, Charlotte	*Elgin Magazine*, 1831 *The Courant*, 23 July 1868 & 2 September 1932 *Northern Scot*, 3 September 1932 Fishermen's Memorial, Lossiemouth
Banton, George	*Banton,* Peter R. Brown (1995), British Deaf History Society Publications
Barnett, Algernon J.M.	*Ephphatha*, June-August 1953
Bather, Arthur H.	*Hansard,* 23 March 1885 (Vol. 240, Col. 2028) *Quarterly Review of Deaf-Mute Education*, 1892
Beale, George	*Peeps into the Deaf World* *British Deaf Times*, Nov/Dec 1917 *British Deaf Times*, May/June 1923 *Deaf Quarterly News*, April/June 1928
Beale, Henry	*The British Deaf Times.* 1921
Blenkarne	*Deaf Heritage in Canada*
Bilibin, Alexander	*The Volta Review* 1946-48 *Tommy,* Arthur F. Dimmock (1991) Scottish Workshop Publications
Blackwood, Alexander	*Edinburgh Deaf and Dumb Benevolent Society Centenary 1835-1935,* commemorative brochure.

207

Bloomfield, Frederick   *The British Deaf News;* Nov/Dec 1982

Blount, Hiram   *Peeps into the Deaf World*
Chosen Vessels
The British Deaf Times Jan/Feb 1936
The British Deaf Monthly Nov 1898, and June 1899
Ephphatha Apr/Jun 1934, No.10

Bone, Edward   *Survey of Cornwall*, Richard Carew (1595) British Library Collection

Burke, James   *Encyclopaedia of Boxing* 1983 edition, Robert Hale & Co., London
The Deaf American, January 1972

Burns, John   *A Historical and Chronological Remembrancer*, 1775

Burns, Matthew
Robert   *Deaf and Dumb Times* 1890
Deaf and Dumb Magazine 1883

Burnside, Helen   *British Deaf Times* 1913
Ephphatha 1896

Campbell, Duncan   *The History of the Life and Adventures of Mr. Duncan Campbell,* Daniel Defoe (1720), Raymond Lee Collection
Secret Memoirs of the late Mr. Duncan Campbell (1732), Raymond Lee Collection

Carmichael, John   *Deaf History Journal*, April 2000, British Deaf History Society

Carr, Cyril   *The British Deaf Monthly*, Dec.1897
*The Spring Hill School Magazine;*Dec.1933, Dec.1940, Dec.1944,

Cavendish, William S.   *The Dukes,* Brian Masters 1980, Bland & Briggs, London.
The House - A Portrait of Chatsworth, The Duchess of Devonshire (1982), Papermac

Clemo, Jack   *Sunday Telegraph Magazine,* 11 January 1987

Cooley, Thomas   *History of Deaf Artists in Ireland: Thomas Cooley.* Paper given by David Breslin at 2nd European Symposium on Deaf History, April 1996.

Creasy, John   *Bermondsey 1792*, Raymond Lee & John A. Hay (1993), National Union of the Deaf

Crosse, Richard   *Richard Crosse, Miniaturist and Portrait-Painter,* Basil S. Long (1929), Walpole Society, London.

Davidson, Thomas   *The British Deaf-Mute* March 1895,
Ephphatha 1897,
Peeps into the Deaf World
Our Deaf and Dumb (1896),

Dent, Rupert Arthur   *The British Deaf Times,* 1910
Peeps into the Deaf World

Drysdale, Alexander   *Deaf and Dumb Times,* May 1880
                             Britain's Deaf Heritage
                             The Lamb Collection, Dundee Local Studies Library

Duff, John   *Farrar's History of Limerick, 1787*

Dyott, John   *Staffordshire Mercury,* 12 November 1971
                             The Siege of Lichfield, Rev. W. Greasley (1923), Constable, London

Edmond, Arthur   *Royal School for Deaf Children Magazine, Margate* 1982

Edward, George   *Peeps into the Deaf World*

Edwards, Leslie   *Leicester & County Mission to the Deaf Annual Report,* 1945
                             The Silent World, September 1950
                             The Deaf News, November 1951
                             Ephphatha, December 1951-February 1952 issue.

Fagan, Lawrence   Admission book, Claremont Institution for the Deaf and Dumb

Fairbairn, Sir Arthur   *Notable Deaf Persons*
H.   *Oldham Deaf-Mute Gazette,* July 1904

Farrar, Abraham   *Notable Deaf Persons*
                             Peeps into the Deaf World

Fenning, Oliver   Pupils' Roll, Annual Reports and Minutes Books from The Brighton
                             Institution for the Instruction of Deaf and Dumb of the Counties of
                             Sussex, Hampshire and Kent.
                             Correspondence with Mrs. E. Wills neé Fenning

Fleming, Sir John A.   *The Inventor of the Valve: A Biography of Sir Ambrose Fleming,* J.T.
                             MacGregor-Morris (1954), The Television Society, London.

Fyfe, David   *British Deaf News,* December 1967

Gaudy, Sir John &   *Egerton mss,* British Library Collection
Framlingham   Will, probate and other family records, Norfolk County Records Office

Gawen, Joseph   *Deaf History Journal,* August 1998, British Deaf History Society

Geikie, Walter   *Walter Geikie 1795-1837,* Raymond Lee (1996), British Deaf History
                             Society Publications

Gilbert, William   *British Deaf News,* February 1990 & May 1998

Goodricke, John
The Cambridge Illustrated History of Astronomy, Royal Astronomical Society
Peeps into the Deaf World
Soundbarrier, June 1986
Various original presentation papers by John Goodricke held by The Royal Society, 6 Charlton House Terrace, London SW1Y 5AG
Various hand-written text books by John Goodricke, York City Archives

Gorham, Charles
The Deaf and Dumb Times, 1889-1891.
Deaf Quarterly News 1922
The British Deaf-Mute, 1893
The Deaf Advance, Brian Grant, The Pentland Press, Edinburgh 1990.
BDDA Minute papers, 1890-1893.

Gostwicke, Sir Edward
Philocophus, or Deafe and Dumbe Man's Friend, John Bulwer, British Library Collection
Dorothy Osbourne's Letters, British Library Collection

Graham, Sir James
Silent World, 1954

Gray, William
Edinburgh Deaf and Dumb Institution Annual Reports, 1820-24
Congregational Roll, Albany Deaf Church, Edinburgh, 1830
Annual Reports & Minutes of the Board of Directors of the Institution for the Deaf and Dumb, Halifax, 1858-1870
The Frat 36 (issue no. 5), Dec.1938, USA
A Short History of the School of the Deaf, Halifax 1856-1961, K C Van Allen, 1964
Notable Deaf Persons
Deaf Heritage in Canada

Griffiths, William A.
British Deaf Times, May/June 1923, Nov./Dec. 1923
The British Deaf-Mute, August 1893
Peeps into the Deaf World

Groom, Jane Elizabeth
An Evangelist Among the Deaf and Dumb, H.H., RNID Library
A Future for the Deaf and Dumb in the Canadian North West J.E. Groom (1886), Doncaster Archives.
Deaf Heritage in Canada

Hague, Joseph
Touch, Touch and Touch Again, Doreen E. Woodford (2000), British Deaf History Society Publications

Harvey, Kate
Deaf History Journal, April 1999, British Deaf History Society

Healey, George F.
The Deaf Quarterly News, Jan-Mar 1928
Our Monthly Church Messenger, 1894
Voluntary Welfare Societies for Adult Deaf Persons (1840-1963), unpublished thesis, K. Lysons

Heaviside, Oliver
The Heaviside Centenary Meeting, 18 May 1950. IEE Publication.
Low Neighbours and Bad Drains: Oliver Heaviside FRS, Charles Dickens and Camden Town, David Sealey in Camden History Review vol. 20. (1996)

Hepworth, Joseph   *Peeps into the Deaf World*

Herriot, James   *Deaf History Journal* December 1998, British Deaf History Society
                        Deaf History Journal Supplement II. 1997, British Deaf History Society
                        Quarterly Review of Deaf-Mute Education, 1898, RNID Library.

Hodgson, Edwin A.   *The Deaf American* September 1978. National Association of the Deaf
                        (USA)
                        The Fanwood Journal October 1933. New York Institution for the Deaf

Hogg, George E. H.   *British Deaf Times,* June 1906

Hossell, Leigh   *Ephphatha* October 1896
                        The British Deaf Times 1906.

Howe, James   *The Man Who Loved to Draw Horses* A.D. Cameron (1986) Aberdeen
                        University Press

Isted, Ambrose   *Deaf History Journal* August 1998, British Deaf History Society

Kickham, Charles J.   *Catholic Encyclopaedia*, The Encyclopaedia Press Inc. (1914), New York,

Kirk, Edward A.   *The Leeds Beacon,* Anthony J. Boyce (1996), British Deaf History Society
                        Publications

Kitto, John   *Deaf and Dumb Magazine*, 1873
                        Notable Deaf Persons

Landseer, Thomas   *Deaf History Journal* August 2000, British Deaf History Society

Lowe, John William   *Notable Deaf Persons*
                        John William Lowe Raymond Lee (1995) British Deaf History Society
                        Publications

Lucas, Samuel Bright   *Ephphatha,* 1899 & Winter 1920

Mackenzie, F.H   *Peeps into the Deaf World*

Mackenzie, George A.   *British Deaf Times,* August 1910
                        The Deaf News, July-August 1951

MacLellan, A. & D.   *The Messenger,* January 1906

Macleod, Murdoch   *The British Deaf Monthly,* May 1900
                        The Deaf News, May-June 1951

Maginn, Francis   *The Deaf and Dumb Times* 1891
                        Ephphatha, 1896
                        The British Deaf Times, 1917
                        Peeps into the Deaf World

Martineau, Harriet	*Peeps into the Deaf World* *Chosen Vessels* *The British Deaf Times* Jan/Feb 1936 *The British Deaf Monthly* Nov 1898 and Jun 1899 *Ephphatha* Apr/Jun 1934
McDougall, William	*The Messenger,* January 1906 *The Deaf News,* May-June 1950
Miles, Dorothy	*Notable Deaf Persons* The Dorothy Miles Archives
Mitchell, William F.	*Ships of the Victorian Navy,* Conrad Dixon (1987), Ashford Press
Muirhead, Alexander	Oxford University Museum of Natural history *Scottish Biographical Dictionary,* Chambers, 1992. *Scottish Daily Record,* February 2000.
O'Keefe, Robert J.	*The Deaf and Dumb Magazine,* March 1876
Oxley, Kate	*The Deaf Quarterly News,* Oct-Dec 1928 *The British Deaf Times,* January-Feb 1930 and March-April 1951 *A Man with a Mission,* K. Oxley (1954), Hill Ainsworth Ltd. Extracts from Yorkshire Institution for the Deaf and Dumb archives.
Patrick, George Percy	*The Deaf and Dumb Times*, 1891 *The Deaf and Dumb Magazine*, 1876 *Peeps into the Deaf World*
Pattison, Thomas	*The History of the New South Wales Schools for Deaf Children and for Blind Children,* Walter, J. (1960) *British Deaf Monthly*, July 1899.
Paul. James	*Peeps into the Deaf World*
Payne, Benjamin H.	*Ephphatha* 1895 *Ephphatha* 1915 *The Deaf Quarterly News* 1926.
Pearce, Richard Aslatt	*Britain's Deaf Heritage* *Chosen Vessels* *Ephphatha,* Jan. 1897, Feb. 1897, Spring 1922 *Peeps into the Deaf World* Selwyn Oxley Collection *The Deaf and Dumb Times* Aug. 1889 Pupils' Roll, Annual Reports and Minutes Books from The Brighton Institution for the Instruction of Deaf and Dumb of the Counties of Sussex, Hampshire and Kent
Pitcher, Bernard	*Deaf History Journal* Supplement V August 1999, British Deaf History Society

Plantagenet, Princess Katherine	*Britain's Deaf Heritage*
Poole, Jane	*Deaf History Journal Supplement 1 1997*, British Deaf History Society
Popham, Alexander	*A West Country Family: the Pophams from 1150* F.W. Popham (1976), Olivers Printing Works, Exeter. *Country Life*, March 1940
Princess Joanna	*The Scots Peerage*, (2nd. & Revised Edition), edited by John P Wood, 18xx Vol. III of '*The proceedings of the Society of Antiquaries of Scotland*', 1862 *Margery's Son, Until He Finds It,* Emily Holt (1879) Vol. XXIX of the *Proceedings of the Society of Antiquaries of Scotland,* R Brydall, 1894/95 *Peeps into the Deaf World* *Dalkeith, its Castle and its Palace*, Francis Stewart (1925) *St Nicolas Buccleuch Parish Church Supplement*, A V Norman (1961) *Black Douglas*, Nigel Tranter (1968) *Britain's Deaf Heritage*
Rowland, Edward	*The British Deaf-Mute*, March 1893
Scott, Charlotte Angas	*Women of Mathematics*, Kenschaft, Patricia (1987), Greenwood Press, USA *Charlotte Angas Scott*, Stephanie Chaplin (1998) on the *Biographies of Women Mathematicians Website*, Angas Scott College, Georgia, USA. *Notable American Women 1607-1950*, Marguerite Lehr (1971)
Scott, George & Robert Menzies	*British Deaf News* 1960 *British Deaf News* June 1998
Shaw, Kathleen T.	*Silent World* 1955
Smith, John	*The Deaf and Dumb Magazine* 1880
Steel, Elizabeth	*Deaf Crime Casebook*, Peter W. Jackson (1997), Deafprint Winsford
Strathern, Alexander F.	*Deaf and Dumb Times* 1891
Sutcliffe, Thomas	The late Bernard Allery's notes (Elaine Lavery collection) *Ephphatha*, Sept-Nov 1950 *British Deaf News*, Winter 1966 and April 1996 *Hearing*, December 1974 *The Challenge of Deafness* T. Sutcliffe (1990)

Tait, George

Annual Reports of Edinburgh Deaf and Dumb Institution, 1842-1849
Treasurer's Accounts & Cash book, Edinburgh Deaf & Dumb Institution, 1842-1849
Annual Reports of Halifax Deaf & Dumb Institution, Nova Scotia
Autobiography of George Tait, etc 1877-1896, George Tait (1897), Halifax, NS
Notable Deaf Persons
Deaf Heritage in Canada

Tavaré, Frederick L.

British Deaf Monthly, February 1900

Thomson, Alfred R.

Silent World, 1959
Tommy, Arthur F. Dimmock (1991) Scottish Workshop Publications

Thorpe, Raymond B.

Deaf History Journal August 1997 British Deaf History Society
Torpy, Raymond Banks Thorpe (1995 - privately published). Raymond Lee Collection

Tonna, Charlotte E.

Personal Recollections, C. E. Tonna (with updates to 1850)
Sketch of Charlotte Elizabeth Tonna, Mrs. Balfour
Memoir of Charlotte Elizabeth Tonna, Anonymous
Introduction to Collected Works, Harriet Beecher Stowe (1844)
The Story of John Britt; the Happy Mute

Turner, Joseph

Annual Reports of Edinburgh Deaf and Dumb Institution, 1815, 1817, 1818, 1824, 1827.
Memoirs of My Youth Alexander Atkinson. (1865).
Anecdotes and Annals of the Deaf and Dumb C. Orpen (1836)

Whalley, Daniel

File ZAB799, Northampton County Records Office

Widd, Thomas

Notable Deaf Persons

Williams, Richard R.

The Deaf and Dumb Magazine May 1880

Wilson, Arthur J.

Peeps into the Deaf World
Ephphatha, 1898
Arthur James Wilson, Arthur F. Dimmock (1996) British Deaf History Society Publications

Wise, Dorothy S.

Peeps into the Deaf World
Ephphatha, Summer 1919

Wood, John Philip

Deaf History Journal April 1998 British Deaf History Society

Wright, David J. M.

Deafness, an autobiography by David Wright, dated 1992
International Authors and Writers Who's Who 1995-96, 14th Edition
The Oxford Companion to English Literature, Edited by M. Drabble, 2000
Volta Review Mar. 1938 and Apr.1951